THE BUSINESS
OF CONTEMPORARY
LAW PRACTICES

ASPEN COURSEBOOK SERIES

THE BUSINESS OF CONTEMPORARY LAW PRACTICES

Christopher L. Meazell

Executive Director, Innovation Hub and Professor of Practice

Wake Forest University School of Law

Wolters Kluwer

Published by Wolters Kluwer in New York.

Wolters Kluwer Legal & Regulatory U.S. serves customers worldwide with CCH, Aspen Publishers, and Kluwer Law International products. (www.WKLegaledu.com)

Cover image: Caitlin Margaret Kelly, *Eva Peron Was Here No. 5*. Copyright © Caitlin Margaret Kelly. Reproduced with permission from the artist.

To contact Customer Service, e-mail customer.service@wolterskluwer.com, call 1-800-234-1660, fax 1-800-901-9075, or mail correspondence to:

Wolters Kluwer
Attn: Order Department
PO Box 990
Frederick, MD 21705

SUSTAINABLE FORESTRY INITIATIVE

Certified Chain of Custody
Promoting Sustainable Forestry

www.sfiprogram.org

Printed in the United States of America.

1 2 3 4 5 6 7 8 9 0

ISBN 978-1-5438-1718-8

Library of Congress Cataloging-in-Publication Data

Names: Meazell, Christopher L., author.
Title: The business of contemporary law practices / Christopher L. Meazell,
   Executive Director, Innovation Hub and Professor of Practice, Wake
   Forest University School of Law.
Description: New York : Wolters Kluwer, [2021] | Series: Aspen coursebook
   series | Includes bibliographical references and index. | Summary:
   "Coursebook for law school courses on the business of law, law practice
   management, and professional development" — Provided by publisher.
Identifiers: LCCN 2021022330 (print) | LCCN 2021022331 (ebook) | ISBN
   9781543817188 (paperback) | ISBN 9781543841381 (ebook)
Subjects: LCSH: Practice of law — United States. | Practice of law — Economic
   aspects — United States. | LCGFT: Casebooks (Law)
Classification: LCC KF300 .M43 2021 (print) | LCC KF300 (ebook) | DDC
   340.068 — dc23
LC record available at https://lccn.loc.gov/2021022330
LC ebook record available at https://lccn.loc.gov/2021022331

About Wolters Kluwer Legal & Regulatory U.S.

Wolters Kluwer Legal & Regulatory U.S. delivers expert content and solutions in the areas of law, corporate compliance, health compliance, reimbursement, and legal education. Its practical solutions help customers successfully navigate the demands of a changing environment to drive their daily activities, enhance decision quality and inspire confident outcomes.

Serving customers worldwide, its legal and regulatory portfolio includes products under the Aspen Publishers, CCH Incorporated, Kluwer Law International, ftwilliam.com and MediRegs names. They are regarded as exceptional and trusted resources for general legal and practice-specific knowledge, compliance and risk management, dynamic workflow solutions, and expert commentary.

For my students—past, present, and future

SUMMARY OF CONTENTS

CONTENTS

Part III: Private Practice   43

Chapter 4: Law Firms   45

CHAPTER 5: ESSENTIAL LAW FIRM ECONOMICS   61

CHAPTER 6: LAWYER COMPENSATION   77

PREFACE

Why write a book about the business of contemporary law practices?

It is now beyond serious debate that contemporary law practice has fundamentally changed as a result of a confluence of factors, including economic downturns, the advent of technology, and a leveling of information and metrics, resulting in a power shift to clients—the consumers of legal services. Client focus, understanding, and service are more important than ever. A recurring comment from law school alumni is that recent law graduates lack an understanding of business fundamentals and an appreciation of the business drivers underpinning the practice of law.

Today's graduates face a changed world, one in which flexibility and adaptability are the keys to success. In order to thrive in such an environment, it is critical to understand—on a systemic basis—how the commercial aspects of the private practice of law have evolved over time and how that change has accelerated in recent years and will continue to do so. As law schools have responded by teaching more "business-oriented" perspectives on the practice, this will be a standard part of legal education, expected by employers, for newly minted lawyers.

This book provides an overview with relevant but not excessive detail. It goes beyond the traditional nuts-and-bolts law practice management class with the goal of providing a solid foundation for understanding, adapting to, and thriving in the world of private law practice. The book includes substantial attention to the "non-legal" subject of business fundamentals and financial literacy. This will simultaneously provide a baseline business-world fluency for new lawyers to better understand and communicate with clients and prepare students for the various nontraditional environments they may find themselves in.

The approach to the material varies depending on the subject matter but strives to balance enough high-level information for students to gain an appreciation for unfamiliar subject matter with a more immersive experience in particular areas to show the depth of thought required. There are also a number of historical references—I find that the history and development of law practice is interesting and a necessary professional background—but overall the book is driven by the present and future, with sections devoted to practice and implementation examples.

Finally, it is beyond the scope of this, or any, book to be a comprehensive resource for every aspect of private practice. Your professor will likely have invaluable personal practice experience to draw from, and that expertise will greatly inform and enhance the content of this book.

Why did I write this book?

This book is born of my blended life in business, law practice, and academia. I have taught an array of business, law practice, and media-related law school courses for many years. I have practiced law for more than 20 years in very different environments, from a specialized media-industry boutique, where I founded and managed my own small satellite office of four lawyers, to the largest law firm in Washington, D.C., and today with one of the pioneer "new model" firms. I have represented individuals with personal matters, start-ups with intellectual property protection issues, and Fortune 500 companies with bet-the-company litigation. Prior to law school, I was in the music business—at its peak—for over a decade. I hope that this combination of law practice and management experience with a student-centered understanding of the law school environment will help bridge the gap between academia and the contemporary practice of law.

ACKNOWLEDGMENTS

This book is the sum of so many influences, recalled or not, that it would be impossible to list them all. I thank my colleagues over the years at Dow Lohnes, Covington & Burling, and the Potomac Law Group, particularly Peter Coffman, who gave me my first assignment as a new associate, became an instrumental mentor, and has remained my dear friend to this day. I am grateful for my students and colleagues at Wake Forest who have taught me at least as much as I have them.

This book would have never taken off from the conception stage without research assistance from John Van Swearingen. It would have never landed without the patience and editorial hand of Betsy Farrell.

Most of all, I am loved by a wonderful family, without whom this book would be meaningless.

Textual Material

American Bar Association, Model Rules of Professional Conduct. Copyright ©2021 by the American Bar Association. Reprinted with permission. All rights reserved. This information or any or portion thereof may not be copied or disseminated in any form or by any means or stored in an electronic database or retrieval system without the express written consent of the American Bar Association.

—. Rule 5.4: Professional Independence of a Lawyer.
—. Rule 5.7: Responsibilities Regarding Law-related Services.
—. Rule 7.1: Communications Concerning a Lawyer's Services.
—. Rule 7.2: Communications Concerning a Lawyer's Services: Specific Rules, (a).
—. Comment to Model Rule 7.2.
—. Model Rule 7.3: Solicitation of Clients, (a) to (d).

Wilmer Cutler Pickering Hale and Dorr LLP, "Slice of History: Reginald Heber Smith and the Birth of the Billable Hour." WilmerHale blog post dated August 9, 2010. Retrieved from https://www.wilmerhale.com/en/insights/publications/slice-of-history-reginald-heber-smith-and-the-birth-of-the-billable-hour-august-9-2010. Reprinted with permission.

INTRODUCTION

Every time has its own version of "today's" lawyer, and the characteristics that society finds desirable in that lawyer may vary. Being a lawyer is many things. It is part of a continuum—depending on the lawyer, it is a calling; a career; a path to upward social and financial mobility; a means of service; a duty; or a joyous, challenging, and, yes, sometimes miserable experience. Traditionally, law schools have prepared lawyers for the substantive and philosophical aspects of the profession through classes on torts, contracts, property, procedure, and jurisprudence, but left most if not all of the "professional" dimensions of lawyering to the post–law school world. As law practice in the United States continues to simultaneously become more differentiated and more concentrated, it is more important than ever that students enter the professional ranks armed with at least a baseline understanding of the economics and business dynamics of the profession. You do not need to have CFO-level management and organizational skills, at least not yet, to adapt and find your own path to success in this profession.

I suggest that contemporary lawyers need to be smart, flexible, creative, and talented, but also intensely aware of the world and the people around them. The pace of change in today's world is dizzying and constantly injects uncertainty into the law practice environment. This can be daunting, particularly for lawyers, who tend to be risk averse by nature. You can take some comfort in knowing that these core attributes and the concurrent demands of an evolving world, however, are not dramatically different from those attributes possessed and the demands successfully faced by "yesterday's" lawyers. The key lies in understanding how to best apply those traits and abilities to your practice environment as you transition into your professional lives.

H.P. Lovecraft—the father of science fiction—said: "The oldest and strongest emotion of mankind is fear, and the oldest and strongest kind of fear is fear of the unknown."[1] The future is somewhat unknown by definition, but the law and lawyering has been around in some fashion since the organization of human societies, and appreciating some of its history and current contours will illuminate the lawyer's place in the twenty-first century and help you to conquer at least some of that fear.

This book begins with two foundational topics: Part I provides a brief historical backdrop and some modern context for the private practice of law, and Part II is an introduction to business fundamentals and vocabulary. Together, they provide the footing to approach a more in-depth examination of private practice throughout the balance of the book. Part III explores what private law firms are

---

[1]H.P. Lovecraft, Supernatural Horror in Literature (1927).

and how they operate in the current environment; Part IV introduces corporate, or "in-house," law departments; and Part V concludes with a look at "New Law" business models and technology.

The law itself is built on the past, but the new constantly presses on the old to evolve and live on in the present, and always with an eye to a better future. Law practice is no different.

THE BUSINESS
OF CONTEMPORARY
LAW PRACTICES

BACKGROUND AND HISTORY OF THE AMERICAN LEGAL PROFESSION

I. Introduction

To fully appreciate the world you have entered and to prepare for the pivots, twists, and turns that your career will inevitably take, consider the following:

Roughly half of America's founding fathers were lawyers. Despite the decentralized judicial nature of America's colonial origins, there was always a strong tradition of having courts—however formal or informal—adjudicate civil, criminal, and administrative matters. With those courts came lawyers, and those lawyers handled many of the same tasks they handle today. While some portions of traditional legal practice have since disappeared into other industries, the parallel evolution of American legal philosophy and practice has largely been a story of the legal industry's synergistic expansion alongside American business.

Part I will help orient you to the historical background of the legal profession in the United States as well as situate some of the overall structures and dynamics of contemporary practice. Be patient—an understanding of where we've been and how we got to the present day is a critical part of charting a course for where we fit in the future.

CHAPTER 1

GROWTH OF THE LEGAL PROFESSION IN THE UNITED STATES

Having now grown from its English roots for almost three hundred years, law in the United States can be considered its own—and the product of our collective experience. Our society depends on law and lawyers, and both have developed throughout our history to serve the changing needs of American society. A review of that evolution through the parallel lenses of legal philosophy and practice brings foundational perspective.[1]

I. The Colonial Era—America's Legal Roots in England

A. Legal Philosophy of the Era

The royal courts of England began laying the foundation of the common law in the sixteenth century. William Blackstone was arguably the first philosopher of English common law; a product of the eighteenth-century Enlightenment, he saw the English legal system as a "perfection of reason" to be preserved in perpetuity. Blackstone's Commentaries sought to establish settled rules of English law through the analysis of cases, which he believed ought to be applied without change.

His contemporary, Lord Mansfield, was a judge of the courts, and Mansfield had a less conservative, more activist view of the judiciary and the law: In the minds of Mansfield and his contemporaries, cases could be handled through the abolishment of old doctrines (and the creation of new law) when necessary.

---

[1]For comprehensive histories, see Lawrence Friedman, A History of American Law (3d ed. 2005); Grant Gilmore, The Ages of American Law (1977).

This fundamental question of adhering to clear, existing rules or retaining the freedom to adapt in the face of change remains a threshold of judicial reasoning to this day.

The colonial era in America was marked by fledgling decentralized legal systems throughout the colonies, but there was no documentation of cases or public record, and therefore no legal system or philosophy to analyze and provide reliable source material.

B. The Practice of Law

Before the advent of jurisprudence, legal academia, or professionalization, law was not yet a heavily intellectual field. During this era, most attorneys worked in law only part time, often concurrently working in trades or as merchants, or serving in the military. In the colonies, though competent bars were establishing themselves in major communities in the years preceding the American Revolution, the absence of legal education and a decentralized apprenticeship model tended to foster public distrust and disfavor of the profession. But formal legal education would soon develop, and the very first law schools in colonial America came to exist out of the law offices widely sought for apprenticeships.

II. The Era of Independence—The Birth of American Common Law

A. Legal Philosophy of the Era

The American Revolution resulted in the birth of a new American nation eager to sever itself from the legal traditions of England, which were often seen as overly formal and complicated. The anti-English political environment, coupled with the federal structure of the Constitution, created a decentralized and uncertain legal climate rife with questions about structure and scope. Interstate travel as we know it did not yet exist, and the Commerce Clause was undeveloped. The federal regulatory schemes we now accept as commonplace were unthinkable in young America.

The law generally was not commonly seen as a regulatory force, but rather a promotional and enabling force to spur development in America. For example, while banks are commonly seen as a target of regulatory laws in today's society, the law of early America was scrambling to figure out how to charter new banks as fast as possible to meet the demands of expansion, particularly in the West. Legislatures of the early states had to charter roads, railroads, and canals to ensure the growth of their economies. The law also provided the framework for the chartering of private businesses; in 1800, there were only a few hundred chartered corporations in the entire United States.

B. The Practice of Law

By 1820, enough had occurred in the American legal experience that the judiciary, for the most part, had a stable and well-respected station in the government; there were enough opinions and decisions published to establish an American common law independent of English cases. Pervasive Mansfieldian attitudes toward precedent and judicial law creation spurred conflict between those who preferred federal uniformity in substantive law and those who preferred an anti-federalist state-focused system. The movement for federal codification of law—first raised by Jeremy Bentham in 1811, then by Justice Story in 1821, albeit with different models—began without tangible success.

Treatises on law, a unique development unlike anything in the English tradition, were published for the first time in the early nineteenth century. However, the profession itself remained somewhat unintellectual; no state yet required formal higher education before admission to the bar. According to none other than Abraham Lincoln, self-education via reading English commentaries and American legal treatises was the best means of attaining a legal education. Major reforms, however, were on the horizon.

III. The Post–Civil War Era—Langdell and the Advent of Formal Legal Education

A. Legal Philosophy of the Era

The postbellum reconstruction of the American South curiously coincided with a massive philosophical shift in American law. The United States government was evolving dramatically; the decades leading up to World War I saw the creation of the "big government" federal model, replete with rising government employment, growing bureaucracy, and increasing economic regulation. The tension between the judicial and the legislative philosophies of the era is perhaps best exemplified by the conflict concerning the establishment of the federal income tax.

In 1870, Christopher Columbus Langdell, the first dean of Harvard Law School, dramatically and irreversibly altered the norm of legal education by approaching legal study as a science. More specifically, Langdell believed that, given enough time to study the body of case law, enduring "legal truths" could be deduced by scholars, and thus the natural "rule of law" could eventually be known. This approach fundamentally simplified and restructured the evolution of doctrine, like contract law and tort law, into their modern forms. Also, and perhaps as importantly, the West National Reporter was established in the 1880s, which allowed case digests to replace treatises as the "stock-in-trade" of working attorneys.

B. The Practice of Law

There were just over twenty thousand lawyers in the United States during the antebellum era, but those ranks swelled fivefold by the turn of the nineteenth century. This era marked the onset of sophisticated corporate practice—the new "Wall Street lawyer" was empowered by the New York Codes of Civil Procedure to handle cases without ever setting foot in the traditional lawyer's venue, the courtroom. The larger firms in major markets began the now-standard practice of paying attorneys' salaries. However, evolution of legal practice remained geographically divided; lawyers in the "frontier" regions continued to work in a more traditional, generalized practice during this time.

The advent of office technology had a negative impact on the need for clerks and apprentices; coupled with the growing prestige of certain law schools, formal legal education grew rapidly as a means of access to the bar. State bar associations, meant to insulate professionals from political machines and maintain standards, started forming in the postbellum era, with the first established in 1869 in New York. The American Bar Association (ABA) formed in 1878 with 75 members from several states, but it did not really rise to a central role in the profession until after the turn of the twentieth century.

IV. The Early Twentieth Century—Social Sciences and the Codification Movement

A. Legal Philosophy of the Era

The philosophies and attitudes of the social science movement made a strong impact on the legal community. A new emphasis on conducting "empirical research" emerged—unlike Blackstone and Langdell, legal thinkers of this era were skeptical of judicial opinions, which these thinkers deemed unlikely to reveal meaningful information beyond the subject of the opinion and the judge's limited knowledge or experience. Meanwhile, legal scholarship reformers at elite schools reshaped their law programs to echo the format of traditional university programs.

The pre–World War II "New Deal" era was characterized by progressive legal attitudes, which meant that the proactive use of legislation to address social problems was viewed as a preferable alternative to bringing legal issues to the still-conservative judiciary. Strict formalism in American law declined during this era, coinciding with the nation's shift from a laissez-faire economic model to a modern "welfare" state.

B. The Practice of Law

In the early twentieth century, apprenticeship as a means of accessing the bar was dying out; there were over one hundred law schools in the United States after World War I and, for better or worse, the Harvard-style case method reigned as the dominant pedagogical technique.

Major-market legal practice was still relatively small by today's standards: In 1935 Chicago, the largest firm was 43 lawyers strong. Further, even the most sophisticated large firms were still local firms; the multi-office, multi-state firm model did not yet exist.

Access to the ABA was extended to women in 1918, but the ABA continued to engage in racially based exclusion in the pre–World War II era. In response to this exclusion, African-American lawyers started the National Bar Association (NBA) in 1925. However, many state bar associations were integrated by the middle of the twentieth century, and the ABA would eventually follow.

V. The "Modern" Twentieth-Century Era—Public Policy Concerns and Corporate Regulation

A. Legal Philosophy of the Era

Following World War II, the philosophy of American law was characterized by post–New Deal judicial activism. The Supreme Court, which had largely remained an economically focused government watchdog until this point, became an active champion of personal rights and social causes under Chief Justice Earl Warren. Even as subsequent iterations of the Supreme Court have become more conservative, the Court's role as a protector of rights against government regulation has remained the same.

More broadly and openly than ever, modern courts (all the way down to the state level) became more willing to consider the forward-looking implications of public policy when rendering decisions. A new tradition of clarifying— or "distinguishing"—cases of importance on factual bases has come to replace the older proclivity for overruling cases deemed "outmoded." Perhaps due to the modern legal focus on policy, appellate and high court opinions became far more likely than ever before to feature concurring and dissenting opinions.

B. The Practice of Law

The ABA expanded dramatically throughout the second half of the twentieth century, and despite only around one-third of lawyers attaining ABA membership by the year 2000, the organization has come to assert great influence over the legal industry. In the 1960s, for example, the ABA copied a handful of elite law schools by requiring a four-year degree for membership; this prerequisite soon became the standard for all law schools.

Thanks to the post–World War II era GI Bill, access to legal education expanded beyond the traditional filters of social background and financial ability. The Law School Admissions Test (LSAT), created shortly after World War II, enabled schools to become more selective when choosing students from among this new, larger applicant pool. The legal industry continued to grow: There were around 600,000 lawyers in the United States in the 1980s, but by the turn of the millennium, there were around one million. Additionally, the presence of women and minorities in practice began expanding during the 1960s—women may comprise the majority of lawyers in the twenty-first century.

Specialized practice areas grew along with the growth of the country and of industry; a dramatic example of this is intellectual property (IP) law. While born from the Constitution, IP law took years to truly develop. The 1946 Lanham Act codified the nation's trademark laws, patent law received a major overhaul in 1952, and by 1982, the practice of IP law had become so technical that a separate federal court system was created to help handle its cases. The nation's business laws have also evolved dramatically in the modern era: Between 1953 and 1974, the states adopted the Uniform Commercial Code, effectively creating national legal standards for businesses.

VI. Conclusion

Finally, it is important to note that the practice of law, which has been evolving in America for well over two centuries, effectively segregated itself into three sectors by the end of the millennium. While the majority of attorneys work for private sector law firms, roughly 10 percent of all lawyers now work directly for companies as in-house counsel, and roughly 10 percent of lawyers are employed in the public sector. To further explore division in the industry, the private sector roughly breaks down into two groups: The majority of private sector lawyers work in the large "corporate client sector," where a firm may have hundreds (or even thousands) of attorneys in multiple offices across the nation or globe; those lawyers not in the corporate client sector tend to work with smaller firms devoted to smaller businesses or non-business matters like real estate law, family law, or personal injury law.

While it is still too early to view with any reliable analytical hindsight, the twenty-first century has already brought dramatic, some would say seismic, change to the United States.[2] We have experienced a series of signature events—9/11, the global financial crisis of 2007-2008, the COVID-19 pandemic, the social justice movement—and "disruption" is the order of the day across many business models, including law firms. The judiciary has become highly politicized (some would say weaponized), and legal philosophy is now often entangled in a divisive contemporary political environment. The Supreme Court, charged with the difficult task of resolving the most fundamental and controversial conflicts in the land, has seen a decline in public respect, perhaps rooted in the politicization of the confirmation process and the perceived polarization of the Justices. We have all witnessed a presidential administration that pushed the accepted boundaries of executive power, and we have experienced the gradual relinquishing of freedom and privacy in the name of security and convenience.

Legal education has been forced to reckon with a changing job market and to embrace pedagogical alternatives. Law firms have had to rapidly adjust to meet whatever the prevailing demands of their clients may be—clients who are themselves facing great uncertainty and financial pressures. You, as law students and soon-to-be lawyers, must comprise a reasoned, resilient backbone as our country, our economy, and even our little world of the law business, all face and adapt to the challenges of our own times.

---

[2] *See* Georgetown Law Center on Ethics and the Legal Profession & Thompson Reuters Institute, *2021 Report on the State of the Legal Market* (2021) ("For the past decade (since the Great Recession), the market for legal services has been evolving toward a different delivery model. The evidence of that evolution has been visible in the changing role and expectations of clients, changes in the pricing of law firm services, growth of competition (including from non-traditional law firms), and changes in technology.").

CHAPTER 2

OVERVIEW OF THE LEGAL PROFESSION

There are over one million lawyers in the United States, doing incredibly varied work in numerous fields, which makes it a challenge to generalize about the American legal profession. Moreover, there are 50 states, and, despite sharing common concepts, each has its own legal system, further rendering the concept of a generalized American legal experience a bit elusive. Because the scope of the profession is vast, it is helpful to break down the broad legal profession into smaller segments, or spheres, to contextualize the differentiated number of practice environments. We will also introduce the current state of diversity, equity, and inclusion in the profession.

Industry discussion, survey data,[1] and media coverage of many aspects of the profession often center on legal practice in large firm environments in major cities. While this arguably limited focus may only provide something of a skewed view into the experiences of one, albeit large, segment of the American legal population, the lessons learned therein are often also generally applicable to law practice across the spectrum—and, of course, may be directly applicable to a number of law students. While somewhere around a third of private sector attorneys are solo practitioners, a clear majority of young attorneys in the private sector work in law firms. And as most private firms tend to be in the corporate client sector, observations centered on the firms in this sector will likely have some pragmatic value to many young attorneys headed into private practice.

I. Private and Public Spheres

Writ large, the profession breaks down into several spheres. One of the largest divides is between those lawyers who work in private firms and companies,

---

[1]Both the American Bar Association (ABA) and the National Association for Law Placement (NALP) compile extensive survey data about many aspects of the practice and profession. *See, e.g.*, *Legal Profession Statistics*, https://www.americanbar.org/about_the_aba/profession_statistics/; *Research & Statistics*, www.nalp.org/research.

and those who work in government and in nonprofits. The former is generally referred to as the "private sector" or "private practice," while the latter is generally referred to as the "public sector" or "public interest." While this book is aimed more toward private practice, a high-level overview may aid in understanding.

Private practice lawyers typically represent individuals or companies. Examples of private practice environments include law firms large and small, and in-house positions with companies.

Public practice takes place in legal services and law reform organizations, as well as in government agencies at all levels. It encompasses charities; educational and public international organizations; private public-interest law firms (as well as private law firms performing pro bono work); and representation on behalf of individuals who cannot afford private attorneys (usually in "legal aid" or "legal services" organizations).

Lawyers in private practice at law firms are generally paid (directly or indirectly) by their clients—and depend on paying clients to fund their business and incomes. However, private practice attorneys working for companies ("in-house counsel") and public practice attorneys working in government or nonprofits are usually paid by salary—their clients are generally not paying for their legal representation(s) per se. Salaries tend to be lower in the public interest sphere than in private practice, although the discrepancies may be small depending on the location.

The following table may help contextualize where a lawyer's income comes from:

Sphere	Source	Examples	Who Pays?
Private—Firm	Fee for Services	Corporate Work Family Practice	Client (from Assets)
Private—Firm	Contingency	Plaintiffs' Personal Injury Litigation	Client (from Recovery)
Private—Corporation	Revenue from Operations	In-House Counsel	Employer
Public—Organization	Grants	Public Interest	Donors
Public—Government	Government	Department of Justice	Taxpayers

Generalizations about private practice and public interest attorneys abound—for example, that one group works longer hours than the other, or that new attorneys will gain more experience or on-the-job training in one than in the other. You should approach such generalizations with a good degree of skepticism—there is tremendous variation among the different types of practice settings within and across all these categories.

II. Criminal and Civil Spheres

A second divide lies between the "criminal" and "civil" spheres, which are further subdivided into fields or practice areas.

A. Criminal Sphere

Criminal law—the body of law relating to crimes—involves litigation brought on behalf of the government (state or federal) against an individual, group, or corporation, seeking to hold the latter accountable for the commission of crimes. Most lawyers in criminal law either represent the government (prosecutors, sometimes called district attorneys, or, at the federal level, U.S. Attorneys), or those charged with crimes (defense attorneys). Defense attorneys can be in private practice—paid either by their clients or by the government on behalf of indigent clients—or work for a government-funded public defender agency.

While the balance of the book will focus largely on private practice, you should have an appreciation for the prosecutorial side of public criminal practice as it manifests itself over various jurisdictions. The term "federalism," particularly in the context of the American political experience, recalls the classic concept of a two-tiered system of government: the limited-but-supreme federal government above, and the states below. However, while there is one legal framework for the federal government, each state is a separate and unique legal system unto itself. For the purposes of this brief discussion, we will consider state legal frameworks in a collective sense.

1. The United States Attorney General (USAG)

The USAG is the head of the U.S. Department of Justice (DOJ). While the USAG was created as a part-time role in 1789, the power of the position has grown dramatically over the years: The DOJ was created in 1870 to assist the USAG, and New Deal–era policies placed the DOJ in charge of substantially all federal litigation. Of the over forty thousand attorneys working in various roles throughout the federal government, around eleven thousand work for the DOJ under the USAG. The USAG, therefore, manages the largest law firm in the world.[2]

The USAG is a cabinet-level position appointed by the President, which adds some unique concerns to the position, including that the USAG must answer directly to the President in connection with the promulgation of the President's executive agenda. The promotion of certain legal policy is complicated, however, by the large, decentralized nature of the DOJ; there are six divisions within the DOJ (antitrust, civil, civil rights, criminal, environmental, and tax) that, at times, may represent competing interests. Additionally, even matters of criminal

---

[2]A wealth of information is available at the United States Department of Justice website, www.justice.gov. Entry-level positions with DOJ are typically filled through the Attorney General's Honors Program, https://www.justice.gov/legal-careers/entry-level-attorneys.

enforcement by the 94 United States Attorneys' offices throughout the country, all nominally under the USAG's control, are handled with a certain independent level of prosecutorial discretion. Thus, the federal bureaucracy that puts the largest litigation firm in the world under the control of the USAG renders that same control somewhat difficult to assert.

Finally, though the USAG oversees furthering the President's executive agenda, the USAG has little interpretive authority over the law for the purposes of helping the other executive agencies establish their administrative policies. This "quasi-legislative" role is fulfilled by the numerous general counsel offices serving the other executive agencies, often leaving the DOJ with the role of representing policies in litigation that it had no role in establishing.

2. State Attorneys General

At the state level, the attorney general (State AG) serves as the chief legal advisor and chief law enforcement officer for the state government and typically operates at the intersection of law and public policy. State AG departments prosecute state law violations, represent the state in litigation and other disputes, and provide legal advice to state agencies and the legislature. In all but a handful of states, the State AG is an elected official, which affords them substantial influence over law enforcement policies and priorities.

States may also have distinct ways of administering their executive branch legal functions. One of the most notable distinctions lies between two models of criminal law enforcement: Some states opt to have locally elected prosecutors handle prosecutions within local jurisdictions, while others have a statewide prosecutor's office handle all state- and local-level prosecutions. Also, states have varying limits on a State AG's ability to initiate or take over local prosecutions. However, it is worth noting that even where a state has both state-level and local-level prosecutors, the relationship between both entities is generally cooperative.

The State AGs also perform tasks that federal agency general counsel typically handle beyond the scope of the USAG, such as providing legal advice to state government agencies. State AGs can also perform a quasi-legislative role insofar as they may be called upon to write legislation.

3. Utilization of Private Attorney Assistance at the Federal and State Levels

In 1978, due to controversy surrounding the federal government's ability to appoint private counsel, the U.S. Office of Legal Counsel issued an opinion on the subject to the President and USAG that clarified the broad authority granted to the USAG. The statute authorizing the USAG's appointment of outside counsel, 28 U.S.C. §543, set the scope of appointments within the vague boundaries of "when the public interest so requires."

Such appointments may be prosecutorial in nature, such as the appointment of a private attorney to a "strike force." Appointments can also be defense-oriented: If a federal employee is the subject of an ongoing federal criminal investigation, and that employee is also the subject of some other criminal or civil action in which the DOJ would normally represent that employee, a private attorney may be appointed. When these types of representative appointments are made, the DOJ sets strict conditions on the private attorney's retention agreement and limits fees collectable to only those actions in the interests of the United States at large. There are no contingency fee agreements for private counsel appointed or retained under the authority of the USAG.

State AGs are typically provided with the power to hire private counsel, but the statutes involved vary in the amount of authority granted: California, for example, enumerates specific circumstances in which the State AG can retain private counsel, whereas Maryland provides the State AG with broad discretion. Many states permit appointed private counsel to represent the state on a contingency fee basis. State AGs may also appoint private counsel as special attorneys general when the state requires some sort of specialized legal expertise.

B. Civil Sphere

Civil law is often contrasted with criminal law, but the category is vast and differentiated. It refers to all legal disputes and relationships between and among non-governmental entities, as well as those with government acting in its non-prosecutorial role. A look at the practice areas section of any large law firm website will reveal the breadth of the civil sphere.

> The ABA currently lists the following specialty groups, which encompasses both spheres:
>
> Administrative Law & Regulatory Practice
> Affordable Housing & Community Development Law
> Air & Space Law
> Antitrust Law
> Business Law
> Civil Rights & Social Justice
> Communications Law
> Construction Law
> Criminal Justice
> Dispute Resolution
> Diversity & Inclusion
> Entertainment & Sports Industries
> Environment, Energy & Resources
> Family Law
> Franchising
> Government & Public-Sector Lawyers
> Health Law
> Infrastructure & Regulated Industries Section
> Intellectual Property
> International Law
> Judicial Division
> Labor & Employment Law

Law Practice
Law Student Division
Legal Education & Admissions to the Bar
Litigation
Public Contract Law
Real Property, Trust & Estate Law
Science & Technology Law
Senior Lawyers Division
Solo, Small Firm & General Practice Division
State & Local Government Law
Taxation
Tort Trial & Insurance Practice
Young Lawyers Division

Often, civil lawyers describe their practice by reference to a type of law or an industry of specialization. So, for example, bankruptcy, intellectual property, and personal injury each refer to areas of legal doctrine focusing on, respectively, financial distress, rights in ideas or intellectual production, and harm to individuals. These areas of practice exist on their own, and clients may come from many different industries. On the other hand, for example, some law practices may focus on a broad range of legal issues as they may be applicable to particular industries, such as media and entertainment, food and drug, or energy. More helpful in understanding law practices in the civil sphere, however, may be the distinction between transactional practice and litigation.

1. Transactional Hemisphere

Perhaps the two largest classes of lawyers are those oriented toward transactions and those oriented toward litigation. While both are vast, transactional practice typically involves researching, preparing, and reviewing the documents that form the basis of deals and agreements, ranging from contracts for large corporate mergers and acquisitions (M&A, in the parlance) to the closing documents for the purchase of a house. Transactional practice includes as well the myriad specialties in regulatory compliance, taxation, and numerous other areas. While often contentious, transactional work takes place outside of the courtroom.

2. Litigation Hemisphere

Litigators resemble more closely the kinds of lawyers we often see depicted in the media. They are the ones who seek to resolve disputes, both in and out of courtrooms: breached contracts, the commission of crimes, defective consumer products, etc. Litigators spend much of their time researching the law, investigating the facts, exchanging information and documents with opposing counsel, analyzing the merits of the case based on the law and facts, and negotiating potential settlements. Upwards of 90 percent of all lawsuits settle before going to trial (although this varies depending on the specific area of law and the resources of the parties), and most litigators spend much more in-court time arguing procedural and substantive motions than in trial, making actual trial time a rare and valuable experience for a young lawyer.

While there is some overlap between these two large areas, most lawyers (especially in larger firms) concentrate their practices on one or the other. Solo and small firm practitioners tend to be more generalists and may often engage in a mix of transactional work and litigation.

III. Diversity, Equity, and Inclusion (DEI)

Students must recognize that identities such as race, sex, gender, age, and disability constitute overly broad conceptions that are necessarily influenced by, and in turn influence, culture and attitudes. The intersectionality of these identities, moreover, adds complexity to people's lived experiences. For purposes of our discussion, however, these commonly used identifiers provide a starting point to try to understand DEI and accommodation practices across the profession.

Despite the known and tangible benefits DEI brings to businesses, the legal profession has struggled to make progress with diversity and representation for decades. People with different backgrounds and experiences can bring more perspectives, which can lead to different problem-solving methods.

The ABA[3] and NALP have tracked the representation of women and persons of color in law firms over a recent ten-year period. It may be useful to review the change over time of the representation of those groups in law schools and law firms before exploring the barriers and potential pathways to diversity, equity, and inclusion that women and persons of color face:

2009 Statistics	Law Schools— 1Ls	Summer Associates	Associates	Partners
Women	47.71%	46.62%	45.66%	19.21%
Persons of Color	25.32%	24.04%	19.67%	6.05%
Women of Color	13.77%	12.90%	11.02%	1.88%

---

[3] *See, e.g.*, American Bar Association, *ABA Profile of the Profession 2020*, https://www.americanbar .org/content/dam/aba/administrative/news/2020/07/potlp2020.pdf.

2019 Statistics	Law Schools—1Ls	Summer Associates	Associates	Partners
Women	54.04%	52.66%	46.77%	24.17%
Persons of Color	31.00%	35.26%	25.44%	9.55%
Women of Color	18.59%	21.16%	14.48%	3.45%

The disconnect between entry and leadership numbers is clear. In its 2019 Report on Diversity in U.S. Law Firms,[4] an annual compilation of legal employer data, NALP highlighted several noteworthy data points, but overall found that the profession is making only incremental progress. Key among its findings, NALP reported that the percentage of African-American associates finally eclipsed the previous high in 2009.

A. Women in the American Legal System

The classical view of the American legal profession asserts that the profession has been dominated by men until recently. Women have always been present in the practice of law: There have been women attorneys since colonial times. Moreover, the first woman admitted to a state bar, the first woman law school graduate, and the first woman judge were all a part of the American legal landscape within only a few years of the Civil War—from which the catastrophic death toll of men opened to some extent previously inaccessible professions to women and even some people of color. Another generation beyond that access, however, saw diminished opportunities.

Still, despite their historic presence in the American legal profession, the story of women in American law has, until recently, been a story of extreme categorical underrepresentation. On a superficial level, that is no longer the case: Women account for about 45 percent of all associate-level attorneys in private practice and represent about one-third of the American judiciary. While neither statistic is at 50 percent, the improvement in industry representation since the 1960s (when women comprised less than 5 percent of attorneys in the United States) is noticeable.

The salient concerns for young women attorneys no longer involve merely gaining access to the legal profession; rather, women attorneys generally see decreasing opportunities for wage growth and management positions as their careers go on. Women currently comprise about 45 percent of law students, and they are hired by law firms at about the same rate. Women attorneys hired out of law school generally make 95 percent of the salary earned by their male counterparts—an exponential improvement over the wage gap in America's past, where, until as recently as 1979, women made only 55 percent of the

---

[4]National Association for Law Placement, *2019 Report on Diversity in U.S. Law Firms*, https://www.nalp.org/uploads/2019_DiversityReport.pdf.

salary of their male peers. Yet this situation remains imbalanced and in need of equitable revision.

Despite starting on near-equal ground, women attorneys generally lose traction over time. Women are, statistically, more likely than men to leave the practice, and some scholarship on the subject has noted that, while men with children may earn more than their peers, women with children earn less. Women are typically less likely to make partner at a firm, and only account for about one-fifth of partner-level attorneys nationwide.

However, at least some research has noted that unhappy women attorneys are more likely than unhappy male attorneys to leave the practice. Women are also more likely to leave their firms before they have been practicing long enough to be considered for partnership. Thus, while the American legal profession may be hiring more women attorneys than ever before, the profession is arguably having a harder time retaining women—especially mothers—to incorporate them into the upper echelons of the profession.

As noted in McKinsey & Company's 2019 Women in the Workplace study:[5] "There are signs the glass ceiling is cracking. . . . But a broken rung prevents women from reaching to the top." And the American Bar Association's Commission on Women in the Profession echoes this statement as applied to law firm life: "The statistics reveal a disheartening picture. In 2018, women comprised only 19.5 percent of equity partners and 30.5 percent of nonequity partners in the nation's 200 largest firms, according to an annual survey by the National Association of Women Lawyers (NAWL), based in Chicago. That's only a 3 percent increase of equity partners from 12 years earlier—a sluggish upward trajectory[.]"[6] At this rate, women will achieve gender parity in equity partnerships in 160 years, according to a 2015 analysis.[7]

B. Race and Ethnicity in the American Legal System

Unexceptionally similar to almost every other aspect of American society, the legal profession largely excluded racial minorities until after World War II. Post–Civil War reconstructionist policies had led to Black people being elected and serving in various positions of power, but in the Southern states, this lasted only until the Union army left. By way of example, Macon Allen, the first Black lawyer in the United States, was from Maine: He became a lawyer in Maine in 1844 and in 1873 became an elected judge in South Carolina; however, he left South Carolina after Reconstruction and relocated to the District of Columbia.

Today, the American legal profession is as racially and ethnically diverse as it has ever been, but that's not saying much. As of 2015, the profession remained

---

[5]McKinsey & Company, *Women in the Workplace 2019*, https://www.mckinsey.com/~/media/McKinsey/Featured%20Insights/Gender%20Equality/Women%20in%20the%20Workplace%202019/Women-in-the-workplace-2019.pdf.

[6]Cynthia L. Cooper, *Broken Rungs on the Career Ladder: A New Analysis of Problems Encountered by Women Lawyers in Private Practice* (Jan. 21, 2020), https://www.americanbar.org/groups/diversity/women/publications/perspectives/2020/january/broken-rungs-the-career-ladder-new-analysis-problems-encountered-women-lawyers-private-practice/.

[7]The American Lawyer, *Special Report: Big Law Is Failing Women* (May 28, 2015), https://www.law.com/americanlawyer/almID/1202727354967/.

almost 90 percent white, with Black attorneys and Latinx attorneys comprising only about 5 percent of the profession each.

The experience of racial and ethnic minorities undoubtedly adds value to the profession: A major public university surveyed 25 years of law school graduates and found that racial and ethnic minorities were more likely than white alumni to start their careers in public service or with public interest organizations. Additionally, racial and ethnic minorities dissatisfied with the legal profession are more willing to stay working in law than equally dissatisfied white attorneys. This increased dedication to the profession is, in the view of some scholars, likely linked to the social disadvantages aspiring minority attorneys are more likely to face.

Corporate clients (as well as many government entities) are demanding a diverse roster of lawyers, in part because of their own accountability measures based on evidence that the companies who invest in DEI realize higher cash flow, outperform non-diverse organizations, and build their brand and consumer trust. Studies show that diverse teams also outperform their peers by a significant margin. A suggested set of best practices includes management setting active goals to promote women; requiring diverse slates for hiring and promotion opportunities; putting evaluators through unconscious bias training; establishing clear evaluation criteria; and funneling key experience opportunities to women.

The Minority Corporate Counsel Association has concluded that "[c]hange that will affect profits will drive the case for diversity in law firms. Without an understanding of how diversity impacts the bottom line, diversity programs are short-lived, inadequately funded and not taken seriously by either the firm management or those responsible for implementing diversity initiatives."[8]

In reporting on its Creating Pathways to Diversity initiative, MCCA described the following barriers to success:

1. **Little understanding of the link between diversity and the bottom line or its connection to strategic business initiatives.**

   The lack of an established business case for diversity explains why it is not fully supported by law firm management.

2. **Myth of the meritocracy.**

   The legal profession still traditionally views its institutions as being governed by a "meritocracy"—where success is the result of an individual's "innate" ability to perform well in such areas as law school GPA or law review participation. While these credentials are acceptable measures of academic performance by a law student, they have yet to be proven reliable yardsticks to measure success as a practicing attorney. This cultural bias frames diversity negatively, as coming at

---

[8]Minority Corporate Counsel Association, *Creating Pathways to Diversity: A Set of Recommended Practices for Law Firms* (2002), https://www.mcca.com/wp-content/uploads/2017/04/Book-2Blue.pdf.

the *expense* of quality of legal service instead of *enhancing* quality legal service.

3. **Revolving door for incoming attorneys of color.**

   Diversity at the associate level is not reflected in the senior partnership or management of most firms. Consequently, a steady stream of minority associates enters the pipeline but leaves within four years. That leaves a shrinking core of minority senior associates and an even smaller number of minority partners.

4. **Lack of senior partner commitment and involvement in the planning and execution of diversity initiatives.**

   Partners drive law firm culture and change. Without the participation of management, inadequate resources are committed to the diversity program. Each initiative then depends on the free time of interested attorneys, often women or people of color, who are already overburdened but are still assigned to spearhead internal diversity initiatives and recruit diverse candidates, while meeting the demands of day-to-day practice.

5. **Insufficient infrastructure and resources.**

   Many of the participants said their firms had a diversity committee or council and/or a recruiting committee with a diversity component, as well as other committees dealing with various aspects of recruitment and retention. But in many cases, there was no central focus or coordinated firm-wide set of goals. Instead, these structures were decentralized and sometimes lacked the authority to make a real difference. Results were not measured regularly nor were they tied to the compensation of the attorneys responsible for implementing each initiative. In fact, because hours spent on diversity management are non-billable, staff members who are assigned this responsibility often take a negative financial hit.

6. **Attrition of women attorneys driven by lack of viable work/life programs.**

   Many female attorneys are unable to maintain family commitments and high pressure, time-intensive legal careers. They also note the lack of role models and the strained relationships with clients and senior firm management.

7. **Stereotypes and assumptions.**

   There was evidence from the focus group data that stereotypes and assumptions about women and minorities still exist, stifling their career growth and a firm's diversity progress. Participants said because of family demands, it is still assumed that a woman will not be as committed to her profession as a man and that she will either leave or ask for "special treatment." Such stereotypes in law firms often do become "self-fulfilling prophecies."

8. **Emphasis on entry-level recruitment of minority attorneys.**

    Most of the initiatives that participants described focused on entry-level recruitment. Even when these efforts were successful, any gains that a firm made often were wiped out within a few years due to the attrition of the same people they had spent so much effort and money to hire.

9. **Good intentions but little willingness to examine specific issues at each firm historically.**

    Most law firms do not conduct an internal audit on firm hiring, culture, or promotion practices. Neither do diversity plans usually focus on internal causes that historically might have contributed to attorney attrition, particularly among women and attorneys of color. For example, a firm that hires exclusively from Ivy League schools or the alma mater of firm partners has unnecessarily limited its selection pool of minority candidates. To increase its staff of attorneys of color and to better understand the graduating pool of law students of color, a firm may have to build relationships with law schools that regularly graduate a large number of minority law students.

10. **External consultants design and implement a diversity training program that is not owned or understood by the firm's senior management.**

    A training program that is not custom-designed but conducted in an "off-the-shelf, one-size-fits-all" manner for the organization will be an expensive failure. Typically, no staff members are designated to monitor the firm's progress toward the program's diversity goals. Such one-shot approaches fall short of expectations, further frustrating employees who want change to occur.

MCCA's study also revealed the following five critical success factors:

1. **Understanding the business case for diversity.**

    To ensure senior partner commitment and firm-wide buy-in, a firm must develop a written plan that clearly makes the business case for diversity. Law firms that grasp the needs and economic potential of an increasingly diverse marketplace and workforce will change to expand their firm's market share, strengthen relationships with current corporate clients, and retain talented diverse staff.

2. **Senior partner commitment.**

An effective diversity program must be directed by a senior partner who is held accountable for the program's success and who is given the authority and resources to implement a firm-wide diversity program. Active involvement by management will ensure adequate resources are allocated to implement and regularly monitor the diversity program.

3. **Collaboration between partners, staff, and knowledgeable experts.**

Successful programs are collaborations between external diversity experts and internal staff, including an advocate who is part of senior management. This team should be responsible for the implementation, evaluation, and follow-up of the diversity program.

4. **Firm-wide ownership and participation.**

The entire firm shares ownership of the implementation and results of diversity initiatives, similar to other firm-wide commitments. Budget resources are provided to facilitate the entire firm's involvement and ownership in the diversity program.

5. **Confidential resources for all attorneys.**

A firm should earmark resources that allow all attorneys to voice their concerns, doubts, and ideas in a confidential or even anonymous forum, where they are not fearful of retaliation or retribution from senior management. Firms that are receptive to the issues raised by all attorneys will be able to change their culture, policies, or practices. Those that stifle feedback will have reticent and unhappy associates who may depart whenever the first good opportunity knocks.

Despite this MCCA study now being almost 20 years old, the conclusions remain as true today as when they were written.[9]

---

[9]MCCA's Pathways to Diversity Research Reports address issues of race/ethnicity, gender, sexual orientation, disability status, and generational differences in addition to tackling topics such as diversity demographics, diversity best practices in law departments, diversity metrics, cross-gender and cross-race mentoring, and career advancement. The series is available at Pathways Research, https://www.mcca.com/resources/pathways-research/.

C. Understanding the Experiences of Diverse People, Such as Those Who Identify as LGBTQ+

A comprehensive look at DEI is well beyond the scope of this book, but all attorneys need to be considerate, compassionate, and vigilant against discrimination in all forms. Consider, for example, even a few obvious elements that are relevant at least to practicing as an attorney and creating a legal career as an LGBTQ+ person:

The social nature of building one's legal career in a traditional sense (attending events, hosting dinners, participating in off-work activities or committees, etc.) often precludes LGBTQ+ attorneys from participating unless they can safely come out as LGBTQ+ in the workplace and community.

It is extremely difficult for transgender or gender nonbinary people to be open about their identities while practicing law, and in particular, for transgender people to undertake a social and/or medical transition while working in the field. Again, outdated and "traditional" perspectives mean that in their everyday practice, in and out of the courtroom, with peers, opposing counsel, judges, partners, and others, they are constantly being questioned and often disrespected through being misgendered, deadnamed, and asked about very personal information, such as their "real" gender, even in professional settings.

. . .

There are also no clear answers or guaranteed paths to success for DEI in law firms. Nor is DEI something that can simply be "fixed" and then forgotten. As you start your career, you should be mindful that DEI is an ongoing process that will require careful consideration and attention, no matter what sphere or practice area you may be in. When strategically planned and intentionally executed, a comprehensive DEI approach can make the legal profession and the representation of clients more effective and can even make a law firm more profitable.

IV. Conclusion

The two chapters in Part I have exposed and sensitized you to various issues impacting the practice of law at a high level and over a long timeline. Knowing that the economic and political drivers that move society and the law will continue to shift, and often at an alarming rate, choosing your "sphere," and operating with decency within it, will be a good start to your success in the profession.

BUSINESS FUNDAMENTALS

Introduction

If you are like many (if not most) law students, you likely have little background in or appreciation for basic business terminology and principles. Part II will provide a foundational understanding of business principles upon which we can then overlay the function of a law practice. Additionally, and perhaps more importantly, this part will help you to better understand and communicate with business clients as well as be better prepared for the various nontraditional work environments many of you may find yourselves in.

As you think about business, however, always bear in mind that despite the rapidly increasing focus on the economic aspects of law firms, the practice of law firmly remains both a profession and a business. Clients are the lifeblood of private practice, and they provide the revenue to keep the doors open. A lawyer without clients is a lawyer without income, but a lawyer without ethics or reputation won't be a lawyer for long.

It is important to understand, however, that "clients"—at least in some views—are not the same as "customers."

HISTORICAL NOTE: A DISTINCTION BETWEEN CUSTOMERS AND CLIENTS

All businesses are dependent on revenue, and revenue comes from customers. You may have heard the old adage that "the customer is always right." For the most part, the words "customer" and "client" are used interchangeably in an everyday sense. In the legal profession, however, we must always bear in mind the often-subtle distinctions between the two. It is helpful to trace the roots of both words to illuminate this distinction.

The origin of the word "customer" is the Latin *consuetudinem*, coming from one's habit or custom—someone's customary practice to do something repeatedly. Here, think of a person who bought bread at a Roman market on a regular basis (or, today, who orders the same drink from their corner coffee shop every morning). By the early fifteenth century, the word had come to mean "a buyer" or "a person with whom one has dealings."

The root of "client," however, is the Latin *cliens*, a word more closely related to the idea of a follower or retainer—one who entrusts another with their protection. In English, a client was originally a lawyer's customer.

As you will see in courses on professional responsibility, in the legal profession, "client" is also a magical status that carries with it the application of ethical duties and responsibilities as well as the protections of the laws of privilege.

Once an attorney-client relationship is formed, it may be challenging for a lawyer to unilaterally withdraw from the relationship. The coffee shop proprietor, on the other hand, may simply choose to no longer sell to a given customer.

Also, the client may not always be right . . .

CHAPTER 3

BUSINESS AND FINANCIAL STATEMENT LITERACY

We begin by demystifying *business* and *finance*—topics studiously avoided by many in the legal profession, from students to senior partners. Yet law firms and many of their clients are businesses and their economic prosperity rests on basic financial principles. By conceptualizing what businesses are and how they manage to remain in business, you will be able to better grasp how and why decisions are made, and how you and your work fit into those decisions.

I. Business and the Profit Equation

A *business* is an organization engaged in commercial, industrial, or professional activities—typically through the production of a good, offering of a service, or retailing of already manufactured products.

A business can be a for-profit entity or a nonprofit organization that operates to fulfill a charitable mission. A business name must be registered with the state, and this name is often referred to as the "doing business as" or DBA name. One of the pivotal steps in forming a business is determining the legal structure of the business and the associated tax implications. Different businesses require various permits and licenses to operate legally. And, finally, a business has legal obligations such as treatment of employees and responsibility for the conditions in which those employees work.

A comprehensive guide to entity selection and tax and business planning is beyond the scope of this book. As background, however, the most basic structure for a business is a sole proprietorship. The owner of the business is the sole individual to whom the assets and debt obligations belong. Alternatively, multiple individuals with shared duties can operate a business, and this business structure is a partnership. A third path is incorporation, which releases its owners from financial liability for business obligations; however, a corporation is subject to varying taxation rules for the owners of the business. For this reason, a fourth business structure, called a limited liability company (LLC)—or its kin, the limited liability partnership (LLP), professional limited liability corporation (PLLC), and others, which may vary by jurisdiction—is available, which combines the tax benefits of a partnership and liability protections of a corporation. Businesses include everything from a small owner-operated company, such as a family-owned hardware store, to a Fortune 500 multinational conglomerate. Typical law firm business structures are discussed in Chapter 4.

Businesses exist on a fundamental profit equation:

Revenue

−

Expenses

=

Profit or (Loss)

This compares the money earned from selling goods and services, and other activities, against the costs and outlays incurred to operate the business. What remains is the profit or (loss).

II. Business Models

A business model is the way in which a business generates revenue and makes a profit from its operations. No model is innately superior to another, and the success or failure of the application of a particular model is typically driven by ability, execution, and sometimes luck.

Typical components of a business model include:

PRODUCT: What are you selling?

TARGET MARKET: To whom are you selling?

ADVANTAGE OR VALUE PROPOSITION: Why are you better or different than competitors?

RESULT: How does the model result in profit?

The two primary levers of a business model are pricing and costs: A business can raise prices and it can find inventory at reduced costs. Both actions can increase profits. Examples of commonly referred to business models and some commonly known counterparts include:

Razor & Blades	(Gillette; Epson)
Cheap Chic	(Target, IKEA)
Franchise	(Fast Food and Hotel Chains)
Subscriptions	(Magazines, Music Streaming Services, Health Clubs)
Captive Audience	(Movie Theaters, Theme Parks)
Premium	(Tiffany, Mercedes-Benz)
Flat-Fee	(Southwest Airlines, All-Inclusive Resorts)
Nickel & Dime	(Legacy Airlines, Car Dealerships)

In addition to a model, there must be an execution strategy. Sometimes this is reflected in a business plan.[1] The plan is about numbers, projections, and differentiation: What makes a business viable and even unique?

The term "moat," commonly attributed to legendary investor Warren Buffett, represents the idea of a business that possesses a sustainable competitive advantage that allows it to generate a profit (often a large one) for the foreseeable future. Like the moats that surrounded medieval fortresses to prevent attack, an economic moat acts to ward off competitors and protect the business. Moats can be established by, for example, economies of scale, network effects, intellectual property, brand identity, or legal exclusivity.

Questions: From your perspective as a consumer, how would you summarize the models of the businesses referenced above? How do you think they make money?

III. Financial Statement Literacy

Corporate *finance* involves the management of assets, liabilities, revenues, and debts for a business. A full understanding of accounting and financial statements is also far beyond the scope of this book, but you should understand that accounting is essentially financial scorekeeping and financial statements are the scorecards.

Financial statements are key indicators of the overall health and sustainability of a business. For public companies, their release can swing stock prices—and lawyers who understand the pressures client businesses are under to "make their numbers" and how their legal issues affect those results are valuable partners.

Every business follows generally accepted accounting principles (GAAP), which at least theoretically allows for analogous comparison and analysis between businesses. Accounting can show, or at least approximate, such things as the financial status of a business; what assets a business has; what debts and liabilities a business has; how much cash a business generates; and, at the end of the day, how much money a business makes.

---

[1]The U.S. Small Business Administration provides clear and accessible guidance and examples of business plans as part of its Business Guide module. *See* U.S. Small Business Administration, *Write Your Business Plan*, https://www.sba.gov/business-guide/plan-your-business/write-your-business-plan. Many bar associations provide law firm–related business plan advice and templates as well. *See, e.g.,* New York City Bar Association, *Writing a Business Plan for Law Firm—Law Firm Business Plan Sample*, https://www.nycbar.org/member-and-career-services/small-law-firm-overview/small-firm-resources/writing-a-business-plan-for-law-firm.

There are four basic financial statements that provide the foundation for understanding a business:

- Balance Sheet or Statement of Financial Position
- Income Statement or Profit and Loss Statement (P&L)
- Statement of Cash Flows
- Statement of Equity

These statements are, for public companies, required to be audited by third parties and to be periodically filed with the Securities and Exchange Commission (SEC). They will also appear as part of annual reports that public companies must (and private ones may) provide to shareholders to describe their operations and financial conditions.[2] These filings and reports also contain extensive explanatory materials, notes, discussion, and analysis that serve to provide context for the raw numbers (and offer a way to gain insight into your client's business).

A. Key Terminology

Before exploring financial statements further, you should first familiarize yourself with some key terminology:

- **Accounts Payable (A/P):** Amounts owed by the entity to pay off short-term debts to creditors.
- **Accounts Receivable (A/R):** The converse of A/P—customer accounts, bills, or invoices that are owed to the entity but have yet to be paid.
- **Assets:** Tangible and intangible items of value owned by the entity.
- **Cash Flow:** The net amount of cash transferred in and out of the entity, including inflows a company receives from its ongoing operations and external investment sources, as well as all cash outflows that pay for business activities and investments during a given period.
- **Expenses:** The costs of running the business. Operating expenses (OPEX) are incurred through normal business operations, such as rent, equipment, inventory costs, marketing, payroll, insurance, and research and development (R&D). Capital expenses (CAPEX) include costs related to acquiring, maintaining, or upgrading capital assets such as property, plants, buildings, technology, or equipment.
- **Income:** The overall amount of money taken in by a business.
- **Liabilities:** Financial debts or other obligations undertaken to run the business.
- **Loss:** When expenses are greater than revenue, this results in a loss.
- **Net Income:** Profit after the payment of all expenses, including taxes.
- **Profit:** When revenue exceeds expenses, this results in a profit. Profits can be distributed to the business owners/shareholders as dividends or reinvested back into the business to fund future growth.
- **Retained Earnings:** Profits not paid out as dividends but retained by the company to be reinvested in its core business, or to pay debt.

---

[2]Examples of corporate SEC filings and annual reports are readily available from investor relations and other publicly available websites.

- **Revenue:** Income gained from conducting business activities. Often called sales.
- **Shareholder Equity:** The owners' economic interest in the business—the residual value of a firm's earnings and assets after the payment of all debts and liabilities.

B. Balance Sheet (or Statement of Financial Position)

This financial statement summarizes a business's assets, liabilities, and remaining equity at a point in time and is based on a fundamental formula (ALE):

Assets = Liabilities + Equity

These three balance sheet segments give owners and investors an idea as to what the company owns and owes, as well as the amount invested by shareholders. The balance sheet gets its name from the fact that the two sides of the equation above—assets on the one side and liabilities plus equity on the other—must balance out. That is, a company must pay for all the things it owns (assets) by either borrowing money (taking on liabilities) or taking it from investors (issuing shareholders' equity).

By comparing current balance sheet totals with historical data, one can identify trends and read the trajectory of a business's growth and expenditures. Balance sheets can indicate whether an entity is structurally sound and may be employed to compare debt to equity and reveal borrowing levels. Because a balance sheet represents only a snapshot in time, however, it is most useful when considered as part of a suite of financial statements.

The basic components of a balance sheet are described below:

1. Assets

Assets, what the business owns, are generally divided by "time" (current versus long term) and "type" (tangible versus intangible).

a. Current Assets

Current assets are generally those that can be reasonably deemed to be convertible into cash within a year (or within a business's normal operating cycle). They are important to businesses because they can be used to fund day-to-day operations and pay ongoing expenses. They are important to lenders and investors because they provide information about how "liquid" a company may be and, should the business experience a downturn, how the business might weather hard times, or what might ultimately be left in the event of business failure or bankruptcy. Depending on the nature of the business, current assets can range from barrels of crude oil, to baked goods, to foreign currency.

On a balance sheet, current assets will normally be displayed in order of liquidity, or the ease with which they can be turned into cash. There are many potential asset classifications that may be used on a balance sheet. For our purposes here, we will focus on a select, but illustrative, few:

Cash and Cash Equivalents (CCE): Cash is money in the form of currency and "demand" deposit accounts such as checking and savings. Cash equivalents are investments that can readily be converted into cash (usually in less than 90 days) and should not be subject to price fluctuations, for example, certificates of deposit and some preferred shares of equity (depending on the maturity date). Marketable securities are financial instruments that are very liquid and can quickly be converted into cash at a reasonable price.

Stocks and Bonds (Investments): A **stock** is a type of security that signifies ownership in a corporation. There are two main types of stock: common and preferred. Common stock usually entitles the owner to vote at shareholders' meetings and to receive dividends, while preferred stock generally does not have voting rights, but has a higher (often fixed) claim on assets and earnings than common stock shares. A **bond** is a debt investment in which an investor loans money to an entity (typically corporate or governmental), which borrows the funds for a defined period at a variable or fixed interest rate. Bonds are used by companies, municipalities, states, and sovereign governments to raise money and finance a variety of projects and activities. When companies or other entities need to raise money to finance new projects, maintain ongoing operations, or refinance other existing debts, they may issue bonds directly to investors instead of obtaining loans from a bank. The indebted entity (issuer) issues a bond that contractually states the interest rate (coupon) that will be paid and the time at which the loaned funds (bond principal) must be returned (maturity date).

Accounts Receivable: As noted above, accounts receivable are customer accounts, bills, or invoices that are owed to the entity but have yet to be paid. Because some accounts will never be paid in full, there is often an "allowance for doubtful accounts," which is subtracted from accounts receivable based on a good faith estimate of the likelihood of collection.

Inventory is included as a current asset, but may be reported, classified, and valued in various ways. For example, a manufacturer of blue jeans might classify its stock of cotton as "raw materials"; dyed but unfinished jeans as "work in progress" (WIP for short); and ready-to-sell, finished clothing as "finished goods." Depending on the market, the raw cotton and finished goods would likely be more liquid (readily saleable to third parties) than WIP.

b. Long-Term or "Fixed" Assets

Assets that cannot feasibly be turned into cash in the space of a year, or a business's operating cycle, are classified as **long-term assets**. These also depend on the nature of the business, but generally include land, facilities, equipment, copyrights, and other illiquid investments.

Property, Plant & Equipment (PP&E): PP&E represents tangible, fixed assets that cannot be easily liquidated: buildings, vehicles, infrastructure, etc. The value of PP&E can range from very low to extremely high compared to total assets.

Goodwill: The value of a company's brand name, solid customer base, good customer relations, good employee relations, and any patents or proprietary technology represent goodwill. Goodwill is considered an intangible asset because it is not a physical asset like buildings or equipment. The value of goodwill typically arises in an acquisition when one company is purchased by another company. The amount the acquiring company pays for the target company over the target's book value usually accounts for the value of the target's goodwill.

Intangible assets are those that are non-physical, but identifiable. Think of a company's proprietary computer software, copyrights, patents, and domain names. These aren't things that one can touch, exactly, but it is possible to estimate their value to the enterprise.

Fixed assets are typically reported net of depreciation. Depreciation and amortization reflect the common idea of gradual loss of value in an asset over time. Depreciation captures the decline in the value of tangible assets and applies to expenses incurred for the purchase of assets with useful lives greater than one year. Amortization is very similar to depreciation in theory, but it applies to intangible assets such as patents, trademarks, goodwill, and licenses rather than physical property and equipment. Tax treatment and classification of such assets may vary widely depending on accounting practices and IRS rules.

Thus, a small business might report its assets as follows:

ASSETS			
		FY-2019	FY-2020
Asset Type	Description	Prior Year	Current Year
Current Assets	Cash and cash equivalents	500	600
Current Assets	Investments	1,000	1,200
Current Assets	Inventories	750	700
Current Assets	Accounts receivable (net of doubtful accounts)	2,500	2,000
Fixed Assets	Property and equipment	8,000	8,000
Fixed Assets	Goodwill	500	500
Fixed Assets	Other intangibles	0	300
Fixed Assets	Less accumulated depreciation (negative value)	(100)	(85)
Total Assets		**13,150**	**13,215**

2. Liabilities

After assets, a balance sheet accounts for the liabilities of the business. Liabilities are also segregated by time, into current and long term.

a. Current Liabilities

Short-term debt refers to any financial obligation that is due either within a 12-month period or within the current fiscal year. There may also be a portion of long-term debt included in this account. This portion pertains to payments that must be made on any long-term debt throughout the year.

Accounts payable is an accounting entry that represents an entity's obligation to pay off a short-term debt to its creditors. On many balance sheets, the accounts payable entry appears under the heading "current liabilities."

Payroll is the sum of all compensation a business must pay to its employees for a set period or on a given date. It is usually managed by the accounting department of a business; small-business payrolls may be handled directly by the owner or an associate. Payroll can also refer to the list of employees of a business and the amount of compensation due to each of them. It is a major expense for many businesses.

Income tax payable is a type of account in the current liabilities section of a company's balance sheet comprised of taxes that must be paid to the government within one year. Income tax payable is calculated according to the prevailing tax law in the company's home country. The taxes are calculated on the company's net income according to its corporate tax rate; if a company is due to receive a tax benefit from its revenue agency, the amount of income tax payable will decrease.

b. Long-Term Liabilities

Long-term debt consists of loans and financial obligations lasting over one year. Long-term debt for a company would include any financing or leasing obligations that are to come due in a greater than 12-month period.

A **capital lease** is a contract entitling a renter to a temporary use of an asset, and such a lease has economic characteristics of asset ownership for accounting purposes. The capital lease requires a renter to add assets and liabilities associated with the lease if the rental contract meets specific requirements. In substance, a capital lease is considered a purchase of an asset, while an operating lease is handled as a true lease under generally accepted accounting principles (GAAP). Unlike operating leases, which do not affect a company's balance sheet, capital leases can have a profound effect on companies' financial statements.

Our same small business might report liabilities like this:

LIABILITIES			
		FY-2019	FY-2020
Liability Type	Description	Prior Year	Current Year
Current Liabilities	Accounts payable	400	350
Current Liabilities	Short-term debts	600	700
Current Liabilities	Payroll and salaries	500	550
Current Liabilities	Income taxes payable	100	100
Long-term Liabilities	Long-term debt	1,000	850
Long-term Liabilities	Capital lease	400	400
Total Liabilities		**3,000**	**2,950**

3. Equity

Equity is the remaining amount of assets available after all liabilities have been paid. It is commonly calculated as a business's total assets less its total liabilities. It represents the owners' economic interest in the business and is commonly divided among a number of shareholders.

When it all comes together, our small business's simplified balance sheet might look like this:

BALANCE SHEET		
	FY-2019	FY-2020
Asset Type	Prior Year	Current Year
Current Assets	4,750	4,500
Fixed Assets	8,400	8,715
Current Liabilities	1,600	1,700
Long-term Liabilities	1,400	1,250
Total Assets	13,150	13,215
Total Liabilities	3,000	2,950
Equity	10,150	10,265

For a more complicated example, a Fortune 500 company's balance sheet might look like this:

THE COCA-COLA COMPANY AND SUBSIDIARIES
CONSOLIDATED BALANCE SHEETS
(In millions except par value)

December 31,	2019	2018
ASSETS		
Current Assets		
Cash and cash equivalents	$ 6,480	$ 9,077
Short-term investments	1,467	2,025
Total Cash, Cash Equivalents and Short-Term Investments	7,947	11,102
Marketable securities	3,228	5,013
Trade accounts receivable, less allowances of $524 and $501, respectively	3,971	3,685
Inventories	3,379	3,071
Prepaid expenses and other assets	1,886	2,059
Total Current Assets	20,411	24,930
Equity method investments	19,025	19,412

(*continued*)

December 31,	2019	2018
Other investments	854	867
Other assets	6,075	4,148
Deferred income tax assets	2,412	2,674
Property, plant and equipment—net	10,838	9,598
Trademarks with indefinite lives	9,266	6,682
Bottlers' franchise rights with indefinite lives	109	51
Goodwill	16,764	14,109
Other intangible assets	627	745
Total Assets	$ 86,381	$ 83,216
LIABILITIES AND EQUITY		
Current Liabilities		
Accounts payable and accrued expenses	$ 11,312	$ 9,533
Loans and notes payable	10,994	13,835
Current maturities of long-term debt	4,253	5,003
Accrued income taxes	414	411
Total Current Liabilities	26,973	28,782
Long-term debt	27,516	25,376
Other liabilities	8,510	7,646
Deferred income tax liabilities	2,284	2,354
The Coca-Cola Company Shareowners' Equity		
Common stock, $0.25 par value; authorized—11,200 shares; issued—7,040 shares	1,760	1,760
Capital surplus	17,154	16,520
Reinvested earnings	65,855	63,234
Accumulated other comprehensive income (loss)	(13,544)	(12,814)
Treasury stock, at cost—2,760 and 2,772 shares, respectively	(52,244)	(51,719)
Equity Attributable to Shareowners of The Coca-Cola Company	18,981	16,981
Equity attributable to noncontrolling interests	2,117	2,077
Total Equity	21,098	19,058
Total Liabilities and Equity	$ 86,381	$ 83,216

C. Income Statement (or Profit and Loss)

The **income statement** reports a company's financial performance over a specific accounting period. Financial performance is assessed by giving a summary of how the business incurs its revenues and expenses through both operating and non-operating activities. It also shows the net profit or loss incurred over a specific accounting period, resulting in the business's "bottom line." Unlike the balance sheet, which covers one moment in time, the income statement provides performance information about a time period. It begins with sales and works down to net income and earnings per share (EPS).

While the balance sheet shows fundamental soundness, the income statement may be of greater interest (particularly to investors) because it shows recent performance and, when viewed over a series of years, can aid as a predictive tool for the future. It tells the story of what happened to the company over a certain period of time.

Revenue (what the company sold to customers)

–

Expenses (what it cost to run the company)

=

Net Income (what is left over for the owners)

R – E = NI

The income statement is divided into two parts: **operating** and **non-operating**.

The **operating** part of the income statement discloses information about revenues and expenses that are a direct result of regular business operations. For example, if a business creates sports equipment, it should make money through the sale and/or production of sports equipment.

The **non-operating** part discloses revenue and expense information about activities that are not directly tied to a company's regular operations. Continuing with the same example, if the sports company sells real estate and investment securities, the gain from the sale is listed in the non-operating items section.

1. Revenue, Expenses, and Income

Revenue is the amount of money that a company receives during a specific period, including discounts and deductions for returned merchandise. It is the "top line" or "gross income" figure from which costs are subtracted to determine net income. Revenue is known as the **top line** because it is displayed first on a company's income statement. Expenses are then deducted from revenue in order to obtain net income, or profit—the **bottom line**.

Cost of sales (or cost of revenue or cost of goods sold (COGS)) is the cost of creating the products that a company sells; therefore, the only costs included in the measure are those that are directly tied to the production of the products, such as the cost of the materials used in creating the product along with the direct labor costs used to produce the product. It excludes indirect expenses such as distribution costs and sales force costs. The exact costs included in the COGS calculation will differ from one type of business to another.

Selling, general, and administrative costs are the costs that occur during the daily operations of a company and are not directly related to the manufacturing of the product. These are the expenses related to the selling, promoting, and delivering of a product as well as managing the company and the costs a company must incur to open the doors each day. Often these expenses are reported in subcategories, such as sales and marketing, R&D, and general and administrative.

"Non-operating" income and expenses are derived from activities not related to core operations, for example, dividend income, profits and losses from investments, gains or losses incurred due to foreign exchange, and asset write-downs.

Next, if a company paid interest on borrowings, it is recorded in the income statement as an **interest expense**. **Taxes** are usually the last expense line item listed on the income statement.

This results in **net income** (or loss), which is the residual income after the deduction of all expenses from revenue.

The stacked formula looks like this:

Sales/Revenue or the Top Line
(COGS (direct costs))
= Gross Profit
(SG&A, R&D, Marketing (indirect costs))
= Operating Income
(Interest Expense)
= Income Before Taxes
(Tax Expense)
= Net Income or the Bottom Line

2. Earnings Per Share (EPS)

EPS is a measurement derived from net income divided by the number of shares outstanding; however, both the numerator and denominator can change depending on how you define "earnings" and "shares outstanding." Basic (aka "primary") EPS is calculated using the number of shares that have been issued and held by investors. These are the shares that are currently in the market and can be traded. Diluted EPS is a more complex calculation that determines how many shares would be outstanding if all exercisable warrants, options, etc., were converted into shares at a point in time. Diluted EPS results in a more conservative number than basic EPS.

A Fortune 500 company's income statement might look like this:

THE COCA-COLA COMPANY AND SUBSIDIARIES
CONSOLIDATED STATEMENTS OF INCOME
(In millions except per share data)

Year Ended December 31,	2019	2018	2017
Net Operating Revenues	$ 37,266	$ 34,300	$ 36,212
Cost of goods sold	14,619	13,067	13,721
Gross Profit	22,647	21,233	22,491
Selling, general and administrative expenses	12,103	11,002	12,834

(*continued*)

Year Ended December 31,	2019	2018	2017
Other operating charges	458	1,079	1,902
Operating Income	**10,086**	**9,152**	**7,755**
Interest income	563	689	679
Interest expense	946	950	853
Equity income (loss)—net	**1,049**	1,008	1,072
Other income (loss)—net	34	(1,674)	(1,763)
Income Before Income Taxes	**10,786**	**8,225**	**6,890**
Income taxes	1,801	1,749	5,607
Consolidated Net Income	**8,985**	**6,476**	**1,283**
Less: Net income (loss) attributable to noncontrolling interests	65	42	35
Net Income Attributable to Shareowners of The Coca-Cola Company	$ **8,920**	$ **6,434**	$ **1,248**
Basic Net Income Per Share	$ **2.09**	$ 1.51	$ 0.29
Diluted Net Income Per Share	$ **2.07**	$ 1.50	$ 0.29
Average Shares Outstanding—Basic	4,276	4,259	4,272
Effect of dilutive securities	38	40	52
Average Shares Outstanding—Diluted	4,314	4,299	4,324

3. Earnings Before Interest, Taxes, Depreciation, and Amortization (EBITDA)

One concept derived from the income statement is earnings before interest, taxes, depreciation, and amortization (EBITDA), which is a non-GAPP metric that measures operating results before costs of capital structure and taxes. EBITDA thus tries to eliminate the effects of financing and accounting decisions. It is a common valuation benchmark used as a proxy for the earning potential of a business. It is often utilized in connection with takeovers, mergers and acquisitions, partnership buyouts, and other transactions requiring valuation.

D. Statement of Cash Flows

The statement of cash flows provides aggregate data regarding all cash inflows a company receives from its ongoing operations and external investment sources, as well as all cash outflows that pay for business activities and investments during a given period. It is a cousin to the income statement and is separated by categories of business activity:

1. Activities

Operating activities are the company's primary business activities, such as the production and delivery of goods and services. Examples of operating cash flows are cash collected from customers, salaries, insurance, and tax payments.

Investing activities relate to asset acquisition or disposal. Cash out for investments made, and cash in for sale of investments.

Financing activities relate to the receipt and repayment of funds provided by creditors and investors. This could be the issuance of debt or securities, repayment of debt, or distribution of dividends. Cash in from capital raised, and cash out for repayment of debt, repurchase of stock, or payment of dividends.

A Fortune 500 company's cash flow statement might look like this:

THE COCA-COLA COMPANY AND SUBSIDIARIES
CONSOLIDATED STATEMENTS OF CASH FLOWS
(In millions)

Year Ended December 31,	2019	2018	2017
Operating Activities			
Consolidated net income	$ 8,985	$ 6,476	$ 1,283
Depreciation and amortization	1,365	1,086	1,260
Stock-based compensation expense	201	225	219
Deferred income taxes	(280)	(413)	(1,252)
Equity (income) loss—net of dividends	(421)	(457)	(628)
Foreign currency adjustments	91	(50)	292
Significant (gains) losses—net	(467)	743	1,459
Other operating charges	127	558	1,218
Other items	504	699	(252)
Net change in operating assets and liabilities	366	(1,240)	3,442
Net Cash Provided by Operating Activities	10,471	7,627	7,041
Investing Activities			
Purchases of investments	(4,704)	(7,789)	(17,296)
Proceeds from disposals of investments	6,973	14,977	16,694
Acquisitions of businesses, equity method investments and nonmarketable securities	(5,542)	(1,263)	(3,809)
Proceeds from disposals of businesses, equity method investments and nonmarketable securities	429	1,362	3,821

(*continued*)

Year Ended December 31,	2019	2018	2017
Purchases of property, plant and equipment	(2,054)	(1,548)	(1,750)
Proceeds from disposals of property, plant and equipment	978	248	108
Other investing activities	(56)	(60)	(80)
Net Cash Provided by (Used in) Investing Activities	(3,976)	5,927	(2,312)
Financing Activities			
Issuances of debt	23,009	27,605	29,926
Payments of debt	(24,850)	(30,600)	(28,871)
Issuances of stock	1,012	1,476	1,595
Purchases of stock for treasury	(1,103)	(1,912)	(3,682)
Dividends	(6,845)	(6,644)	(6,320)
Other financing activities	(227)	(272)	(95)
Net Cash Provided by (Used in) Financing Activities	(9,004)	(10,347)	(7,447)
Effect of Exchange Rate Changes on Cash, Cash Equivalents, Restricted Cash and Restricted Cash Equivalents	(72)	(262)	241
Cash, Cash Equivalents, Restricted Cash and Restricted Cash Equivalents			
Net increase (decrease) in cash, cash equivalents, restricted cash and restricted cash equivalents during the year	(2,581)	2,945	(2,477)
Cash, cash equivalents, restricted cash and restricted cash equivalents at beginning of year	9,318	6,373	8,850
Cash, Cash Equivalents, Restricted Cash and Restricted Cash Equivalents at End of Year	6,737	9,318	6,373
Less: Restricted cash and restricted cash equivalents at end of year	257	241	271
Cash and Cash Equivalents at End of Year	$ 6,480	$ 9,077	$ 6,102

2. Free Cash Flow

A commonly used non-GAAP term as applied to an income statement is "free cash flow" (FCF), which is an additional measure of a company's financial performance, typically calculated as operating cash flow minus capital expenditures. FCF represents the cash that a company can generate after spending the money required to maintain or expand its asset base.

E. Statement of Equity

The statement of equity is used to show how the owner's equity has changed in a given period of time. The company profits may be distributed to shareholders in the form of dividends or retained for reinvestment in the business. For example, the statement of equity might reflect sold or repurchased stock or membership interests. It might also include dividend payments or other distributions. A Fortune 500 company's statement of equity might look like this:

THE COCA-COLA COMPANY AND SUBSIDIARIES
CONSOLIDATED STATEMENTS OF SHAREOWNERS' EQUITY
(In millions except per share data)

Year Ended December 31,	2019	2018	2017
Equity Attributable to Shareowners of The Coca-Cola Company			
Number of Common Shares Outstanding			
Balance at beginning of year	**4,268**	4,259	4,288
Treasury stock issued to employees related to stock-based compensation plans	**33**	48	53
Purchases of stock for treasury	**(21)**	(39)	(82)
Balance at end of year	**4,280**	4,268	4,259
Common Stock	$ **1,760**	$ 1,760	$ 1,760
Capital Surplus			
Balance at beginning of year	**16,520**	15,864	14,993
Stock issued to employees related to stock-based compensation plans	**433**	467	655
Stock-based compensation expense	**201**	225	219
Other activities	**—**	(36)	(3)
Balance at end of year	**17,154**	16,520	15,864
Reinvested Earnings			
Balance at beginning of year	**63,234**	60,430	65,502

(*continued*)

Year Ended December 31,	2019	2018	2017
Adoption of accounting standards	546	3,014	—
Net income attributable to shareowners of The Coca-Cola Company	8,920	6,434	1,248
Dividends (per share—$1.60, $1.56 and $1.48 in 2019, 2018 and 2017, respectively)	(6,845)	(6,644)	(6,320)
Balance at end of year	65,855	63,234	60,430
Accumulated Other Comprehensive Income (Loss)			
Balance at beginning of year	(12,814)	(10,305)	(11,205)
Adoption of accounting standards[1]	(564)	(409)	—
Net other comprehensive income (loss)	(166)	(2,100)	900
Balance at end of year	(13,544)	(12,814)	(10,305)
Treasury Stock			
Balance at beginning of year	(51,719)	(50,677)	(47,988)
Treasury stock issued to employees related to stock-based compensation plans	501	704	909
Purchases of stock for treasury	(1,026)	(1,746)	(3,598)
Balance at end of year	(52,244)	(51,719)	(50,677)
Total Equity Attributable to Shareowners of The Coca-Cola Company	$ 18,981	$ 16,981	$ 17,072
Equity Attributable to Noncontrolling Interests			
Balance at beginning of year	$ 2,077	$ 1,905	$ 158
Net income attributable to noncontrolling interests	65	42	35
Net foreign currency translation adjustments	45	53	38
Dividends paid to noncontrolling interests	(48)	(31)	(15)
Acquisition of interests held by noncontrolling owners	(84)	—	—
Contributions by noncontrolling interests	3	—	—

(*continued*)

Year Ended December 31,	2019	2018	2017
Business combinations	59	101	1,805
Deconsolidation of certain entities	—	—	(157)
Other activities	—	7	41
Total Equity Attributable to Noncontrolling Interests	$ 2,117	$ 2,077	$ 1,905

IV. Financial Statements for Law Firms

So far, we have considered this material from a general business viewpoint, as this is the way your clients will see and use financial statements. Like other businesses, of course, law firms also utilize financial statements for financial management, and technology has made firm financial analysis easier and more accessible than ever.[3] As we cover the particulars of law firm businesses in later chapters, bear in mind that a law firm's financial statements may look different in a number of respects. Particularly, law firm financials are not geared for the investing public and are not subject to the same auditing and disclosure requirements that their clients' financials may be. This allows them to be more specifically tailored to the firm's operations and business concerns. Nevertheless, the internal purposes of the financial statements remain largely the same.

For example, in a law firm setting, a balance sheet could provide an accurate snapshot of the partners' equity positions, bank balances, property, and vendor and other debts. An income statement could show firm management what client revenue has been earned or received and what expenses have been accrued or paid. A law firm's cash flow statement can provide a firm with a more accurate picture of its cash position than either a balance sheet or income statement can provide. By allowing management to understand where its cash is going, and coming from, operations can be smoothed out, which is particularly true for firms that work on a contingency fee basis or advance substantial client expenses such as expert witness fees. A statement of equity also could be used to readily show partner profits and distributions over time.

V. Conclusion

Congratulations! You've made it deeper into this wilderness than many lawyers do in a lifetime. Finance professionals will often handle the details, but with this background you are better equipped to explore what a private practice law firm's business looks like.

---

[3]Chapter 10 will discuss some of the technological aspects of financial software and systems dedicated to law practices.

PART III

PRIVATE PRACTICE

Introduction

In Part III we will explore the contours and environments of private practice law firms. From sole practitioners to global mega-firms and everywhere in between, you need good people, a business model, revenues, and, hopefully, a profit.

Private practice in the United States continues to undergo constant and significant shifts—law firms have been forced by circumstance to make radical changes throughout their business models, services, staffing, delivery methods, overhead, client mix—and the list goes on. Yet the core combination of legal skills, management skills, and client-relation skills remains at the heart of every successful law practice. As we study what have historically been the operating forms and parameters that have guided private practice for decades, also be mindful of opportunities for evolution and the future. We will explore that dynamic in later chapters.

CHAPTER 4

LAW FIRMS

A *law firm* is, to give a definition, simply one or more lawyers who share some or all of the following: space, clients, expenses, and revenues. Law firms are, however, much more—living entities with cultures of their own. Historically, firms began when sole practitioners joined together for efficiency and camaraderie. Today, private firms run the gamut from small affiliations to global conglomerates.

Figuring out what private practice environment makes sense for you can be a mysterious and challenging process. We will try to shed some light on the various environments and hope to give you some good information against which to make decisions. Know, too, that law practice is an ever-evolving process—which is one of the great advantages and joys of the profession. Law practice can and will mean and involve many different things to you throughout your life.

I. Structures

A. Going Solo

According to the 2020 ABA Profile of the Legal Profession report,[1] few new law graduates—less than 1 percent—start solo practices immediately upon graduation, while nearly half begin their careers in law firms. But we'll start with the most basic proposition: Should you start your own firm (either alone or with a colleague)? Some of the considerations and questions you should ask yourself are discussed next.

How self-sufficient are you? If you are someone who requires input and prodding from others to overcome work inertia, working for yourself might be a struggle. Managing the *law* side of a practice is challenging enough on its own. Balancing that with the *business* side, particularly in a solo environment where the buck truly stops with you, requires a high level of self-awareness and constant attention.

---

[1]American Bar Association, *ABA Profile of the Profession 2020*, https://www.americanbar.org/content/dam/aba/administrative/news/2020/07/potlp2020.pdf.

What is your risk tolerance, and do you have enough money saved to survive for 6 to 12 months without significant, stable cash flow? The good news in a solo practice is that you are your own boss. The bad news is the same—you are your own boss. You alone are responsible for the success or failure of your business. You will also not be drawing a steady paycheck or reliable salary; there may be long stretches where work or collections are slow and you will not have money coming in. Managing expenses is a critical element of success.

Are you disciplined? It takes constant and repeated effort to build and maintain a solo practice. You will have to set schedules and stick to them. With no one chaining you to your desk, there is nothing keeping you from calling it a day at 2 p.m. on Friday afternoon. You simply must keep your practice in focus and free from distraction. Much like the challenge of catching up in a 1L torts class where you've fallen behind, "catching up" on case files is very hard to do.

If you have a significant other, are they on board and supportive? Building a solo practice can be time-consuming and distracting.

Do you have a business plan? You must have a path to financial viability. What area of the law are you competent in? How are you going to get clients? What does the competition look like?

For those of you who are contemplating starting your own practices, pay particular attention to Chapters 5, 7, and 10. There are many detailed resources and how-to guides available, and most state bar associations and the ABA maintain excellent materials dedicated to starting a solo practice.[2] And, of course, seek advice from someone with an established solo practice in your market. Sole practitioners are sometimes thought of as "lone wolves," yet they are often among the most outgoing and helpful lawyers in the profession.

Many sole practitioners are very successful and happy with their practice. Many wouldn't have it any other way. But it is not for everyone.

B. Partnership Forms

Law businesses typically operate as "firms" of various types. As you may know from your other courses, there are various legal forms that a business can take, from sole proprietorships to corporations. Most law firms are partnerships of some sort, but that is an oversimplification.

At a high level, partnership-model business forms break down into "true" partnerships or limiting entities, the choice of which is largely driven by the number of lawyers, tax considerations, and complexity tolerance. While they are creatures of state law, the classic law firm forms include the following:

1. Sole Proprietorship
2. General Partnership
3. Limited Liability Partnership (LLP)
4. Professional Service Corporation: Professional Association (PA) or Professional Corporation (PC)
5. Professional Limited Liability Company (PLLC)

---

[2] *See, e.g.,* Washington State Bar Association, *Start Your Practice,* https://www.wsba.org/for-legal-professionals/go-solo.

The primary factors that distinguish these forms are (1) ownership structure; (2) tax treatment; and (3) personal liability of owners for business debts.

1. Sole Proprietorship

A sole proprietorship exists when there is a one lawyer who owns the business and its assets. That owner may have employees, but the firm has no legal identity apart from the owner-lawyer. This is an easy form to administer and carries no separate income tax—the profits and losses of the firm are passed through to the owner-lawyer and taxed at the same rate as any other personal income. A big drawback of the sole proprietorship is that the owner-lawyer is personally liable for business debts and liabilities, and her assets are at risk to firm creditors.

2. General Partnership

A general partnership is the original form for lawyers working together, and is nothing more than an association of two or more owner-lawyers who come together to practice. A general partnership is a separate entity, but it is not completely separate from the owner-lawyers. Often, there will be a written partnership agreement, but that may not be a requirement under applicable state law. From a tax perspective, there is no partnership income tax, and profits and losses flow through to individual partners as with a sole proprietorship. The partnership may be liable for other taxes such as sales and property tax. A general partnership also shares a drawback with the sole proprietorship form: Partners are personally liable for all debts and obligations of the partnership, and this liability is joint and several. This means that not only are individual partners responsible for their own business debts and obligations, but they are responsible for those of their partners as well. Taking on liability for one's partners may be workable in small setting, but as firms grow, they want to limit the risks among the partners—hence the legal creation of the limited liability forms.

3. Limited Liability Partnership (LLP)

A limited liability partnership limits or eliminates personal liability of partners without affecting the tax treatment of the partnership. LLPs are usually simple to form: The owners file a declaration or statement stating that the partnership is a limited liability partnership and then include the letters "LLP' in the firm name. This is a very popular "best-of-all-worlds" choice among lawyers. Some states, however, do restrict the availability and scope of limited liability partnerships, such as by limiting liability only for negligence claims or restricting them to professional associations.

4. Professional Service Corporation: Professional Association (PA) or Professional Corporation (PC)

Some states also have dedicated professional business forms for licensed professionals such as lawyers. Often denominated professional corporations (PC) or professional associations (PA), these specialized forms allow professionals to take advantage of the corporate form. Typically, all shareholders in a PC or PA must be licensed to practice, and shareholders have limited liability for negligence of other shareholders or employees.

5. Professional Limited Liability Company (PLLC)

Another popular choice is the professional limited liability corporation, a hybrid business form that provides limited personal liability for the owners—like a corporation—and the pass-through tax advantages of a partnership.

Technically, the owner-lawyers in many of these limited liability forms are called "members" or "shareholders" rather than "partners," but long habit and custom leads to the practice of casually referring to the owner-lawyers in almost any law firm as "the partners."

Regardless of what legal form the firm may take, the decision to practice together is informed by several desires and variables, from the social aspects—lawyers may simply enjoy working with and around other people—to business needs. Partners may join to take advantage of practice and client synergies—a real estate and tax practice, for example.

When considering whom you want to partner with, you might think about not only complementary practices, but an alignment of work styles and goals. A success-driven, career-first person may not necessarily align well with a more laidback, this-is-my-job type person. Eventually, the partners' expectations may diverge to the point of unsustainability. You should also consider an alignment of abilities both in substantive areas of practice and in business generation.

Small differences can grow to large conflicts. It is almost always advisable to make sure to document the practice with a partnership or membership agreement.

C. An Example Consideration—Office Space

A key consideration is where to locate a firm. Often this decision is driven by clients and where the business is. Do you need to be in a large metropolitan area, with its attendant higher costs and greater levels of competition? Do you want to be in a smaller setting?

Do you need to be in the downtown or central business district of that city? Within walking distance to the courthouse? Office space is a large expense—what do your clients expect?

The pandemic experience of 2020 has normalized working remotely, but it remains to be seen whether many clients will consider that a stable, trustworthy practice environment going forward. Remember that most clients don't *want* to hire a lawyer in the way they may want to hire someone to remodel their kitchen. Rather, they *need* to hire a lawyer to respond to an urgent situation—their kitchen is on fire (so to speak). Certainly, for clients who are individuals or small businesses, whatever is driving them to hire a lawyer may be the most important thing in their lives or businesses at that time, and they need to feel like they have hired someone they can trust. For many people, office space is a projection of stability and success that may provide them comfort.

Firms must of course balance this against extravagance. Many a client has walked into an upscale law office and remarked (or at least thought), "I see where my money is going." Many lawyers, however, believe that the open projection of success is essential to business development, and "trophy" office space may be just what they require. A virtual office and meeting in a coffee shop may work for some practices and clients, but there will undoubtedly be limitations on growth with that model.

II. People

While there is no way to encapsulate what firms across the spectrum may look like, as a general matter a firm might be structured like this:

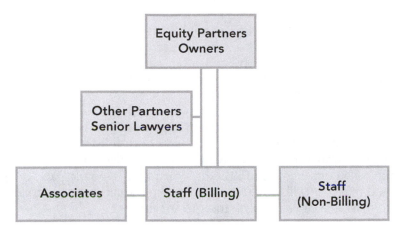

A. Equity Partners

The equity partners/owner-lawyers are the capital stakeholders and are ultimately responsible for the operation of the firm.

Becoming an equity partner often involves a capital contribution or buy-in, and new owners may be allocated shares or an ownership percentage. The number of shares can form the basis for a payout of profits (or allocation of losses in a down year). Equity partners have voting rights, which may be defined by the partnership agreement. In some firms, those voting rights are equal—"one partner, one vote"—and in others, they are apportioned unequally based on seniority or may parallel each partner's ownership percentage. There is no absolute one way this is done, and firms may agree to administer voting and other rights according to the terms of their partnership agreement. Equity partners, or subcommittees thereof, may also make decisions such as whether to elect or admit new partners, whether to terminate or de-equitize existing partners, whether to open or close an office, how to select management and staff committees, and how to set lawyer compensation and approve the firm's budget and expenses.

Some firms may have just one owner-lawyer. For example, a plaintiff's personal injury firm, even with a roster of 15 attorneys, may be the business of one key, face-of-the-firm lawyer.

The promotion of lawyers to partner status is one of the most important decisions a firm must make. It is critical for culture and business continuity to keep talent at the top, but the wrong decisions can carry consequences for years.

B. Other Partners—Senior Lawyers

Some firms have additional tiers of partners, sometimes referred to as "non-equity" or "income" partners. These are senior lawyers with the title of partner, but who are paid on a fixed basis rather than via a percentage of profits (the details of compensation models will be discussed in more depth in Chapter 6). Some firms give non-equity partners voting status, some do not.

Often, but not always, this is an interim status. A lawyer is promoted to partner to recognize her achievement and success within the firm, and the title is a reward of sorts. It can provide a sense of personal accomplishment for the lawyer as well as project the lawyer's elevated status to the firm's clients and the public. At some firms, this is a trial period—the lawyer is charged with demonstrating what she can do in terms of the business development skills required to take on an equity role. Conventional wisdom holds that many clients will not entrust important matters to a lawyer who is not a "partner" at their firm, and thus the title can provide a means for more junior, but experienced, lawyers to flex their client- and business-development muscles. The length of time one spends in a non-equity status varies widely by firm.

Firms will also use a non-equity role as a transition to equity to protect the lawyer from the vagaries of equity payouts and what can be dramatic shifts in income and tax liability. Many lawyers who have been fully focused on their substantive practice for many years and living on a fixed salary and bonus, with taxes and benefits taken out, may be surprised to learn that an equity partner's pay can fluctuate and that they will have to estimate and pay quarterly taxes to the IRS in addition to making a capital contribution to the firm.

C. Counsel

Counsel, whether or not modified by a prefix such as "Of," "Special," or "Senior," is a common law firm title, but it can mean many different things in different firm environments.

At a high level, counsel may include lawyers who typically are paid on a salary basis and who do not have a substantial or voting role in firm management. Counsel may be subject matter specialists, who are called upon for discrete projects, or they may be senior or semi-retired lawyers who no longer want to take on the duties and responsibilities of partnership. Counsel may be new lateral hires from government, business, or other firms who are in an interim status on the way to partnership. "Of counsel" is often used for an outside relationship of some sort; it can be more like a consultancy or sometimes describes an alternative work arrangement. Sometimes firms may need to hire a "counsel" lawyer who resides in a state where the firm does not do business or cannot have a resident partner due to multijurisdictional taxation issues.

In sum, the various uses of the titles "partner" and "counsel" make it difficult to predict exactly what a lawyer's role is within a given firm. You would thus be wise not to make assumptions about a lawyer's experience, qualifications, influence, or lifestyle based solely on what title they carry or where they may fall on the firm masthead.

D. Associates

The role of an associate is one that the overwhelming majority of students going into private practice will hold. As such, we will spend some time looking at this role in depth. It will provide useful background to consider the answers to two fundamental questions:

- Why might you want to be an associate at a law firm?
- Why might a law firm want to hire an associate?

The answers turn on both present and future needs.

	You	Firm
Present Needs	Income & Training	Efficiency & Leverage
Future Needs	Experience & Exposure	Growth & Diversification

Fresh out of law school, you likely lack the substantive knowledge and connections to simply launch a firm of your own. The time-tested way for young lawyers to gain experience is by working at a law firm and gaining the on-the-job training and work ethic commonly needed to succeed in the profession. Your most immediate need may also be to have an income to live on (and perhaps to pay off your student loans). An associate position fulfills both present needs nicely.

In the longer view, an associate position provides you with a body of work experience to build on and prepare you for your next professional step, be that through promotion within your first firm, a lateral move to another firm or practice area, a move to a business or corporate role, or even launching your own firm. Simply being associated with an established law firm will open doors and provide introductions that you would not otherwise have access to outside of that environment.

From the firm's perspective—and as we will discuss in more detail later in the book—it is fundamentally undesirable and inefficient to have its senior lawyers performing every task on a client's matter. Associates provide the means to accomplish many time-intensive tasks, such as due diligence in a merger, initial drafts of litigation briefs, and research, in a cost-effective manner. And, as there are only so many hours in the day, having associates allows law firms to take on, and staff, larger and more lucrative projects.

While actual experiences may vary, associates at a mid-size or larger law firm can expect to spend much of their time working in the following areas:

- Researching and analyzing complex legal issues and writing briefs for a supervising lawyer in the firm
- Analyzing and summarizing complicated legal documents, including contracts, and suggesting edits to those documents
- Performing discovery of various electronically stored data and hard copies of information in preparation for litigation
- Performing due diligence in legal matters concerning contracts, agreements, and mergers and acquisitions

At the more senior associate level, those areas might expand to include the following:

- Appearing in a court or before other judicial bodies
- Negotiating with outside parties on contractual issues and legal disputes, including settlement conferences
- Anticipating and mitigating potential legal problems, and developing strategies to avoid litigation and reduce potential areas of risk
- Managing junior associates

And, in the firm's long view, continuity and growth can only be achieved by bringing along new lawyers to ultimately succeed those who retire. Many firms pride themselves on having their own culture, and they promote from within to preserve and enhance it.

In a larger law firm environment, the typical promotion cycle—often called the "track"—for associates is seven to ten years of service before being considered for partnership (which, as noted above, can mean different things at different firms). Conventionally, the track is broken into segments along the following lines: Track years one to three are "junior" associates; years four to six are "mid-level" associates; and years seven and up are "senior" associates.

From an economic perspective, management may conceptualize associate roles and development like this:

Junior Associates: Junior associates provide a support function to partners on small and large matters. Entry-level associates may be given assignments that train new lawyers and lead to professional growth, but firms frequently do not realize a substantial profit from the work of junior associates. As such, successful junior associates are viewed as those who (a) do good work that generally does not need to be written off; (b) are good team players and fit within the firm culture; and (c) if interacting with clients, are liked by those clients. At the junior level, it can also be essential to have support from more senior associates, and, ideally, to develop a mentor relationship.

Mid-Level Associates: After a few years of practice, successful associates will have developed substantive knowledge that allows them to add value and to begin being profitable members of the firm, while continuing the positive practice traits from the early years. At many firms, business and client development will start at this stage.

Senior Associates: Senior associates are experienced and profitable to the firm. At this stage, they are being assessed as to whether they will make good partners. Becoming a partner may depend in large part on the senior associate's potential to bring in new clients to fuel the continued growth and health of the firm—something that is generally not taught by the firm and that associates should be looking for opportunities to do from their mid-level years on. Getting and keeping clients is highly competitive, and the most sought-after law firm lawyers are typically those who excel at getting and keeping high-value clients.

The "Cravath System"[3] arose from one of the first Wall Street firms and is described as "a self-sustaining meritocracy" or, more colloquially, "up or out." This process reflects the basic understanding that not all associates who start at a firm can, will, or even want to be partners at that firm. Firms, particularly larger ones, must constantly assess their needs regarding the number of available associates to have on board. As associates progress through their career paths, it is incumbent on both the associates and the partnership to proceed against this understanding and to not mislead or harm each other. An associate for whom the partnership has no long-term plans should be made aware of this and given an appropriate amount of time to transition into a role at another firm or

---

[3]See Cravath, Swaine & Moore LLP, *The Cravath System,* https://www.cravath.com/cravathsystem/.

business. Likewise, an associate with no intention of remaining should not take advantage of a firm's substantial investment in training and experience.

E. Other Lawyers

Firms may also employ other lawyers not categorically discussed above—there may be "off-track" associates, who are not on the standard route of up-or-out progression. There may be staff attorneys or "discovery lawyers" who are hired on a contract basis for a particular task or project. They may, of course, be full or part time. Typically, expectations and responsibilities are limited for contract lawyers, who may be placed on a project basis through an agency.

F. Non-Lawyers

1. Billing Staff

Most firms have employees who are not lawyers (or at least not practicing ones) but for whom the firm charges clients to work on their matters. These are billing staff, and may include, for example, paralegals, law clerks, various specialists, and patent agents. People in these roles typically track their time along with the lawyers in the firm, and their work is paid for by clients. Given the generally lower salary requirements as compared to lawyers, billing staff can provide a lucrative profit opportunity for the firm.

2. Non-Billing Staff

Finally, but no less importantly, firms employ non-lawyers in roles that support various functions at the firm but for whom the firm does not directly charge clients for their work on a matter. Rather, they are paid a salary and are part of the overhead incurred by the firm. These roles include administrators; support staff; filing personnel and librarians; event coordinators; and recruiting, accounting, marketing, business development, operations, and other personnel.

Here is some good advice for new associates: Do not think that because you earned a law degree you may treat firm staff with anything other than courtesy and professional respect. If you are rude or demeaning, you can pick up a poor reputation almost overnight, and you will lose the critical guidance and support that staff can provide a junior lawyer navigating the ins and outs of a new firm.

III. Ancillary Services

Our discussion of structures would not be complete without addressing the availability of non-legal services to law firms. These are often referred to as *ancillary services*, a growing and important area. Ancillary services provide necessary support to the primary activities or operations of an organization or system—in our examination, a law firm. But ethical rules provide tight restrictions in the law firm environment.

A. Restrictions on Ancillary Services

1. ABA Model Rule 5.7

Rule 5.7: Responsibilities Regarding Law-Related Services

Law Firms and Associations

(a) A lawyer shall be subject to the Rules of Professional Conduct with respect to the provision of law-related services, as defined in paragraph (b), if the law-related services are provided:

(1) by the lawyer in circumstances that are not distinct from the lawyer's provision of legal services to clients; or

(2) in other circumstances by an entity controlled by the lawyer individually or with others if the lawyer fails to take reasonable measures to assure that a person obtaining the law-related services knows that the services are not legal services and that the protections of the client-lawyer relationship do not exist.

(b) The term "law-related services" denotes services that might reasonably be performed in conjunction with and in substance are related to the provision of legal services, and that are not prohibited as unauthorized practice of law when provided by a nonlawyer.

Model Rule 5.7 applies to lawyers providing "law-related services" if the services are provided under similar circumstances to the provision of legal services — for example, a lawyer who is also a CPA would be subject to the Rules, as would a lawyer providing services through an entity controlled by a lawyer and others who does not properly inform clients of the nature of the services.

When law-related and legal services are provided in distinct circumstances, such as when a law firm owns a real estate brokerage, the lawyer must ensure that the client understands that brokers do not owe him the same ethical responsibilities as lawyers.

2. ABA Model Rule 5.4

Model Rule 5.4 further prohibits lawyers from sharing legal fees with a non-lawyer or from forming a partnership with a non-lawyer, if any of the activities of the partnership consist of the practice of law.

Rule 5.4: Professional Independence of a Lawyer

Law Firms and Associations

(a) A lawyer or law firm shall not share legal fees with a nonlawyer, except that:

(1) an agreement by a lawyer with the lawyer's firm, partner, or associate may provide for the payment of money, over a reasonable period of time after the lawyer's death, to the lawyer's estate or to one or more specified persons;

(2) a lawyer who purchases the practice of a deceased, disabled, or disappeared lawyer may, pursuant to the provisions of Rule 1.17, pay to the estate or other representative of that lawyer the agreed-upon purchase price;

(3) a lawyer or law firm may include nonlawyer employees in a compensation or retirement plan, even though the plan is based in whole or in part on a profit-sharing arrangement; and

(4) a lawyer may share court-awarded legal fees with a nonprofit organization that employed, retained or recommended employment of the lawyer in the matter.

(b) A lawyer shall not form a partnership with a nonlawyer if any of the activities of the partnership consist of the practice of law.

(c) A lawyer shall not permit a person who recommends, employs, or pays the lawyer to render legal services for another to direct or regulate the lawyer's professional judgment in rendering such legal services.

(d) A lawyer shall not practice with or in the form of a professional corporation or association authorized to practice law for a profit, if:

(1) a nonlawyer owns any interest therein, except that a fiduciary representative of the estate of a lawyer may hold the stock or interest of the lawyer for a reasonable time during administration;

(2) a nonlawyer is a corporate director or officer thereof or occupies the position of similar responsibility in any form of association other than a corporation; or

(3) a nonlawyer has the right to direct or control the professional judgment of a lawyer.

Thus, in most of the United States,[4] a lawyer and a non-lawyer such as an accountant cannot form a partnership to advise clients and cannot share profits and losses if any activities of the partnership consist of the practice of law. The accountant cannot have an ownership stake in the law firm, but the law firm can have an ownership stake in the ancillary business. Moreover, the lawyer cannot pay the non-lawyer a percentage of legal fees for a matter or a portion of a contingent case recovery.

B. Examples of Ancillary Services

Under a law-related or ancillary business model, a law firm operates an ancillary business providing professional services to clients.[5] The firm and its lawyers must make sure that clients understand that the ancillary business is separate and distinct from the firm and does not offer legal services. There may be some sharing of fees and management responsibilities in the ancillary business under the Rules of Professional Conduct, but perils still await the unwary in this area. Some of the challenges in implementing this business model might

---

[4]Arizona and Utah are on the forefront of what could become a trend by allowing non-lawyer ownership or investment in law firms under certain circumstances.

[5]The ancillary services model is also often considered a part of what is called "multidisciplinary practice," which is generally conceived to encompass an entity that includes lawyers and non-lawyers and has as one, but not all, of its purposes the delivery of legal services to a client other than the organization itself; or that holds itself out to the public as providing non-legal, as well as legal, services. This would include law firms joining with a professional firm—say in accounting—to provide services, with a direct or indirect sharing of profits. There is also a burgeoning industry of professional service firms operated by non-lawyers seeking to provide legal services to the public—while use of this form has grown in the United Kingdom, it remains under development in the United States.

include concerns about data security and risk of breaching client confidentiality; difficulties keeping operating standards in parallel with main firm operations; and an ever-present concern about the unauthorized practice of law by ancillary employees.

Yet, even with the restrictions and challenges that come with operating an ancillary services business, there remain several compelling reasons that firms pursue this model. Ancillary services can provide supplemental or complementary support to the legal side of the business. They can provide clients with access to specialized expertise in a centralized fashion while offering firms a means to provide alternative billing arrangements such as flat or reduced-fee services. A successful ancillary business can also act as a market differentiator and a branding advantage, and attract talent to the firm.

Some examples of law-firm ancillary services are described below:

1. Financial Planning and Accounting

Firms may employ CPAs, enrolled agents, and certified financial planners to assist clients with financial preparation and planning. This is a means to offer cost-effective consultation services for individuals and corporate clients.[6] The Big Four accounting firms have made great strides in incorporating the provision of legal services to their massive rosters of accounting clients. The United Kingdom and Australia have authorized "multidisciplinary practices," which let attorneys share profits without restriction with other professions. With the flexibility to offer discounted, fixed fees, these businesses have been able to win a substantial amount of corporate legal work related to services they already offer, such as employment, compliance, commercial contracting, and due diligence in mergers and acquisitions.

2. Consulting

A consulting model may facilitate access to specialized knowledge not readily or typically available within a firm, such as those situations where financial, tax, or industry-specific expertise is required.

3. E-Discovery and Document Review

Businesses providing e-discovery and document review can compete with stand-alone legal service providers and present an opportunity for firms to retain the former profit centers of work surrounding large due diligence and litigation projects. Providers in this area include legal staffing agencies, outsourced providers, and in-house centers.[7]

---

[6]*See, e.g.*, Duane Morris LLP, *Tax Accounting Group*, https://www.duanemorris.com/site/taxaccounting.html#tab_Services (Duane Morris LLP Tax Accounting Group rates are "typically 30% less than the largest CPA firms and compare favorably to mid-sized firms").

[7]*See, e.g.*, Womble Bond Dickinson, *BullDox*, https://www.womblebonddickinson.com/us/services/wbd-advance/bulldox.

4. In-House Professionals

Service providers in this area can provide field-specific subject matter expertise to attorneys. They can examine patient medical histories, spot issues including alternative causation theories and missing information in tort cases, and aid in preparing expert witnesses in litigation. For example, Robins Kaplan LLP employs a number of financial and economic consultants, investigators, medical professionals, and science advisors.[8]

Regardless of their nature, remember that use of ancillary services involves ethical responsibilities. There is always a risk that clients may misunderstand the lawyer's role and assume that the legal and ethical responsibilities in a normal attorney-client relationship, such as attorney-client privilege, the exercise of independent judgment, and the avoidance of conflicts, are present when they are not.

IV. Partnership Decisions

Place yourself in a future where you are part of a management committee tasked with making hard partnership decisions while considering the challenges involved in juggling work-life balance, firm culture, and the bottom line as you work through the following scenarios:

MANAGEMENT SCENARIO 1: NEW PARTNERS FOR HOLMES & WATSON, LLP

Holmes & Watson (H&W) was founded by two trial lawyers over 50 years ago and has grown to become a diversified, general practice firm of 60 lawyers. H&W has a single office in a large metropolitan area and, while not the largest firm in town, enjoys a strong reputation. H&W typically represents regional business and individuals in various matters and divides itself internally into four practice groups: litigation, corporate, intellectual property, and tax. H&W has only three classifications of lawyers: associates, counsel, and (equity) partners. The partnership "track" is flexible, but partnership decisions are typically made after seven or eight years of work at H&W. H&W does not currently offer ancillary services, but there has been some discussion about whether that model might make sense in the firm's future.

You are a partner on the H&W committee considering which associates and counsel should be offered partnership this year. Four lawyers are under consideration, but the committee can only promote one or possibly two of them.

For this exercise, break into small groups and discuss which of the following candidates you would suggest promoting, and why. Then discuss your deliberations as a class.

---

[8] *See* Robins Kaplan LLP, *Professionals*, https://www.robinskaplan.com/professionals.

Here is some brief background information regarding the four candidates:

Ann is counsel in the litigation group. She has not previously been considered for partnership because she works part time (50% hours/salary). Ann attended the state flagship public law school and joined H&W after her graduation ten years ago. She went part time as a sixth-year associate following the birth of her second child. She has always met her part-time hours commitments and originates a respectable amount of her own business. Ann has also consistently received favorable reviews, from both H&W partners and clients. (Indeed, her reputation and professionalism were key reasons why she was allowed the exception of a part-time schedule in the first place.) While she has never worked in a leadership role at the firm, she is active in the community and chairs the local arts council. The head of the litigation practice has indicated that she likes Ann personally and professionally but doesn't consider her indispensable to the future of the practice.

Bette is a sixth-year corporate associate. She has been recommended by the head of the corporate practice for early consideration because she has been wooed by one of H&W's competitors as a lateral partner. (Apparently, she impressed them as opposing counsel in a large merger transaction.). Bette is from the D.C. area, graduated from a top-ranked national law school seven years ago, clerked for a federal judge, and then joined H&W. Bette has worked hard to involve herself in the local start-up and tech culture and has shown promise in cultivating new client relationships in that sector. Bette is well liked within the firm but often comes across as overly driven, ambitious, and arrogant. She sometimes complains that the local legal and tech scenes are "minor league."

Chris is a counsel in the tax group. Originally from China, he graduated from the University of the State Next Door School of Law nine years ago and has an advanced degree in tax from a major program. Chris joined H&W right after his tax degree and has worked in the tax practice ever since. His hours and work are always solid, and he originates a decent amount of his own business through connections with the local accounting community. Chris is shy and something of a loner at work; he often works remotely but is always responsive.

Donna is a seventh-year associate in the intellectual property practice. She graduated from the prestigious local prep school and has dual degrees from Ivy League universities (which she will constantly remind you of). After law school she practiced briefly at a major firm in New York City before returning home and joining H&W. Donna comes from a long line of local lawyers—her father was the state attorney general and her sister is the general counsel for a large corporation. Through her connections, she originates a large amount of business for an associate, but her work ethic at H&W has always been somewhat limited. Donna has open political ambitions, and it is loudly whispered in the halls that she only views H&W as a stepping stone to bigger things.

MANAGEMENT SCENARIO 2: WHAT TO DO WITH UNDERPERFORMING EXISTING PARTNERS?

This scenario involves the flip side of Scenario 1. The background facts remain the same, but the situation faced by your committee involves demotion of existing partners rather than promotion of counsel/associates.

You have been charged with determining whether one or more current partners should be moved to a counsel position. Four lawyers are under consideration.

For this exercise, break into small groups and discuss which of the following candidates, if any, you would suggest moving to a counsel role, and why. Then discuss your deliberations as a class.

Here is some brief background information regarding the four candidates:

Walter is a hard-working litigator who has spent his entire career at H&W and made partner six years ago. Walter has had limited success in business development, however, and originates only a very small amount of work. Most of Walter's time is spent supporting the H&W lead trial lawyer and head of the litigation practice, who enthusiastically supported Walter's partnership promotion but has remained neutral on this decision. On the one hand, he says that much of Walter's work could be performed by other lawyers at the firm, but on the other, if Walter were to leave the firm there would be some risk of upsetting current clients and, of course, the potential loss of Walter's originations.

Xavier is a lawyer in the corporate practice who has been with H&W for many years, through good times and bad. Many years ago, he was one of H&W's largest rainmakers, due largely to his relationship with Pluto, Inc., one of the region's largest software companies, which generated not only a lot of transactional work, but also tax and litigation work that was handled by H&W. Three years ago, however, the Pluto work started to drop off. At that point, H&W decided to take on a lateral partner who represented Pluto's main competitor and the partnership voted to cut ties with Pluto to take on the new work (which was about twice what Pluto provided). Xavier obviously was unhappy about the decision, but he soldiered on with his other clients. His originations have dropped by about half since the breakup with Pluto. Lately, however, he has taken to grumbling about his compensation and complaining about management's decision to "kill his business." He has a few enemies among the partners and very few allies.

Yvonne is a partner in the intellectual property practice. She graduated from an Ivy League law school and practiced with a major Silicon Valley firm before joining H&W five years ago as counsel. Yvonne was made a partner three years ago and has consistently originated over $1 million in business every year since; she was recently named to the local "Rising Stars" list of young lawyers. Yvonne, however, can be insufferable to those she deems beneath her. She is sarcastic and demeaning to staff and even smaller clients (she is now on her seventh administrative assistant in three years). What's more, she has a biting wit to accompany a nasty temper and, it is rumored, a bit of a drinking problem. Associates dread working for her and one just left H&W due to what they considered her harsh management style.

Zelda has been with H&W for over 30 years. She was the firm's tenth law-yer, started and still heads the tax practice, and serves on the management committee. Historically, Zelda originated over $1.5 million in business, but her largest client was broken up in a hedge fund acquisition several years ago and she has only been able to pull in around $300k/year from her remaining clients. Zelda is well liked and has a high profile in the local community. She has resisted pivoting her practice to another area, however, maintaining that she "is" tax law in our fair city and that the business will come back. Some of the partners believe Zelda is grossly overpaid and no longer pulling her weight.

V. Conclusion

There are many variations and nuances among law firms, but they all share common attributes, chief among which is that they are organized around people. This "human capital" forms the core of a firm's identity and, ultimately, will determine its success or failure. Understanding how the people in a firm, and their roles, fit together to form a cohesive whole is an important backdrop for self-awareness and evaluation of your place within a particular firm environment—and, hopefully, finding the right fit for your career.

CHAPTER 5

ESSENTIAL LAW FIRM ECONOMICS

I. The Past, Present, and Future

A. The Law Firm–Centric View of the World

For many decades, private law firms operated on a tightly controlled business model that was, in large part, centered on the senior partners at those firms. Their personal relationships with clients drove the business, and the firms were largely able to set the terms of those relationships. Legal knowledge and information was not widely dispersed through digital platforms and the Internet, and clients required lawyers for almost every task that was remotely related to their legal affairs. This arrangement allowed firms to control pricing and delivery of legal services in a manner that best suited their interest; this was a law firm–centric view of the world.

While concerns about the inefficiencies and asymmetry of this model have always been present, it proved to be remarkably resilient. Recently, however, the role that law firms play in the overall business ecosystem is being constantly reevaluated.

B. Impact of the Great Recession

The Great Recession of 2008 was a devastating shock to the system for many businesses, including law firms. The sudden collapse of financial institutions—previously thought to be invulnerable—and the threat to the entire economy were unprecedented events in the lifetimes of most law firm leaders. Facing dire economic crises of their own, clients demanded new levels of efficiency, predictability, and cost-effectiveness from their lawyers. Calls were made for shared sacrifice from firms, to become partners with their clients rather than mere service providers. In-house legal departments faced slashed budgets, which in turn led to slashed revenues at many firms. This led to a rise in alternative fee arrangements and budget-based pricing pressures rarely before encountered by lawyers.

As a result, firms were forced to adapt—with varying degrees of success. This era led to greater segmentation among the country's larger law firms in terms of economic performance and profits. Many firms merged with or were absorbed into competitors in a bid to try to survive. Many firms, however, were unable or slow to respond to these demands, and they suffered or perished.

Corporate law departments turned away from outside counsel and kept a larger portion of their matters inside the company's law department, resulting in contracted work opportunities and lost market share for many firms. This era also led to acceleration of the nascent growth of legal technology and alternative service providers.

In retrospect, however, law firms' responses to the Great Recession were largely reactive and failed to fundamentally result in sustained, proactive change in the traditional law firm business model.

C. Toward a Client-Centric View of the World

1. Clients Take Control

In the years since, firms are finally facing what may be inevitable systemic changes to the business of law under the historically accepted model. Pressures from clients and non–law firm competitors are reshaping the delivery of legal services—at least in certain segments of the market. Clients today feel more in charge of the relationship than ever and are utilizing cost control techniques with law firms that were once reserved for more truly arm's-length business or vendor relationships. These techniques include implementing competitive procurement procedures for certain matters—putting cases out for bid—often in concert with not only corporate legal departments but also corporate procurement departments; strict budgeting, billing, and forecasting requirements; and increased reliance on splitting various tasks in major matters among different service providers, including multiple law firms, project managers, legal service providers, and staffing firms.

Today, more than ever, the client, large or small, has options and is in control of the relationship.

2. A Roadmap: Outside Counsel Guidelines

One control technique that clients are using with more frequency is the implementation of outside counsel guidelines. While as an associate, it is unlikely that you would directly be involved in this process, knowing what's contained in the guidelines and the thinking behind it can help illuminate client concerns and the bigger picture. Also, and equally important, while such guidelines are predominantly used in larger corporate settings, the issues and concerns raised therein pertain to almost any lawyer-client business relationship. As such, analyzing an example of such guidelines is instructive on a number of levels. While the content of such guidelines will vary from company to company, the topics they address are relatively uniform and provide a ready means of considering the parameters of the business relationship between clients and their lawyers. An example follows.

EXAMPLE OF OUTSIDE COUNSEL GUIDELINES— "NEWCO"

Purpose and Scope

These Guidelines apply to outside counsel representing or advising Newco, including any Newco subsidiary or business unit, and employees in their official capacity (collectively, "Newco") in connection with ongoing legal matters. To the extent that any of these Guidelines conflict with or contradict any provision of an engagement letter or other agreement between Newco and outside counsel, these Guidelines prevail unless otherwise explicitly agreed by Newco in writing. Newco will not be liable to outside counsel for any professional fees or disbursements incurred that are inconsistent with these Guidelines without prior written approval by Newco.

Newco encourages the development of a cooperative relationship with outside counsel to achieve our business goals. Although Newco requires all outside counsel to comply with these Guidelines, we recognize that exceptions to these Guidelines may be warranted under certain circumstances and we will address them on a case-by-case basis.

Contacts with Company

Newco will designate one point of contact for outside counsel. In most cases, this point of contact will be Jane Doe, Associate General Counsel, unless otherwise designated in writing.

Staffing and Supervision

Newco expects you to staff our matters in a high quality and cost-efficient manner. We encourage delegation of appropriate tasks to junior and staff attorneys and the use of paralegals for tasks that do not require an attorney. We will not pay for services provided by attorneys that customarily are handled by clerical staff. Outside counsel should avoid engaging in unnecessary legal or factual research and holding unnecessary internal multi-lawyer conferences.

Ideally, attorneys and staff assigned to one of Newco's matters should remain assigned to the matter until completion. If it is necessary to transition work to another attorney or other personnel at your firm, Newco should not be billed for time spent educating replacement personnel or reading them into the matter.

While we understand that a firm may want to include law clerks, interns, summer associates, first-year associates, or trainees on our matters, you may not bill us for the time spent by these individuals without advance approval.

You must also obtain our prior approval before:

- Engaging another firm as local or special counsel
- Retaining an expert
- Hiring an investigator or other consultant

- ■ Hiring a third-party vendor (such as for e-discovery)
- ■ Hiring contract attorneys

Budgets
Newco requires that outside counsel consider cost-effectiveness when making estimates and evaluations. Outside counsel must provide a reasonably detailed budget and other cost estimates at the beginning of any matters that involve over $20,000 in total expected billings. Outside counsel may not begin working on a matter until the company approves the budget, unless otherwise authorized to do so in writing.

Newco may request status and progress reports periodically. Outside counsel may not bill Newco for time spent on budgeting and status or progress reports.

If outside counsel exceeds the approved budget, Newco will not pay any invoices until Newco and outside counsel adjust the budget. Adherence to the budget is a key measurement for outside counsel's performance.

Legal Fees
Fees for professional legal services must be established in advance of the engagement for each specific matter. We expect hourly billing rates to remain constant for the duration of a matter, absent circumstances where prior approval has been granted. Newco will not accept hourly billing rate increases during an engagement, including both annual rate increases and seniority/step increases for associates. By way of example, a third-year associate's hourly rate will remain the same even when that associate progresses to fourth-year status while working on a Newco matter. Newco shall receive a 10 percent discount off your regular billing rates.

Newco encourages proposals for alternative fee arrangements when appropriate for a case or project.

Expenses
Newco will reimburse outside counsel for the actual cost, without any markup, of the following types of disbursements if reasonable and necessarily incurred in your representation of Newco:

- ■ Photocopying or printing at no more than five cents per page
- ■ Actual charges for overnight and hand delivery messenger services, only when such delivery methods are necessary for time sensitive matters or to meet imminent deadlines
- ■ Actual item-specific charges billed to the firm for each long distance, mobile, or conference call, or long distance outgoing facsimile (if separately charged)
- ■ Actual charges for the use of outside consultants, vendors, and experts

You may not bill us for your firm's overhead or administrative costs, including each of the following types of expenses, which Newco views to be overhead costs that are included in the law firm's hourly rate or other fee arrangement:

- Electronic research services (Westlaw/Lexis)
- Word processing, secretarial, or clerical services
- Ordinary postage charges
- Local telephone calls and outgoing facsimile messages
- Incoming facsimile messages
- Time spent preparing bills
- Charges for time in opening files, including charges for identifying and resolving conflicts of interest
- Other law firm staff services, such as proofreading and local staff messengers
- Transportation to and from home (including transportation outside of regular business hours)
- Meals (including working meals and overtime meals)

Travel

Travel, meals, and lodging costs for Newco matters should be reasonable and economical. We expect you to be cost conscious and exercise good judgment when selecting travel, meals, and lodging that Newco will be charged for. We also expect you to carefully and properly distinguish between chargeable business expenses and personal expenses. Newco will not pay for first-class airfare. Out-of-town travel time not spent on substantive legal work is generally not chargeable.

Billing

Invoices should be itemized by task and contain sufficient detail, including:

- An explanation of the task performed, and service provided. Do not include overly general descriptions
- The amount of time spent on the task performed, billed in increments of one-tenth (1/10) of an hour
- Identification of the responsible attorneys and legal assistants
- The matter name and number
- The date of each task performed
- The billing rate for each timekeeper

Time entries that include more than one task ("block billing") will be rejected and may be resubmitted only after each task, including the time spent on the task, is separately identified.

No more than one attorney should bill for in-office conferences, depositions, court appearances, or other events unless Newco has given prior approval.

Invoices also must itemize disbursements and expenses. Newco will not accept an "other" or "miscellaneous" category of expenses on an invoice.

Invoices generally should be submitted within 30 days of the end of the month when services were provided to us. Newco's practice is to pay invoices within 60 days of receipt.

Conflicts of Interest

Newco takes conflicts of interest very seriously and we expect our outside counsel to do the same. We expect you to conduct a conflict check prior to representing our company and to update same periodically during the representation. If a potential or actual conflict of interest arises, you must notify us in writing immediately.

Newco expects that neither you nor anyone in your firm will represent a party adverse to Newco or in any matter while you are representing Newco.

Newco may agree to waive a conflict (or agree to different standards) on a case-by-case basis. However, Newco will not give a blanket waiver of conflicts of interest to law firms.

In addition, due to the competitiveness of our industry, we have a general policy of not engaging law firms who represent our main competitors or take on representations that otherwise may damage the commercial or strategic interests of our company.

Maintaining Confidentiality and Privilege

Newco expects you to maintain the confidentiality of all non-public information that we provide to you, or that you learn during an engagement. We also expect you to comply with all ethical rules and codes regarding the maintenance of confidentiality. Newco expects you to make reasonable efforts to prevent unauthorized access to Newco's non-public information and to protect Newco's non-public information from inadvertent or unauthorized disclosure.

Outside counsel should represent us in a manner that preserves the attorney-client privilege. Newco generally does not waive the attorney-client privilege, and if we do, such waiver is not effective unless and until you receive Newco's consent in writing.

Media Contacts and Publicity

Newco typically does not publicly comment on litigation, potential transactions, regulatory proceedings, or other legal matters. If you are contacted for comments, interviews, or information, do not respond to any such requests without prior written approval from Newco. Instead, please direct the request to Jane Doe, Associate General Counsel.

Diversity

Newco is deeply committed to diversity, both internally and in our outside counsel hiring practices. We believe that a culturally sensitive, diverse workplace is better able to serve our needs and produce better results. Newco expects our outside counsel to make a good faith effort to recruit, retain, and promote qualified women and minorities. We also expect our outside counsel to include women and minority partners and associates when working on our matters.

> **Questions:** What client concerns do you see at the heart of these guidelines? Do you think they are an effective means to address those concerns? How might such an agreement reduce or increase friction between the client and the law firm?

II. Fees and Billing

At whatever stage of the business-model evolutionary scale a firm might operate, like all businesses, firms need to identify where their revenue comes from, what sort of client mix they can best serve, and what practice areas make sense. As a practical matter, in order to collect money from clients, firms must first present them with a bill. Many lawyers consider the invoice as an afterthought, but that is a mistake. Conceptually, whether denominated a "bill," an "invoice," or a "statement of account," this is actually a key communication tool and, when done well, can provide an effective and compelling narrative of the work performed and convey the value delivered. For as long as most lawyers practicing today have been invoicing clients, the primary driver of this form of communication has been based on a simple, yet quite controversial, concept—a unit of time.

A. Billable Hours

1. Origins and Concept

Undoubtedly, you've heard of billable hours, a much-maligned and central feature of the business of law for many years. Common criticisms are that billable hours promote inefficiency while penalizing productivity, are unpredictable, and potentially result in a misalignment of interests between lawyers and their clients. As such, their demise has been predicted for decades. And yet billable hours persist as the predominant unit of productivity in the law business, and it seems likely that timekeeping will remain a core feature of private practice for the foreseeable future. To better to know it as a companion rather than an enemy, it is important to understand why the billable hour occupies such a central place in law business and culture.

Until the 1950s, most legal services were billed on a fixed fee basis. Some state bar associations also published suggested minimum fee schedules for various standardized legal services, such as wills and title searches. These minimum fee schedules were, however, ultimately invalidated as price-fixing in the Supreme Court's 1975 *Goldfarb v. Virginia State Bar* decision.

In the early twentieth century, an attorney named Reginald Heber Smith sought to bring modern accounting and recordkeeping into his practice at Boston Legal Aid. It worked like a charm and efficiency followed. When Smith later practiced at the Hale & Dorr firm, he began to implement similar methods for internal tracking. Believing that it led to fairness, transparency, and client satisfaction, Smith thought time provided the ideal organizing principle for law office organization. And by the 1960s, the unit of time had transitioned to a means of billing clients. The law firm WilmerHale tells the origin story of the superhero/villain billable hour best:

> The next time you're grumbling over your timesheet, you might be interested to know that the credit for its invention can be laid at the feet of one of our own. Reginald Heber Smith, managing partner of legacy Hale and Dorr from 1919 to 1956, is the man who pioneered the rationalization of the modern law firm.
>
> Accurate accounting methods, budgets, a mathematical system of profit distribution, timesheets and—yes—the dreaded billable hour are all among Smith's many contributions to the legal profession. But recent detractors who blame Smith for where the billable hour has taken us might be surprised to know that the earnest and altruistic man himself, living in a gentler age, would have been as shocked as they at today's incarnation of a system that he fully intended to promote fairness, efficiency, client satisfaction, professional ethics, and the advancement of the public good.
>
> Ironically, for an invention that has been criticized for the erosion of law firms' public service, the seed of the idea that was to become the billable hour grew from Smith's experiences in the world of legal aid. In 1913, straight out of Harvard Law School, Smith was invited to become counsel of the Boston Legal Aid Society, where he had volunteered during his summers as a law student. Passionate about redressing the inequities of a legal system that, in his words, effectively "close[d] the doors of the courts to the poor" (Justice and the Poor, 1919, 8), Smith was faced with the challenge of funding and staffing approximately 2,000 legal aid cases per year on a shoestring budget, with the help of only a few assistant counsel, a social service secretary and some clerical assistants.
>
> Smith, drawn to the emerging discipline of scientific business management, took his own management dilemma to the halls of Harvard Business School. There, Professor William Morse Cole and a group of his students set about devising a functional system of accounting and recordkeeping—including a method for tracking statistical information on cases—for the Boston Legal Aid Society. Armed with this information, Smith was able to implement new controls, training procedures and management practices, such as weekly conferences with all attorneys, that greatly improved the functioning of the office. In 1915, the Society cleared an impressive 65% more cases than it had the prior year, and reduced the average net cost of each case from $3.93 in 1913 to $1.63 in 1915.
>
> Smith's tenure at the Society was to last five years, the last two of which he largely spent conducting a national study of legal aid that became the foundation for his magnum opus, Justice and the Poor, published in 1919. That same year, he came to Hale and Dorr—a newly formed firm of six partners—as managing partner, bringing with him the same organizational zeal that had fueled his early success.
>
> While its details remained elusive, Smith sensed that the perfect organizational system lay just beyond his grasp, and was determined to unearth it. "After I came to Hale and Dorr, at the conclusion of World War I, my partners generously granted me permission to see if I could establish records as to time," Smith was to write in 1966 (Memo, reprinted in John A. Dolan's Hale and Dorr: Backgrounds and Styles, 1993, 305), looking back over his career. "It took me quite a while so that in retrospect I am thoroughly ashamed of myself." Indeed, Smith gradually came to realize, it was time itself that provided the ideal organizing principle for law office organization. Even from the vantage point of four decades later, Smith's musings on the timesheet have the air of revelation: "Actually nothing could be simpler than a form on which you wrote the name of the client, the name of the case (because a client may have several cases

in the office at the same time), a brief description of the work you did, and the time you spent doing it." (Memo, 305.)

To Smith, a time-based system had the inexorable logic of a law of nature. "Really my only contribution as [sic] to decide that the minimum time entry should be one-tenth of an hour," he wrote, marveling at the ease with which the details fell into place. "I fixed that for the reason that I can more easily add, subtract, and divide on the decimal system." (Memo, 306.) The timesheet, divided into six-minute increments, was born. Now Smith had to sell it to his partners at Hale and Dorr.

"This simple plan had but one weakness which is that lawyers are individualists," Smith wrote. "[T]hey hate any system; and to keep a detailed record of time seemed to them about as bad as a slave system." (Memo, 306.) Note that Smith's time-based system was not being criticized—as it was by the close of the 20th century—as a "slave system" for driving up work hours at the expense of lawyers' personal lives, public service, health and sanity. What bothered the Hale and Dorr partners—who were generally expected to work a genteel 5.5 hours on weekdays and 2.5 hours on Saturday mornings—was the indignity of being asked to provide any kind of accounting for the way in which they saw fit to use their time within those hours. To them, any system of time measurement smacked of the Taylorist industrial assembly line, its workers performing their tasks like automatons as an officious manager stood by with a stopwatch. Through perseverance, transparency, and his sincere commitment to the health and future of the firm, however, Smith prevailed upon his partners to accept the timesheet, and it eventually became, to them, "as much a matter of habit as getting dressed in the morning." (Memo, 306.)

Initially, the timesheet remained a purely internal metric, used for organizational planning and budgeting. But at some point between the timesheet's inception around 1920 and his completion, in 1940, of a book detailing his fully realized vision, Smith discovered the utility of translating the timesheet into the billable hour. Until that time, according to legal historians, lawyers had relied largely on flat-fee arrangements, or looked to the state bar associations' minimum fee schedules, which set different prices for different services. The beauty of the billable hour, in Smith's mind, was that it provided a fair, logical, transparent and indisputable method for valuing legal services—one that clients could understand and embrace as readily as the lawyers themselves. "This method is especially pleasing to businessmen, all of whom have cost systems of their own," reflected Smith. "You can show him your cost and you can give him your supporting evidence. This at once dispels the notion that you are charging 'all the traffic will bear.'" (Memo, 306.)

In 1940, the American Bar Association published Smith's Law Office Organization, which originally appeared as four separate articles but was reprinted, by popular demand, in the form of a pamphlet that, by the early '90s, had gone through 11 editions. Hale and Dorr, in 1940 a firm of 17 partners and eight associates, had become the proving ground for a system that was to dominate the legal industry, both in the United States and beyond, into the next century. Extrapolated from one firm to an entire industry, however, and fueled by forces that he could never have foreseen, Smith's formula for fairness and efficiency was to become something else altogether.

By the late 1950s, the national bar—lamenting the "economic plight" of lawyers, whose earnings had failed to keep pace with those of other professionals, such as doctors and dentists—had mounted a campaign to promote the billable hour as a business strategy, says law professor Niki Kuckes. By the late 1970s, a decade after Smith's death, pure hourly billing had taken over. "To improve productivity, law firms began adopting policies requiring attorneys to bill a certain number of minimum hours each year," Kuckes writes. "It seemed like a harmless enough step—until the number of those hours began to rise steadily beginning in the '80s." ("The Hours," *Legal Affairs*, Sept./Oct. 2002.) Driven by the Supreme Court's invalidation of the bar on lawyer advertising, and by *The American Lawyer*'s ushering in of the "big-firm star system," adds Scott Turow ("The Billable Hour Must Die," *ABA Journal*, Aug. 2007), the legal profession's "competitive war" had begun.

In Smith's careful hands, the billable hour was never the double-edged sword that now stands accused of cutting out the soul of the legal profession, misaligning the interests of law firm and client, and forcing the industry's breakneck rush to ever greater growth, leverage and profits. Smith, contrary to the arguments of today's critics, never saw profit as the primary motive. "Normally you hope for profit over cost," he wrote in 1966, shortly before his death. But, he continued, "[o]ften, and for good reason because law is a profession, you must fix a bill below cost." (Memo, 306.)

Smith's real goal, ever since his days in legal aid, was "100% efficiency" in the delivery of the best that the legal profession had to offer, whether to pro bono clients, fee-paying clients of the firm, or to society at large. "The goal is to render to clients who need legal advice and assistance a definitely better help than any other firm has ever given at any time anywhere else," Smith wrote in 1941, in his 23rd annual report to the partners of Hale and Dorr. "Our perpetual ambition must be to build up the finest service that it is humanly possible to give." (Dolan, 246.) For all of Smith's pleasure in the neatness and logic of the billable hour, and his satisfaction at the administrative certainties it could bestow, it seems likely that—were he with us today—he might be in favor of jettisoning it in favor of the deeper values that he never lost sight of throughout the whole of his lengthy career.[1]

2. Implementation

a. Timekeeping

As a practical matter, billable hours are reflected in narrative form and logged by the amount of time spent on a given task. The predominant metric is six-minute intervals—"point one," in the parlance. Practical advice for new lawyers in adjusting to timekeeping, whether working on paper, spreadsheet, text files, or software, includes the following:

Make timekeeping a daily habit. It is much more accurate to make time entries on a current rather than a retrospective basis.

Record your time accurately. Many new lawyers, feeling self-conscious about their learning curve and productivity, self-edit and mentally reduce the time they spent on a task before entry. Unless you've been told otherwise, you shouldn't be arbitrarily reducing your time just because you thought it would be best or you were embarrassed about how long it took you to accomplish a task. Of course, you should never inflate the time spent on a task either.

Ensure that the narrative reflects the work involved in the task and the corresponding time entry matches. For example, if you were on a phone call with a client for 20 minutes and your time entry shows "Telephone call with client (1.0),"

---

[1] Wilmer Cutler Pickering, Hale and Dorr LLP, *Slice of History: Reginald Heber Smith and the Birth of the Billable Hour*, https://www.wilmerhale.com/en/insights/publications/slice-of-history-reginald-heber-smith-and-the-birth-of-the-billable-hour-august-9-2010.

there's a good chance that the client can look at her call log history and know something's off, and then perhaps begin to question other entries and start a billing dispute. Such a situation is neither ethical nor pleasant.

Phrase your time narrative in such a way that the reader can appreciate the value in the task. Place yourself in the shoes of the billing partner (your boss) and the client, and consider if you would understand what was done and whether you would pay for it. For example, which description below sounds better to you?

"Review various files and research re same"

or

"Review of new documents received from collection at company data center and research re relevance and admissibility of same"

b. Hourly Rates

Recorded units of time provide the first part of the billing equation—the "X," if you will. The second part is the corresponding billing rate—the "Y." Each lawyer in a firm typically has an hourly rate. Sometimes they vary by individual, sometimes by title or seniority. Where to set an hourly rate is a complex business decision involving what the market will bear, the practice area, the client relations needs, and the firm's financial goals.

In a small firm or solo environment, it may simply be best to refer to your business plan and reverse engineer what your rate needs to be to make your numbers. To arrive at a rough estimate, say (i) you want to make $85,000 (pre-tax) for the year; (ii) you estimate that your expenses will be $2,000 a month; and (iii) you have 50 total hours a month to devote to the practice, including time spent on billable, non-billable, pro bono, business development, marketing, and administration work. You might use the following formula:

$$((Income) + (Expenses \times 12)) / ((Hours/5/3) \times 240)$$
$$((85,000) + (2,000 \times 12)) / ((50/5/3) \times 240)$$
$$109,000/800$$
$$\$136.25/hour$$

The left side of the equation represents the total amount of revenue that you will need to make over the year to pay yourself and your expenses. In this example, that would be $109,000. You divide this gross revenue number by the number of hours you can work in the workdays available in a year (which is estimated as 240 to allow for weekends, vacation, holidays, and emergencies) divided by three. This last operation acts as an estimate of how much of your available time you will actually spend on billable work. This yields a rough estimate of the hourly rate you would need to charge, and collect, to make your revenue targets, here $136.25.

In a law firm setting, this basic formula becomes extrapolated across all the lawyers in the firm. And, as the expenses and income targets grow, the hours and rates must increase significantly. One recent study showed that the largest firms (750+ lawyers) had an average partner billing rate of $575 per hour. Those with 201–750 attorneys were averaging partner billing rates of $380 an hour. And firms of 101–200 lawyers were averaging $295 an hour.[2] Associate rates are almost always proportionately lower, of course.

Hourly rates are typically referred to as "standard rates" (or, more colloquially, "rack," "book," or "retail" rates). Standard rates are often discounted in practice, particularly for clients who do a volume of business with the firm, but, as we'll explore in more detail below, they provide a benchmark for assessing profitability.

B. "Alternative" Fee Arrangements

The Great Recession led to increased interest in "alternative fee arrangements" (AFAs).[3] Alternative to what, you might ask? That largely depends on who you are talking to, but AFAs most commonly are employed as an alternative to traditional hourly billing arrangements. Conceptually, hourly billing is what a building contractor would call a "cost-plus" arrangement, whereby a homeowner agrees to pay the contractor for its costs and expenses, plus an additional payment to allow for a profit. This has the effect of shifting much of the risk of cost overruns from the contractor (lawyer) to the homeowner (client). This type of agreement is often used where accurate estimates of the final cost of a project are difficult to accurately estimate. Conversely, in a "fixed-price" arrangement, the payment amount does not depend on the time and resources required to complete the job, and the risk of cost overruns falls on the contractor (lawyer). AFAs are, in essence, client-relations tools founded on an attempt to reallocate some of this risk from client to lawyer.

The first form of AFA we'll consider, which by some definitions isn't really an "alternative" at all, includes variations on the billable hour theme. These variations represent alternatives to standard rates:

Discounted hourly rates, whereby the client receives a discount off the standard rate. These discounts can take different forms for different matters and may increase or decrease depending on the total amount of work involved. The Example of Outside Counsel Guidelines previously mentioned included such a discount for Newco (10%), which is a commonly encountered discount rate.

Blended hourly rates, whereby a law firm charges an agreed rate for all attorneys staffing a legal matter, regardless of seniority. For example, rather than charging associates at $300/hour and partners at $500/hour, all lawyers are billed at $375/hour.

Capped hourly rates, whereby a firm will limit the highest rate charged on a matter.

While these approaches are commonly deployed, they remain part of a fundamental billing structure that involves multiplying units of time by an hourly rate. Thus, they do not actually modify the essence of the traditional arrangement or alter the incentives of the parties.

Lawyers are creative people, and there are a wide variety of AFAs in use. For illustrative purposes, we'll focus on a few of the more common forms:

---

[2] CounselLink, *2020 CounselLink Enterprise Legal Management Trends Report*, https://counsellink.com/trends/.

[3] *Id.* (AFAs were utilized in approximately 12 percent of matters and 10 percent of billings).

In a **retainer agreement**, the client makes a deposit in return for which the law firm guarantees its availability for a specific period and/or to perform a defined set of work. For example, the client, a financial services business, pays a law firm a $5,000 monthly retainer in return for which the law firm agrees to have two of its securities lawyers on call two days a week to answer questions. This arrangement has some advantages—clients may be more likely to seek legal help when they know the meter isn't running every six minutes, and the law firm has a level of certainty on the monthly revenue associated with the account. Drawbacks might include disagreements about whether a task is included in the retainer. Note that this arrangement differs from an "advance" or "security" retainer whereby the client advances funds to the law firm as a (refundable) deposit against future hourly work.

With **flat** or **fixed fees**, a client engages a law firm to perform a specific task or service (such as a non-disclosure agreement, simple will, or LLC formation for a set price). Fixed fees can also be used for a phase or portion of a larger matter. For example, a client pays a law firm a fixed fee to handle the initial interview phase of an internal investigation. Such an arrangement allows the client to have cost certainty, but the law firm assumes the risk of cost overruns. As a result, lawyers must fully understand the costs of providing services, or risk losing money on the engagement. A drawback is that unforeseen circumstances may lead to conflict around the need for more or higher-quality work on the matter.

A **holdback** involves time-based billing, but the client only pays a percentage (say 80 percent) of the invoiced amount. The remaining 20 percent stays in "holdback," subject to discretionary payment at the end of the matter depending on client satisfaction or predetermined conditions. Holdbacks are required of firms working on many large bankruptcy cases. This is similar to a bonus arrangement, except that in a holdback, the available "bonus" is drawn from a predetermined pool of unpaid billings.

Contingency fees are one of the oldest forms of AFA and are a common feature of many plaintiff-side litigation arrangements. They are often scaled based on a percentage of the amount recovered, and at what phase of the matter. For example, should a case settle before discovery, a firm might receive 20 percent of the proceeds, but if the matter advances through trial the firm's share might increase to 40 percent.

From a law firm perspective, any AFA requires a solid understanding of the costs involved in delivering an effective result and project management skills. Regardless of whether and to what extent a firm employs AFAs, its lawyers are still likely to track their time on an hourly basis, at least for internal measuring purposes.

III. Profitability

As discussed in Chapter 3, profit is revenue less expenses. Whatever the fee arrangement may be, revenue in the door does not itself equate to profits for the firm. There is a long path between a lawyer providing a description of her work and a correlating amount of time spent on the task on a timesheet or billing software entry and that becoming money in the bank. Not all firms manage "by the numbers," but there is an increasing trend toward applying financial metrics to law practices, particularly given the now-widespread adoption of timekeeping and billing software.

A. Realization

Many firms analyze lawyer productivity using a metric known as a "realization rate." This metric represents the proportion of billable hours at standard billing rates to the amount that is actually billed to (or collected from) clients. For example, an attorney's standard rate is $300/hour, and she works 100 billable hours in a month. Thus, her monthly billing at her standard rate is $30,000. However, the partner only invoices the client for $27,000, which is a realization rate of 90 percent (calculated as $27,000 billed divided by $30,000 at standard rates). Realization rates can, of course, be reported by individual, partner, office, or practice group, or firm-wide.

Maintaining high realization rates is important for firm health and management. By way of example, a realization rate of around 92 percent might be considered a current healthy industry standard.

B. Collections

Rare is the lawyer who enjoys collecting money owed to the firm, but it is a necessary task. Cash flow is notoriously uneven in the law business, typically lowest in the first quarter and highest in the fourth quarter. An important factor in law firm profitability is maintaining speed in billing and collections—particularly in the end-of-the-year cycle. Until money is in the door, the owners of the firm must draw on capital contributions or loans to fund firm operations, so reducing the amount of time of this "float" is all to the good.

In Chapter 3, you learned about accounts receivable (A/R). A related concept is "work in progress" (WIP). In a law firm setting, A/R represents invoiced but unpaid lawyer time and WIP represents as-yet-unbilled lawyer time. "WIP turnover" is a concept that measures the amount of time it takes from when work is performed until it is billed. "A/R turnover" is a concept that measures the amount of time it takes from invoice to collection date.

To give an example, Sue records eight hours on a client matter on September 1, when it becomes WIP. It is approved by the billing lawyer and invoiced to the client on October 15, when it becomes A/R. The client pays the invoice on December 15, when it becomes collected. The WIP turnover for this time entry is 45 days. The A/R turnover for this time entry is 61 days. When the turnover periods are combined, however, we see that it took 106 days for Sue's work to become money in the door, a not insubstantial period. This total lag time is sometimes referred to as "lockup." Industry professionals generally consider three to four months of lockup to be a reasonable time for most firms.

This illustration is quite simplified, but you can see that when billing data is aggregated, the application of metrics such as these can provide firm managers with insight into the overall operations of the firm's business and finances.

C. Expenses

Expenses must be paid to turn revenue into profits, of course. Law firm expenses typically fall into the following categories: compensation for lawyers, compensation for support staff, occupancy/office space, technology and equipment, benefits, marketing and business development, library/reference, recruiting, bar dues, and malpractice insurance. The apportionment of these expenses varies by firm, but lawyer income typically represents the vast majority of a firm's budget, followed by technology and office space. A simplified pie chart of expense categories might look like this:

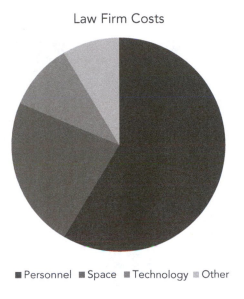

Law Firm Costs

■ Personnel ■ Space ■ Technology ■ Other

IV. Conclusion

While private law firms may have vastly different approaches to practice and strategy, they remain for-profit businesses. The ways in which firms operate and measure their success and profitability may be complex, but having an appreciation for the business environment will greatly inform your experience, business development, and career.

CHAPTER 6

LAWYER COMPENSATION

Lawyer compensation is typically a firm's greatest expense. Money alone almost never equates to career satisfaction, but compensation also represents much more than simply an amont of money. It can be a controllable means for firm management to encourage (or discourage) behavior, and a way to encourage practice habits that advance and contribute to a firm's culture and performance goals. Compensation also carries significant signals, such as power, success, and status, and significant psychological effects. It can also represent a system of hierarchy and rank within a firm.

I. Aspects of Compensation: Decisions and Systems

Most people have a need to feel "fairly" compensated for their work, both in absolute and relative terms. In absolute terms they need to feel they receive a fair return on their efforts, and in relative terms they need to feel that others are not receiving more for less—a person's compensation satisfaction is often driven by its value relative to those whom she considers her peers. In many cases, it is the *relative* number that is more important, both externally (as compared to lawyers in other firm environments) and, perhaps more so, internally (as compared to peers within the firm).

Historically, law firm compensation was invisible to the outside world. But then *The American Lawyer* began to publish rankings, and an arms race was on among large law firms, whose partners were now treated to an annual scorecard showing where they fit in the professional hierarchy. Social media and dedicated websites have since led to real-time transparency about associate pay and bonuses. No matter the size of the firm, handling compensation matters is very important—and tricky. If a firm is, at essence, a team (or at least a group of professionals pursuing a largely similar goal), how a firm compensates its lawyers should be designed to advance that goal. What criteria a firm uses to determine lawyer pay is a fluid topic and is presented in this chapter as high-level background with questions for personal reflection and class discussion.

A. Associates

How much money should you be paid as an associate lawyer? That, of course, depends on a number of variables: responsibilities, industry or practice area, and, of course, geographic location. Most important for an entry-level position, however, may simply be prevailing market conditions. Aside from recruiting-based market demands, the core criteria for associate compensation is typically productivity, as measured on an hours worked and collected basis.

One traditional metric is that a firm should set associate salaries at approximately one-third of the expected revenue that flows from that associate. The concept here is that one-third of that revenue goes to overhead, one-third to the associate, and the remining one-third to the firm's partners as a whole. Because salaries are typically set at the start of the year, when collections are unknown, firms must set salaries based on projections and expectations. This is often based on billable hours projections, and it's one reason why many firms employ bonuses for additional billable hours over and above the base. For example:

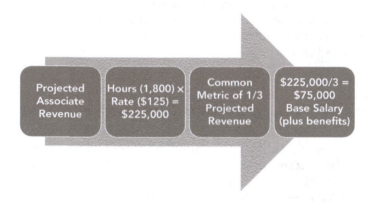

As we saw in Chapter 5, a billable hour doesn't necessarily translate into revenue, and, behind the scenes, firms tend to be conservative with associate hours expectations and must make financial projections based on collections expectations. By way of illustration:

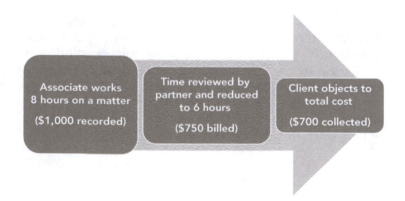

Firms who overpay for associates—that is, they cannot collect revenues at the rates required to turn a profit—cannot sustain the practice for long. And, in some instances, firms may be simply unable to realize any substantial profit in an associate's early years due to the number of hours that are "write downs." These pressures make it more important than ever that entry-level lawyers strive to provide value as quickly as possible.

B. Partners

Determining partner pay is much more nuanced and varied—and, in many cases, creates an interpersonal relationship minefield.

1. Compensation Criteria

Compensation criteria vary from firm to firm, and the decisions made can have a dramatic impact on firm culture, cohesion, and retention. Even at the associate level, having an appreciation for the considerations involved and the drivers of partner productivity can be informative.

Examples of criteria, in alphabetical order, might include:

- **Business Origination:** A lawyer's ability to create and foster client relationships that lead to new business opportunites for the firm. Often a prime compensation marker and tracked in the form of "origination credits."
- **Client Relations and Retention:** How strong are the lawyer's existing client relationships?
- **Collegiality:** Most firms outwardly profess to have a collegial environment. While difficult to measure, whether a firm rewards this trait financially may be more telling.
- **Expertise:** Does the lawyer add to the firm's prominence and general cachet?
- **Marketing and Profile-Raising:** Does the lawyer engage in activities that increase the firm's reach and profile, such as teaching, writing, and speaking?
- **Ownership:** How much has the lawyer invested in the firm by way of capital contributions? Does he have an allocated percentage of profits? Does he have a guaranty of a certain base amount?
- **Pro Bono:** How effectively does the lawyer support the firm's pro bono efforts?
- **Productivity:** As with associates, but more so for partners measured on a client relations, revenue generation basis. May include an allowance for the quality and complexity of the work personally performed and supervised.
- **Seniority:** How long has the lawyer been at the firm?
- **Service (external):** Does the lawyer interact within the community, both for the intrinsic good and for the doing-well-by-doing-good aspects?
- **Service (internal):** Does the lawyer support the firm's internal needs through mentoring, training, committee work, or management?

In Chapter 4, we discussed lawyer titles within a firm. When it comes to compensation, it may be more appropriate to look behind titles and into partner *roles*. There are three general roles that, at a high level at least, convey some of the attributes commonly ascribed to various law firm partners. Most lawyers, of course, are a combination. Colloquially, they carry three colorful names: finders, minders, and grinders.

Finders are partners who devote most of their time and energy to developing new clients and business for the firm. They are constantly on the hunt for new blood to infuse into the firm's economic circulatory system. Characteristics of finders include having a "sales" personality and orientation; spending much of their time with prospective or existing clients or client sources, such as other partners within the firm (to facilitate cross-selling); and having a high public profile—serving on boards, chairing CLE panels, or playing golf with an eye toward cultivating business relationships. Billing hours is not typically a finder priority, and successful finders require a team of lawyers to support the work they bring in.

Minders fill the role of managing and maintaining existing client relationships. This is a role that many senior associates and newer partners naturally fill. Characteristics of minders include projecting stability and trust in the firm; excelling at handling communications and managing deals, cases, and lawyers; and an aptitude for quality control.

Grinders take on the role of actually finishing the work sourced by the finders and managed by the minders. They are sometimes called "service partners," but they actually function as a key component of the work-to-revenue pipeline. Characteristics of grinders include the ability to handle large workloads and functional, efficent, and often specialized legal skills.

2. Compensation Systems

While many firms have complicated compensation systems, most are some variant of a few basic concepts—*subjective versus objective* and *open versus closed*.

In a *subjective* system, compensation decisions are made based on an overall sense of fairness and are derived in part from various benchmark criteria. This type of system tends to foster openness and collegiality. Due to its unstructured nature, however, a subjective system is best employed in firms with a solid organizational culture and sense of identity, and, critically, a strong sense of trust and respect for the ultimate decision makers. As firms grow in size, this last aspect may become less tenable.

In an *objective* system, established criteria are fed into a formula, with the outputs establishing partner compensation levels or ranges. Examples of these inputs might include (a) hours billed an/or collected; (b) business origination and client development; and (c) allocated share of profits. Payout formulas range in complexity, of course.

Many firms employ a hybrid model, whereby some aspects are controlled by formula and others left to the discretion of a managing partner or compensation committee.

In addition to the criteria- and decision maker–based systems, an important consideration is whether the partnership allocations will be *open* or *closed*. In an *open* system, the compensation paid to each individual partner is disclosed to the other partners within the firm. Open compensation is also commonly utilized with associate salaries and is often based on class-level seniority—referred to as *lockstep*. Lockstep compensation models were also historically utilized at the partner level in many firms. As market pressures and lateral markets have grown, however, lockstep has seen a diminishing role at the partner level.

In a *closed*, or "black box," system, only management and the compensation decision makers are aware of each partner's compensation. Proponents of the closed system argue that it fosters collegiality by reducing the relative internal comparison concerns described earlier in this chapter.

3. Draws and Distributions

Most firms also operate on a draw and distribution system, whereby partners "draw" an advance from the firm each month to cover personal bills and expenses. The balance, and often the bulk, of their pay, however, comes in "distributions," which come from firm profits as determined on a periodic basis, at least annually. A partner's draw (advance) is then deducted from the overall share apportioned for the year.

For example, Jane receives a draw of $10,000 on the first of each month throughout the fiscal year. The firm reconciles profits only once—on December 31. The firm has a good year and Jane is apportioned $300,000 of the firm's total profit pool for the year. She would receive a distribution payment of $180,000 representing her share ($300,000) minus draws (totaling $120,000).

Questions:

■ If you were designing a compensation scheme, what concepts and criteria would you draw upon, and why?

■ How might you rank in overall importance the list of criteria noted above?

■ Should a partner's origination credits for a particular client sunset over time or persist indefinitely?

II. Departures, Dissolutions, and Unfinished Business

In the contemporary environment, partners change firms with some frequency. Sometimes, those departures are mutual, voluntary, and uneventful. In other instances, however, departures lead to conflict, crisis, and even dissolution. Partnerships of all kinds, including law firms, are constantly susceptible to competitive pressures, internal dynamics, and volatile financial performance. Small law firms, with fewer decision makers involved, may dissolve when the partners want to pursue other opportunities or simply have disagreements over the firm's direction. And even large, established, and seemingly stable law firms fade or collapse with astonishing frequency—an Internet search will return a graveyard of formerly prominent law firms.[1]

---

[1] *See, e.g.*, Erin Fuchs, *The Eight Most Crushing Law Firm Implosions in the Nation's History* (June 24, 2012), https://www.businessinsider.com/the-eight-most-spectacular-law-firm-collapses-in-history-2012-6#this-firms-fearless-leader-robbed-clients-and-investors-of-400-million-6.

Irrespective of the causes of departures or dissolutions, law firms must deal with client business impacted by the changes. In the former instance, a departing partner may plan to take "her" clients and matters with her to her new firm—sometimes referred to as a "book" or "portable" business. But her partners may have investments in those relationships as well and may not be pleased to lose out on the associated revenue. Sorting this out can be challenging and contentious.

A dissolution is even more complicated—there may be hundreds of clients and thousands of open matters. Dissolved firms likely have creditors to satisfy, and bankrupt firms will have a trustee charged with gathering the firm's assets. The "unfinished business doctrine" (or the "Jewel Rule," as it has become known, from the California case *Jewel v. Boxer*) essentially establishes that absent an agreement to the contrary, partners in a dissolved law firm have a duty to account to the dissolved firm and their former partners for all fees generated from work in progress at the time of the firm's dissolution. This doctrine has been modified by statute in some jurisdictions.

Firms may often try to address these issues in partnership agreements or other contracts. While non-compete agreements are functionally unenforceable in a law firm setting, the following cases provide illustrations of (1) how firms utilize contracts to try to control the results of lawyer defections and (2) the unfinished business doctrine in a dissolution situation.

Frasier, Frasier & Hickman, L.L.P. v. Flynn
114 P.3d 1095 (Okla. App. 4th Div. 2005)

Opinion by RONALD J. STUBBLEFIELD, Judge.

This is an appeal by a former law firm partner, from judgment entered on jury verdict in favor of the plaintiff law firm in its action for breach of contract, deceit and fraud. Based on our review of the record on appeal and applicable law, we affirm.

Facts and Procedural History

Attorney Robert Flynn (Flynn) joined the law firm of Frasier, Frasier & Hickman, L.L.P. (Frasier), as an associate attorney in 1991. He subsequently was admitted to "Class B" partnership. As a "Class B" partner, Flynn became entitled to receive a designated interest in the profits of the partnership. However, he obtained neither equity nor interest in the assets of the partnership, nor did he have the right to participate in the management decisions of the partnership. The "Class B Partnership Agreement," which Flynn executed on January 1, 1995, contained this provision:

> If the undersigned Class B Partner leaves the Partnership, any fees generated by any cases then being handled for any client of the Partnership who chooses to take his case with the departing Class B Partner shall be divided between the Partnership and the departing Class B Partner according to the respective amount of work performed for the client on the case before the client left the Partnership versus the amount of work

performed thereafter; provided that, in no case shall the Partnership's portion of the fee be less than one half (½) of the total fee in a contingent fee case. In any case handled in whole or in part by the undersigned Class B Partner, same will agree to protect any referral fee to any non-Frasier & Frasier attorney. This paragraph shall not limit Partnership's damages in case of a breach of this Agreement.

The partnership agreement also contained a non-solicitation provision, whereby Flynn agreed that he would not solicit business from Frasier's active clients for a period of two years following his departure from the law firm.

In August 2000, Flynn informed Frasier of his intention to leave the law firm. Flynn's departure was not immediate—the parties reached an agreement whereby Flynn continued working for the firm as a contract laborer, paid on a per diem basis. By subsequent written agreement, Flynn formally withdrew from the partnership on October 11, 2000. The parties terminated the working relationship on November 6, 2000, and Flynn subsequently opened his own law practice.

Following his separation from the firm, Flynn continued to handle many of the pending contingency fee cases that had originated with Frasier. These were primarily workers' compensation cases, for which Flynn collected fees when he successfully concluded the cases by settlement or trial. There were some active cases, for which Frasier had advanced substantially all of the litigation expenses, which Flynn resolved just over one month after his departure from the firm.

When paying workers' compensation awards, insurers often issued checks made payable to the client, and to Flynn and Frasier. Flynn requested that Frasier endorse these checks, which it did. Frasier later claimed it did so with the understanding that, after distributing the funds due to the client, Flynn would retain the attorney fees and costs in a trust account, and the monies would remain there until the parties determined how to divide them. However, Flynn used the monies to operate his practice, and later denied telling Frasier that the monies would be placed in a separate trust account.

The parties could not agree on how to divide the generated fees. According to Flynn, as the attorney who "closed the file" he was entitled to one half of the fee generated, regardless of the proportion of post-departure services he provided, because this was "custom" in workers' compensation cases. At the same time, Flynn objected to enforcement of the fee allocation provision of the partnership agreement because it would allow Frasier to retain no less than fifty percent of the fee recovered, even if Flynn devoted more than fifty percent of the efforts toward recovery in the case after his departure.

Frasier filed this action on September 10, 2001, alleging Flynn had breached the terms of the partnership agreement by (1) soliciting clients; (2) failing to divide fees recovered; and (3) failing to reimburse sums advanced. Frasier further alleged that, after he left the firm, Flynn induced Frasier to endorse checks for attorney fees by his promise that the monies would be held in trust pending the parties' agreement on how to divide them. As an affirmative defense, Flynn asserted that the fee arrangement set forth in the partnership agreement violated the fee-splitting prohibition of Rule 1.5(e) of the Oklahoma Rules of Professional Conduct, 5 O.S.2001, ch. 1, app. 3-A; was contrary to public policy; and, therefore, void and unenforceable.

Flynn initially asserted a counterclaim wherein he sought an accounting of all amounts due him under the partnership agreement from the date of execution until the date of his resignation. According to Flynn, although the agreement provided for his compensation at three percent of partnership profits, it did not set forth the manner in which this interest was to be calculated. Frasier later amended its petition to assert claims for fraud and punitive damages. Flynn answered the amended petition but did not reassert his counterclaim.

Both parties filed motions seeking summary adjudication of Frasier's claim for breach of contract. Flynn continued to maintain that the attorney fee provision of the partnership agreement was not enforceable. The Trial Court denied Flynn's motion and adjudicated the contract issue in Frasier's favor. Although the Trial Court found that Flynn was liable for breach of contract, it determined that a jury should decide the amount of Frasier's damages.

Frasier subsequently filed motions in limine, seeking to prohibit any reference by Flynn at trial to the Oklahoma Rules of Professional Conduct or his defense that the fee allocation provision of the partnership agreement constituted unlawful "fee splitting or division of fees." The Trial Court sustained Frasier's motions. Earlier, the Trial Court had entered an order requiring that all unspent attorney fees and costs that Flynn had collected in certain identified cases (a total of 145) be placed in a trust account pending resolution of the matter, with signatures of both parties required for withdrawal of any monies from the account.

At trial, Frasier presented testimony of two of its partners, and called Flynn as a witness. Over Flynn's objection, the Trial Court allowed Frasier to present the testimony of an experienced workers' compensation attorney, Tony Laizure, who gave his expert opinion regarding the amount of fees Flynn owed Frasier. Flynn moved for a directed verdict, again claiming the fee division was void, but also claiming that the expert's testimony regarding the amount of "work performed" by Frasier on the 145 cases prior to Flynn's departure was unreliable. The Trial Court denied Flynn's motion. Flynn presented neither witnesses nor exhibits.

The jury returned a verdict in favor of Frasier, awarding actual damages of $450,000. The jury also found clear and convincing evidence that Flynn had acted intentionally, with malice, and in reckless disregard of others' rights. It awarded punitive damages in the amount of $50,000. Flynn appeals from judgment entered on the jury verdict.

Discussion of Issues

I. The Partnership Agreement

In his first proposition of error, Flynn asserts that the Trial Court erred as a matter of law in determining that the fee allocation provision of the partnership agreement was enforceable. Flynn claims this provision of the partnership agreement violates the Oklahoma Code of Professional

Responsibility because it apportions fees between lawyers not in the same firm without client consent and without regard to the degree of responsibility assumed for the continued representation. The Trial Court's legal conclusion on this issue stands before us for de novo review. When reexamining a trial court's legal rulings, this Court exercises plenary, independent and non-deferential authority. Booth v. McKnight, 2003 OK 49, ¶12, 70 P.3d 855, 860.

Flynn correctly asserts that Oklahoma courts will not aid in the enforcement of an agreement that is unlawful or the object of which is contrary to public policy. Such agreements are void and unenforceable. Webster v. McFadden, 1942 OK 192, 125 P.2d 987; see also 15 O.S.2001 §104. However, despite Flynn's assertion to the contrary, we do not find that the provision of the partnership agreement at issue violates public policy as embodied in the Oklahoma Rules of Professional Conduct.

Rule 1.5(e) of the Oklahoma Rules of Professional Conduct provides:

> A division of fee between lawyers who are not in the same firm may be made only if:
> (1) the division is in proportion to the services performed by each lawyer or by written agreement with the client, each lawyer assumes joint responsibility for the representation;
> (2) the client is advised of and does not object to the participation of all of the lawyers involved; and
> (3) the total fee is reasonable.

5 O.S.2001, ch. 1, app. 3-A.

The parties do not direct us to any Oklahoma decision directly on point, but we have reviewed several cases wherein courts of other jurisdictions determined that similar agreements did not violate the Rules of Professional Conduct. For example, in Tomar, Seliger, Simonoff, Adourian & O'Brien, P.C. v. Snyder, 601 A.2d 1056 (Del. Super. Ct.), appeal refused, 571 A.2d 788 (Del. 1990), the Court examined an agreement reached between an attorney and law firm, while the attorney was still a partner with the firm. The agreement provided that the firm would transfer certain contingent fee cases to the attorney upon his leaving the firm and that he would pay the firm one third of all fees he received in connection with the cases. The Court held that the agreement did not violate the Delaware Lawyers' Rules of Professional Conduct concerning fee splitting and was valid and enforceable. Id. at 1059. The Court rejected the departing attorney's arguments that the agreement violated the ethical rule that fees must be divided in proportion to services rendered in the case and that the client had to be informed of the fee agreement. The Court in *Tomar* noted that the contingent fee cases the departing attorney continued to handle had originated with the firm while the attorney was either an associate or a partner, and there was no "brokering of legal services" such as Rule 1.5(e) was designed to prevent. Id. The Court reasoned:

> By its own terms, Rule 1.5(e) does not apply to lawyers who are in the same firm. It has no application to this case as there is obviously no issue with regard to brokering of legal services. . . .

It is not uncommon for a law firm and a departing attorney to divide the fees resulting from contingent fee cases which the attorney has been handling and will continue to handle after he leaves. . . .

Furthermore . . . the clients did not have to be informed of the fee agreement because they were not affected by it in any way. . . . [T]his fee agreement was simply a part of the overall process of the lawyer's separation from the firm. Id. (citing La Mantia v. Durst, 234 N.J. Super. 534, 561 A.2d 275 (Ct. App. Div .1989), and Baron v. Mullinax, Wells, Mauzy & Baab, Inc., 623 S.W.2d 457 (Tex. Ct. App. 1981)). See also McCroskey, Feldman, Cochrane & Brock, P.C. v. Waters, 197 Mich. App. 282, 494 N.W.2d 826 (1992) (agreement mandating that a percentage of fees obtained by a departing attorney for former firm cases be given to the firm as a way to compensate the firm for its work was found not void as against public policy); Groen, Laveson, Goldberg & Rubenstone v. Kancher, 362 N.J. Super. 350, 827 A.2d 1163 (Ct. App. Div. 2003) (fee-division provision of partnership agreement requiring withdrawing partner to share 50 percent of contingent fees recovered was enforceable); Restatement (Third) of The Law Governing Lawyers, §47 cmt. g (2000).

More recently, in Walker v. Gribble, 689 N.W.2d 104 (Iowa 2004), the Iowa Supreme Court examined a settlement agreement reached between a lawyer and her former partner regarding division of several lucrative contingent fee cases. The case was before the Court on the lawyer's appeal from summary judgment granted in favor of the former partner. The lawyer, making arguments virtually identical to those made herein by Flynn, claimed the agreement she had reached with her former partner was void because it violated the Iowa Code of Professional Responsibility for Lawyers. Id. at 108. The Iowa Supreme Court disagreed, and after finding that clients were not affected by the agreement, determined: "Nothing in the parties' settlement agreement runs afoul of the Iowa Code of Professional Responsibility for Lawyers. It does not violate public policy. It is enforceable." Id. at 116.

We note that Iowa's equivalent to Oklahoma Rule of Professional Conduct 1.5(e) includes this additional provision:

["](B) This disciplinary rule does not prohibit payment to a former partner or associate pursuant to a separation or retirement agreement.["]
Iowa Code of Professional Responsibility DR 2-107. Oklahoma's former DR 2-108(B), 5 O.S. Supp. 1987, ch. 1, app. 3, was identical to this Iowa provision. Oklahoma's Code of Professional Responsibility was superceded in 1988, when the Oklahoma Rules of Professional Conduct were first adopted. See 5 O.S. Supp. 1988, ch. 1, app. 3-A. Rule 1.5(e) of the American Bar Association's (ABA) Model Rules of Professional Conduct, from which Oklahoma Rule 1.5(e) is derived, no longer contains the exclusion regarding "payment to a former partner or associate pursuant to a separation or retirement agreement." However, the official commentary to ABA Model Rule 1.5(e) provides: "Paragraph (e) does not prohibit or regulate division of fees to be received in the future for work done when lawyers were previously associated in a law firm." Model Rules of Prof'l Conduct R. 1.5(e), cmt. 8 (2003). Courts of other jurisdictions with a legislative history similar to Oklahoma's have found "nothing . . .

that would indicate that the deletion of this exclusion was intended to make the fee division rule applicable to the division of fees for pending matters between law firms and departing attorneys." Piaskoski & Assocs. v. Ricciardi, 2004 WI APP 152, ¶28, 275 Wis. 2d 650, 686 N.W.2d 675, 686. See also Norton Frickey, P.C. v. Turner, P.C., 94 P.3d 1266, 1268-69 (Colo. Ct. App. 2004).

We find the authorities set forth above persuasive. We conclude that Rule 1.5(e) of the Oklahoma Rules of Professional Conduct does not prohibit a law firm from sharing fees with a former partner under a separation agreement for work arising from matters that were entrusted to the firm before the partner's departure. There is no evidence herein that the Frasier clients, who followed Flynn upon his departure, were in any way prejudiced by the parties' agreement. They all had signed contracts employing the Frasier firm, each of which contained an attorney fee agreement. Flynn's arguments regarding the alleged adverse effect on clients and disincentive to provide zealous representation are without evidentiary support in the record and totally unpersuasive.

We conclude that the fee division provision of Frasier's partnership agreement is neither illegal nor contrary to the public interests promoting Rule 1.5(e), but instead is valid and enforceable. In view of the undisputed evidence that Flynn violated the provision, we find that the Trial Court did not err in adjudicating, as a matter of law, Flynn's liability for breach of the partnership agreement.

II. *Admission of Expert Testimony Regarding Fee Division*

[The court found no error regarding the admissibility of expert testimony on the issue of fees.]

Conclusion

Flynn's propositions of error are not availing of reversal. We find no error in the Trial Court's rulings of which Flynn complains. Accordingly, the judgment entered on jury verdict must be affirmed.

Affirmed.

RAPP, V.C.J., and GOODMAN, P.J., concur.

Questions: ABA Model Rule 5.6 places per se restrictions on the use of restrictive covenants among lawyers:

Rule 5.6: Restrictions on Rights to Practice
A lawyer shall not participate in offering or making:
(a) a partnership, shareholders, operating, employment, or other similar type of agreement that restricts the right of a lawyer to practice after termination of the relationship, except an agreement concerning benefits upon retirement; or

(b) an agreement in which a restriction on the lawyer's right to practice is part of the settlement of a client controversy.

Comment 1 thereto states: "An agreement restricting the right of lawyers to practice after leaving a firm not only limits their professional autonomy but also limits the freedom of clients to choose a lawyer."

■ How can this be squared with some jurisdictions' acceptance of using contractually imposed financial disincentives to functionally serve as a deterrent to departures?
■ Does a dramatic change in the practice of law since 1961, when Model Rule 5.6 was instituted, require a balancing of the interests of departing lawyers to practice with the interests of the remaining partners to preserve the stability of the law firm?
■ Should lawyers be treated any differently than other professionals, such as medical doctors, who may be subject to reasonable non-compete clauses?

Geron v. Robinson & Cole, LLP et al.
476 B.R. 732 (Bankr. S.D.N.Y. 2012)

Memorandum & Order

WILLIAM H. PAULEY III, District Judge.

These actions arise from an alarming phenomenon—the bankruptcy of a major law firm. The pursuit of pending hourly fee matters as assets of the estate has become a recurring feature of such bankruptcies. But this concept of law firm "property" collides with the essence of the attorney-client relationship. That relationship springs from agency law, not property law. The client is the principal, the attorney is the agent, and the relationship is terminable at will. The question presented is whether a dissolved law firm's pending hourly fee matters are nevertheless its property.

Plaintiff Yann Geron (the "Trustee"), the Chapter 7 trustee of the bankruptcy estate of former law firm Thelen LLP ("Thelen"), brings fraudulent transfer and accounting and turnover claims against Defendants Seyfarth Shaw LLP ("Seyfarth Shaw") and Robinson & Cole LLP ("Robinson & Cole"). Through these claims, the Trustee seeks to recover profits from work that former Thelen partners performed after they joined those two law firms. Seyfarth Shaw moves for judgment on the pleadings under Federal Rule of Civil Procedure 12(c), and Robinson & Cole moves to dismiss all claims against it under Federal Rule of Civil Procedure 12(b)(6). For the following reasons, Seyfarth Shaw's motion is granted in its entirety and Robinson & Cole's motion is denied. Further, this Court sua sponte certifies this order for interlocutory appeal.

Background

Until its dissolution in late 2008, Thelen was a registered limited liability partnership governed by California law, (Voluntary Petition ("Pet.") at 1, In re Thelen LLP, Case No. 09-15631 (Bankr. S.D.N.Y.).) On October 28, 2008—in the midst of the global financial crisis—Thelen's partners voted to dissolve the firm. (Complaint against Robinson & Cole and Partner Does, dated Sept. 14, 2011 ("RC Compl.") ¶20; Complaint against Seyfarth Shaw and Partner Does, dated Sept. 14, 2011 ("SS Compl.") ¶20.) At the same time, Thelen's partners adopted the Fourth Amended and Restated Limited Liability Partnership Agreement (the "Fourth Partnership Agreement"), which was also governed by California law. (RC Compl. ¶20; SS Compl. ¶20.) In connection with the Fourth Partnership Agreement, Thelen's partners voted to wind up Thelen's business under a written Plan of Dissolution. (RC Compl. ¶21; SS Compl. ¶21.) At the time of its dissolution, Thelen was insolvent. (RC Compl. ¶¶23, 28-29; SS Compl. ¶¶23, 28-29.)

Unlike Thelen's previous partnership agreements, the Fourth Partnership Agreement incorporated a so-called Jewel Waiver. (RC Compl. ¶34; SS Compl. ¶34.) Specifically, it provides:

> Neither the Partners nor the Partnership shall have any claim or entitlement to clients, cases or matters ongoing at the time of dissolution of the Partnership other than the entitlement for collection of amounts due for work performed by the Partners and other Partnership personnel prior to their departure from the Partnership. The provisions of this [section] are intended to expressly waive, opt out of and be in lieu of any rights any Partner or the Partnership may have to "unfinished business" of the Partnership, as the term is defined in Jewel v. Boxer, 156 Cal. App. 3d 171 [203 Cal. Rptr. 13] (Cal. App. 1 Dist. 1984), or as otherwise might be provided in the absence of this provision through the interpretation or application of the [California Uniform Partnership Act of 1994, as amended].

(RC Compl. ¶34; SS Compl. ¶34.)

On September 18, 2009, Thelen filed a voluntary petition for relief under Chapter 7 of the Bankruptcy Code in the United States Bankruptcy Court for the Southern District of New York. At that time, Thelen indicated that it "has been domiciled or has had a residence, principal place of business, or principal assets" in the Southern District of New York. (Pet. at 2.) After the Trustee was appointed, he instituted adversary proceedings against Seyfarth Shaw, Robinson & Cole, and several former Thelen partners. The Trustee contends that Thelen's adoption of the Jewel Waiver in its Fourth Partnership Agreement constituted a fraudulent transfer by Thelen. The Trustee now seeks to avoid the fraudulent transfer of Thelen's unfinished business, recover its value, and require Defendants to account for and turn over the profits generated from that work.

Discussion

I. Legal Standard

Courts evaluate motions for judgment on the pleadings under the same standard as motions to dismiss for failure to state a claim. See Bank of N.Y. v. First Millennium, Inc., 607 F.3d 905, 922 (2d Cir. 2010). "To survive a motion to dismiss, a complaint must contain sufficient factual matter, accepted as true, to 'state a claim to relief that is plausible on its face.'" Ashcroft v. Iqbal, 556 U.S. 662, 678, 129 S. Ct. 1937, 173 L. Ed. 2d 868 (2009) (quoting Bell Atl. Corp. v. Twombly, 550 U.S. 544, 570, 127 S. Ct. 1955, 167 L. Ed. 2d 929 (2007)). To determine plausibility, courts follow a "two-pronged approach." *Iqbal*, 556 U.S. at 679, 129 S. Ct. 1937. "First, although 'a court must accept as true all of the allegations contained in a complaint,' that 'tenet' 'is inapplicable to legal conclusions,' and '[t]hreadbare recitals of the elements of a cause of action, supported by mere conclusory statements, do not suffice.'" Harris v. Mills, 572 F.3d 66, 72 (2d Cir. 2009) (alteration in original) (quoting *Iqbal*, 556 U.S. at 678, 129 S. Ct. 1937). Second, a court determines "whether the 'well-pleaded factual allegations,' assumed to be true, 'plausibly give rise to an entitlement to relief.'" Hayden v. Paterson, 594 F.3d 150, 161 (2d Cir. 2010) (quoting *Iqbal*, 556 U.S. at 679, 129 S. Ct. 1937). A court's "consideration [on a motion to dismiss] is limited to facts stated on the face of the complaint, in documents appended to the complaint or incorporated in the complaint by reference, and to matters of which judicial notice may be taken." Allen v. WestPoint-Pepperell Inc., 945 F.2d 40, 44 (2d Cir. 1991).

II. Choice of Law

To prevail on its claims against Seyfarth Shaw, the Trustee must demonstrate that Thelen had an interest in "property." See 11 U.S.C. §§542, 544, 548, 550; see also Cal. Civ. Code §§3439.04-3439.07. According to the Trustee, Thelen's partners transferred "property" to Seyfarth Shaw and Robinson & Cole when they executed the Jewel Waiver. The parties agree that California law defines any "property interest" that Robinson & Cole received. However, the Trustee and Seyfarth Shaw dispute whether California law or New York law defines any "property interest" received by Seyfarth Shaw.

As a preliminary matter, this Court rejects the Trustee's contention that California law applies because Thelen's Fourth Partnership Agreement contained a choice-of-law provision to that effect. Because Seyfarth Shaw was not a party to the Fourth Partnership Agreement, it cannot be bound by that agreement. See Int'l Customs Assocs., Inc. v. Ford Motor Co., 893 F. Supp. 1251, 1255 (S.D.N.Y. 1995) (citing Abraham Zion Corp. v. Lebow, 761 F.2d 93, 103 (2d Cir. 1985)). Further, "a contractual choice-of-law-provision governs only a cause of action sounding in contract, not one sounding in tort[.]" Drenis v. Haligiannis, 452 F. Supp. 2d 418, 425-26 (S.D.N.Y. 2006). Fraudulent transfer claims sound in tort. See *Drenis*, 452 F. Supp. 2d at 418. Accordingly, Seyfarth Shaw is not bound by the agreement's choice-of-law provision.

In the absence of a binding contractual choice-of-law provision, this Court applies the choice-of-law rules of New York to determine which state's law governs the purported property interest at issue. See In re Gaston & Snow, 243 F.3d 599, 600-01, 607 (2d Cir. 2001). Thus, this Court first examines whether an actual conflict exists between the laws of the jurisdiction involved. See Paradigm BioDevices, Inc. v. Viscogliosi Bros., LLC, 842 F. Supp. 2d 661, 665 (S.D.N.Y. 2012). If there is such a conflict, this Court conducts an "interest analysis," and applies the "law of the jurisdiction having the greatest interest in the litigation[.]" Istim, Inc. v. Chemical Bank, 78 N.Y.2d 342, 347, 575 N.Y.S.2d 796, 581 N.E.2d 1042 (1991) (quoting Schultz v. Boy Scouts of Am., Inc., 65 N.Y.2d 189, 197, 491 N.Y.S.2d 90, 480 N.E.2d 679 (1985)) (internal quotation marks omitted).

For the reasons described below, the existence and scope of a dissolved law firm's property interest in pending hourly fee matters vary under New York and California law. This Court therefore examines the competing interests of New York and California in this action. In ascertaining the state with the greatest interest, this Court undertakes a two-pronged inquiry, determining "(1) what are the significant contacts and in which jurisdiction are they located; and, (2) whether the purpose of the law [at issue] is to regulate conduct or allocate loss." Padula v. Lilarn Props. Corp., 84 N.Y.2d 519, 521, 620 N.Y.S.2d 310, 644 N.E.2d 1001 (1994) (citation omitted).

Here, the majority of the significant contacts occurred in New York. The Trustee does not dispute that the majority of the former Thelen partners who moved to Seyfarth Shaw are licensed to practice law in New York. Moreover, Thelen filed its Chapter 7 petition in the Southern District of New York, indicating that it "has been domiciled or has had a residence, principal place of business, or principal assets" in the Southern District of New York. (Pet. at 2.) In view of these contacts, Thelen's status as a California limited liability partnership is inconsequential. See El Cid, Ltd. v. N.J. Zinc Co., 575 F. Supp. 1513, 1518-19 (S.D.N.Y. 1983). And where, as here, regulation of conduct is at issue, the state where the alleged tort took place has the greater interest. See GFL Advantage Fund, Ltd. v. Colkitt, No. 03 Civ. 1256 (JSM), 2003 WL 21459716, at *3 (S.D.N.Y. June 24, 2003); see also Roselink Investors, L.L.C. v. Shenkman, 386 F. Supp. 2d 209, 225 (S.D.N.Y. 2004) ("A fraudulent conveyance statute is conduct regulating rather than loss allocating." (internal citation and quotation marks omitted)). Here, the alleged tort occurred in New York. Accordingly, New York has the greatest interest in this litigation, and New York law defines the property interest—if any—that Seyfarth Shaw received.

III. Unfinished Business Under New York Law

To prevail on its claims against Seyfarth Shaw, the Trustee must demonstrate that Seyfarth Shaw received a property interest of Thelen's. To that end, the Trustee seeks to recover Thelen's purported ownership interest in profits from its former clients' hourly fee matters that were pending when Thelen dissolved. The Trustee also seeks to recover profits from pending contingency fee matters. In opposing these claims, Seyfarth Shaw contends that New York law does not recognize a law firm's property interest in pending hourly fee matters. It is this Court's task "to ascertain what the state law is, not what it ought to be." Klaxon Co. v. Stentor Elec. Mfg. Co., 313 U.S. 487, 497, 61 S. Ct. 1020, 85 L. Ed. 1477 (1941). Accordingly, without guidance from the state's highest court, this Court must "predict how the New York Court of Appeals would resolve the question[.]" Amerex Grp., Inc. v. Lexington Ins. Co., 678 F.3d 193, 200 (2d Cir. 2012) (quoting Highland Capital Mgmt. LP v. Schneider, 460 F.3d 308, 316 (2d Cir. 2006)) (internal quotation marks omitted).

The Trustee bases his claims on the "unfinished business doctrine," which is "[t]he general rule that the business of a partnership that is unfinished on the date the partnership dissolves is an asset of the partnership, and must be concluded for the benefit of the dissolved partnership." Dev. Specialists, Inc. v. Akin Gump Strauss Hauer & Feld LLP, 477 B.R. 318, 2012 WL 1918705, at *11 (S.D.N.Y. May 24, 2012) ("DSI") (citing Stem v. Warren, 227 N.Y. 538, 125 N.E. 811 (1920)). The seminal case applying this doctrine to law partnerships is Jewel v. Boxer, 156 Cal. App. 3d 171, 179, 203 Cal. Rptr. 13 (Cal. App. 1 Dist.1984), where the court noted that "each former partner has a duty to wind up and complete the unfinished business of the dissolved partnership." The court also observed that "[t]he Uniform Partnership Act unequivocally prohibits extra compensation for postdissolution services, with a single exception for surviving partners." Jewel, 156 Cal. App. 3d at 176-77, 203 Cal. Rptr. 13 (citing Cal. Corp. Code §15018(f) (since repealed)). Applying this "no compensation" rule, the court in Jewel held that "absent a contrary agreement, any income generated through the winding up of unfinished business is allocated to the former partners according to their respective interests in the partnership." Jewel, 156 Cal. App. 3d at 176, 203 Cal. Rptr. 13. New York's Partnership Law is a codification of the Uniform Partnership Act ("UPA"), and the "no compensation" rule applies in New York. See DSI, 477 B.R. at 327, 2012 WL 1918705, at *5 (citing N.Y. P'ship Law §1); see also N.Y. P'ship Law §40(6). After Jewel, some courts have characterized a dissolved law firm's unfinished business as a "partnership asset." See, e.g., In re Brobeck, Phleger & Harrison LLP, 408 B.R. 318, 333 (Bankr. N.D. Cal. 2009). The question here is whether New York law sanctions the expansion of such a rule to a dissolved law firm's pending hourly fee matters.

Under New York law, it is well settled that "[a]bsent an agreement to the contrary, pending *contingent fee cases* of a dissolved partnership are assets subject to distribution." Santalucia v. Sebright Transp., Inc., 232 F.3d 293, 297 (2d Cir. 2000) (emphasis added). But New York courts have not expanded the unfinished business doctrine to reach pending hourly fee matters. Rather, the only New York court to consider whether a debtor law firm possesses a property interest in its unfinished hourly fee matters concluded that it does not. In Sheresky v. Sheresky Aronson Mayefsky & Sloan, LLP, 35 Misc. 3d 1201(A), 2011 WL 7574999, at *5 (N.Y. Sup. Ct. Sept. 13, 2011), the state court declined to expand the unfinished business doctrine to pending hourly fee matters, reasoning that "[i]t is logical to distinguish between contingency fee arrangements and cases which are billed on the basis of hourly work." Citing the New York Rules of Professional Conduct, the court refused "to recognize a cause of action for unfinished business for hourly fee cases which has, hitherto, not been recognized by the New York courts." *Sheresky*, 2011 WL 7574999, at *6.

Although *Sheresky* is not binding authority, a New York trial court's interpretation of New York law is entitled to "great weight." In re Brooklyn Navy Yard Asbestos Litig., 971 F.2d 831, 850 (2d Cir. 1992) (internal quotation marks omitted). And this Court finds *Sheresky* persuasive. Unlike in the contingency fee context, applying the unfinished business doctrine to pending hourly fee matters would result in an unjust windfall for the Thelen estate, as "compensating a former partner out of that fee would reduce the compensation of the attorneys performing the work." *Sheresky*, 2011 WL 7574999, at *5. Such an expansion of the doctrine would violate New York's public policy against restrictions on the practice of law. See Cohen v. Lord, Day & Lord, 75 N.Y.2d 95, 96, 551 N.Y.S.2d 157, 550 N.E.2d 410 (1989). Indeed, recognizing a property interest in pending hourly fee matters would clash directly with New York's Rules of Professional Conduct, which state:

> A lawyer shall not divide a fee for legal services with another lawyer who is not associated in the same firm unless: (1) the division is in proportion to the services performed by each lawyer or, by a writing given to the client, each lawyer assumes joint responsibility for the representation; (2) the client agrees to the employment of the other lawyer after a full disclosure that a division of fees will be made, including the share each lawyer will receive, and the client's agreement is confirmed in writing; and (3) the total fee is not excessive. 22 NYCRR 1200.0, DR 1.5(g).

When confronted with two apparently conflicting statutes, New York courts adopt "any fair construction" that yields "a reasonable field of operation for both statutes." Cnty. of St. Lawrence v. Shah, 95 A.D.3d 1548, 945 N.Y.S.2d 443, 446 (3d Dep't 2012) (quoting Con. Edison Co. of N.Y., Inc. v. Dep't of Envtl. Conservation, 71 N.Y.2d 186, 195, 524 N.Y.S.2d 409, 519 N.E.2d 320 (1988)) (internal quotation marks and alteration omitted). Although the Rules of Professional Conduct lack the force of law, cf. Niesig v. Team I, 76 N.Y.2d 363, 369, 559 N.Y.S.2d 493, 558 N.E.2d 1030 (1990), New York courts interpret other laws to harmonize with them where possible. See *Sheresky*, 2011 WL 7574999, at *5.

Further, recognizing a property interest in pending hourly fee matters would contravene New York law's treatment of post-dissolution contingency fee matters. Although New York cases deem pending contingency fee matters to be "assets" of a dissolved firm, they hold that a dissolved firm has "no cognizable property interest in [a] fee" where the "successful settlement of a pending contingent fee case post-dissolution is due to a surviving partner's post-dissolution efforts, skill and diligence [.]" *Santalucia*, 232 F.3d at 298 (quoting Shandell v. Katz, 217 A.D.2d 472,

629 N.Y.S.2d 437, 439 (1st Dep't 1995)) (internal quotation marks omitted). "Thus, in a case where a lawyer departs from a dissolved partnership and takes with him a contingent fee case which he then litigates to settlement, the dissolved firm is entitled only to the value of the case at the date of dissolution, with interest." *Santalucia*, 232 F.3d at 298 (citing Kirsch v. Leventhal, 181 A.D.2d 222, 586 N.Y.S.2d 330, 333 (3d Dep't 1992)). In an hourly fee case, unlike a contingency fee case, all post-dissolution fees that a lawyer earns are due to that lawyer's "post-dissolution efforts, skill and diligence[.]" *Shandell*, 629 N.Y.S.2d at 439 (quoting *Kirsch*, 586 N.Y.S.2d at 333) (internal quotation marks omitted). Accordingly, New York law does not recognize a debtor law firm's property interest in pending hourly fee matters. And recognizing such a property interest would have bizarre consequences. If such an interest exists, it becomes property of the estate upon the filing of a bankruptcy petition. See 11 U.S.C. §541. It would appear, then, that the Bankruptcy Code empowers a debtor law firm to sell its pending hourly fee matters to the highest bidder. See 11 U.S.C. §363 ("The trustee, after notice and hearing, may use, sell, or lease . . . property of the estate [.]"). When this Court asked the Trustee whether a debtor firm could auction off its pending matters, the Trustee was unable to answer definitively. (Hearing Transcript, dated July 31, 2012 ("Hr'g Tr.") at 31 (12 Civ. 1364, ECF No. 17).) And the Trustee's reticence is understandable, as allowing such a sale of "property" is inconsistent with a client's right to choose attorneys. See Demov, Morris, Levin & Shein v. Glantz, 53 N.Y.2d 553, 556, 444 N.Y.S.2d 55, 428 N.E.2d 387 (1981) ("[It is] well rooted in our jurisprudence [] that a client may at any time, with or without cause, discharge an attorney [.]"). Similarly, under the Trustee's interpretation of the unfinished business doctrine, it is unclear whether a client who discharges a debtor law firm and transfers his case to a new firm violates the automatic stay. See 11 U.S.C. §362 (prohibiting "any act to obtain possession of property of the estate . . . or to exercise control over the property of the estate").

These unworkable results militate powerfully against extending the unfinished business doctrine to hourly fee matters. Perhaps for this reason, New York courts have endeavored to cabin the doctrine, holding that "[r]etainers from former clients on new matters—even matters, like appeals, that are related to finished representations—. . . [are] 'new business' and not subject to the duty to account." *DSI*, 477 B.R. at 332, 2012 WL 1918705, at *11 (citing Talley v. Lamb, 100 N.Y.S.2d 112, 117-18 (N.Y. Sup. Ct. 1950)). Given this background, characterizing unfinished hourly fee matters as "property" makes little sense.

In arguing that pending hourly fee matters are nevertheless Thelen property, the Trustee relies heavily on Stem v. Warren, 227 N.Y. 538, 125 N.E. 811 (1920), a hoary case involving architecture partnerships. According to the Trustee, *Stem* stands for the proposition that a partnership's executory contracts may be partnership property even if they are terminable at will. But the Trustee's reading of the case is overbroad. Rather, "under *Stem*, if an executory contract with a third party contemplates that it should survive dissolution, it remains a joint venture asset and the co-venturers have an obligation to perform with the concomitant right to its benefits." Scholastic, Inc. v. Harris, 259 F.3d 73, 89 (2d Cir. 2001). Here, Thelen's hourly fee matters cannot have contemplated post-dissolution survival without infringing a client's right to terminate an attorney at will. See Demov, Morris, Levin & Shein, 53 N.Y.2d at 556, 444 N.Y.S.2d 55, 428 N.E.2d 387. Although the contract in *Stem* was, by its terms, terminable at will, see 227 N.Y. at 544, 125 N.E. 811, contracts for legal services are categorically different from architecture contracts. Clients repose "ultimate trust and confidence" in their attorneys. In re Cooperman, 83 N.Y.2d 465, 472, 611 N.Y.S.2d 465, 633 N.E.2d 1069 (1994). "The attorney's obligations, therefore, transcend those prevailing in the commercial market place," and "[t]he contract under which an attorney is employed by a client has peculiar and distinctive features[.]" *Cooperman*, 83 N.Y.2d at 472-73, 611 N.Y.S.2d 465, 633 N.E.2d 1069 (quoting Martin v. Camp, 219 N.Y. 170, 172, 114 N.E. 46 (1916)) (internal quotation marks and citations omitted).

A pending client matter is not an ordinary article of commerce. Contrary to *DSI*, an hourly fee matter is not akin to "a Jackson Pollack [sic] painting" that a departing attorney "rip[s] off the wall of the reception area [.]" *DSI*, 477 B.R. at 329, 2012 WL 1918705, at *7. The client, not the attorney, moves a matter to a new firm. Thus, the attorney-client relationship is unique, and applying *Stem* to hourly fee legal service contracts would undermine it. New York law does not countenance such a result. See *Sheresky*, 2011 WL 7574999, at *5-6. In *Cohen*, the New York Court of Appeals drew on an ethics opinion from the New York County Lawyers' Association to emphasize New York's commitment to client autonomy: "Clients are not merchandise. Lawyers are not tradesmen. . . . An attempt, therefore, to barter in clients, would appear to be inconsistent with the best concepts of our professional status." *Cohen*, 75 N.Y.2d at 98, 551 N.Y.S.2d 157, 550 N.E.2d 410 (internal quotation marks omitted). This policy applies just as forcefully to client matters.

The Trustee also cites cases from other jurisdictions for the proposition that "every other court confronted with this issue . . . has held that pending cases, regardless of whether they are hourly-fee cases or contingent-fee matters [are] . . . assets of the partnership subject to post-dissolution distribution." In re Labrum & Doak, LLP, 227 B.R. 391, 408 (Bankr. E.D. Pa. 1998) (citing Sufrin v. Hosier, 896 F. Supp. 766, 769 (N.D. Ill. 1995)). But the cases on which the Trustee relies do not represent a consensus view. See *Sheresky*, 2011 WL 7574999, at *5-*6. In *DSI*, the district court nonetheless gave substantial weight to these decisions on the ground that "New York courts must harmonize their rulings with those of other UPA jurisdictions by statute[.]" *DSI*, 477 B.R. at 336, 2012 WL 1918705, at *15 (citing N.Y. P'ship Law §4(4)). This Court respectfully disagrees.

The purpose of UPA is to harmonize partners' duties regarding partnership property, not to delineate the scope of such property. See Welman v. Parker, 328 S.W.3d 451, 458 (Mo. Ct. App. 2010) (explaining that state common law, and not the Uniform Partnership Law, determines "which party is entitled to the contingent fee"); see also *DSI*, 477 B.R. at

334, 2012 WL 198705, at *13 ("There is surprisingly little New York authority on how a court is to determine what property is within or without a partnership.") (quoting Sriraman v. Patel, 761 F. Supp. 2d 7, 18 (E.D.N.Y. 2011)); cf. Butner v. United States, 440 U.S. 48, 55, 99 S. Ct. 914, 59 L. Ed. 2d 136 (1979) ("[T]here is no reason why [property] interests should be analyzed differently simply because an interested party is involved in a bankruptcy proceeding."). The Trustee identifies no provision of UPA that addresses whether pending hourly fee matters are partnership property. And, for the reasons discussed above, recognizing a property right in unfinished hourly fee matters conflicts with New York's strong public policy in favor of client autonomy and attorney mobility. See Cohen, 75 N.Y.2d at 98, 551 N.Y.S.2d 157, 550 N.E.2d 410; see also Denburg v. Parker Chapin Flattau & Klimpl, 82 N.Y.2d 375, 381-82, 604 N.Y.S.2d 900, 624 N.E.2d 995 (1993). Accordingly, the Trustee's contention that the court in Sheresky, 2011 WL 7574999, at *6, failed to engage in the requisite analysis of out-of-state case law is without merit. (Hr'g Tr. at 28.) To the extent that the out-of-state cases suggest a result that is irreconcilable with New York policy, they are not reliable indicators of New York law.

Thus, under New York law, a dissolved law firm's pending hourly fee matters are not partnership assets. And because the Trustee's complaint against Seyfarth Shaw fails to distinguish between pending contingency fee matters and hourly fee matters, the complaint is deficient. See Iqbal, 556 U.S. at 678, 129 S. Ct. 1937.

Accordingly, Seyfarth Shaw's motion for judgment on the pleadings is granted, and the Trustee's claims against Seyfarth Shaw are dismissed. If the Trustee intends to pursue claims against Seyfarth Shaw regarding Thelen's pending contingency fee matters, the Trustee must amend his complaint.

IV. Unfinished Business Under California Law

In contrast to Seyfarth Shaw, Robinson & Cole concedes for the purposes of its motion to dismiss that California law governs any property interest that it received. Robinson & Cole argues that, notwithstanding Jewel and the cases following it, California law no longer recognizes a dissolved law firm's property right in its pending hourly fee matters. Robinson & Cole also maintains that, even assuming the existence of such a property interest, the interest was never transferred to Robinson & Cole. The Trustee responds that California law recognizes pending hourly fee matters as assets, and that Thelen transferred those assets to Robinson & Cole when its partners executed the Jewel Waiver.

Assuming that pending hourly fee matters are "assets," Thelen fraudulently transferred those assets when its partners adopted the Jewel Waiver on the eve of dissolution without consideration. See In re Heller Ehrman LLP, No. 08-32514DM, 2011 WL 1539796, at *5 (Bankr. N.D. Cal. April 22, 2011); see also 11 U.S.C. §101(54) (a "transfer" is "each mode, direct or indirect, . . . of disposing of or parting with— (i) property; or (ii) an interest in property"). Under section 550(a) of the Bankruptcy Code, the Trustee may recover the value of fraudulently transferred property from "(1) the initial transferee of such transfer or the entity for whose benefit such transfer was made; or (2) any immediate or mediate transferee of such initial transferee." 11 U.S.C. §550(a). And when Thelen's former partners brought pending matters to Robinson & Cole, they transferred that "property" to their new firm. Thus—assuming that pending hourly fee matters are "property"—Robinson & Cole may be liable as an "immediate or mediate transferee" of those assets. See 11 U.S.C. §550(a)(1). That Robinson & Cole owes no fiduciary duties to Thelen is irrelevant to its status as a transferee. See *Brobeck*, 408 B.R. at 339 n. 31.

The central question, then, is whether California law recognizes a dissolved law firm's pending hourly fee matters as partnership assets. In *Jewel* and the cases following it, California courts held that such matters were, indeed, assets of a dissolving firm. See *Jewel*, 156 Cal. App. 3d at 176, 203 Cal. Rptr. 13; see also Rothman v. Dolin, 20 Cal. App. 4th 755, 758-59, 24 Cal. Rptr. 2d 571 (Cal. App. 2 Dist. 1993). And *Jewel* applies to registered limited liability partnerships like Thelen. See Fox v. Abrams, 163 Cal. App. 3d 610, 616, 210 Cal. Rptr. 260 (Cal. App. 2 Dist. 1985) (extending the Jewel doctrine to the dissolution of a law corporation because *Jewel* "was not based solely on partnership law but also cited 'sound policy reasons' for its decision"). However, Robinson & Cole argues that California's enactment of the Revised Uniform Partnership Act ("RUPA") in 1994 abrogated the Jewel doctrine. *Jewel* and its progeny relied on UPA's "no compensation" rule. See *Jewel*, 156 Cal. App. 3d at 176-77, 203 Cal. Rptr. 13; see also Rothman, 20 Cal. App. 4th at 757, 24 Cal. Rptr. 2d 571. But RUPA abolished the "no compensation" rule, providing instead that a partner is entitled to "reasonable compensation for services rendered in winding up the business of the partnership." Cal. Corp. Code §16401(h).

Robinson & Cole's argument is persuasive. In applying the unfinished business doctrine to law partnerships, *Jewel* relied expressly on UPA's "no compensation" rule, reasoning that "[t]he Uniform Partnership Act unequivocally prohibits extra compensation for postdissolution services, with a single exception for surviving partners." *Jewel*, 156 Cal. App. 3d at 176-77, 203 Cal. Rptr. 13. But RUPA transformed the law on which *Jewel* relied and eroded the theoretical underpinnings of the Jewel doctrine. Because RUPA entitles partners of a dissolving firm to "reasonable compensation for services rendered in winding up the business of the partnership," Cal. Corp. Code §16401(h), there is no basis to require Thelen's former partners to remit all profits earned from former Thelen matters to the Thelen estate.

Nevertheless, the former Thelen partners' post-RUPA entitlement to "reasonable compensation" does not necessarily mean that Robinson & Cole did not receive Thelen "assets." The question of "reasonable compensation" is fact-intensive, and this Court cannot, on a motion to dismiss, determine whether the former Thelen partners are entitled to retain all profits earned from pending hourly fee matters. Robinson & Cole cites Jacobson v. Wikholm, 29 Cal. 2d 24, 30-31, 172 P.2d 878 (1946), for the proposition that "reasonable compensation" includes profits resulting from a partner's post-dissolution skill and effort, except to the extent that those profits result from the use of the dissolved partnership's capital. Yet, notwithstanding Jacobson, the fact-bound "reasonable compensation" inquiry may not be resolved on a motion to dismiss. See Anderson News, L.L.C. v. Am. Media, Inc., 680 F.3d 162, 185 (2d Cir. 2012) ("Fact-specific questions cannot be resolved on the pleadings." (internal alterations, quotation marks, and citations omitted)). Thus, Robinson & Cole's liability turns on the extent to which the former Thelen partners received remuneration beyond "reasonable compensation." This question can only be resolved on a more fully developed record.

In arguing that dismissal of the claims against it is warranted, Robinson & Cole advances many of the same policy arguments proffered by Seyfarth Shaw. But these arguments are less persuasive in the context of California law because California courts have rejected them. See *Fox*, 163 Cal. App. 3d at 616, 210 Cal. Rptr. 260 (discussing "sound policy reasons" supporting Jewel doctrine); see also *Jewel*, 156 Cal. App. 3d at 179, 203 Cal. Rptr. 13. And New York's commitment to attorney mobility appears to be stronger than California's. Compare *Cohen*, 75 N.Y.2d at 98, 551 N.Y.S.2d 157, 550 N.E.2d 410, with Howard v. Babcock, 6 Cal. 4th 409, 422-23, 25 Cal. Rptr.2d 80, 863 P.2d 150 (1993) (declining to follow *Cohen*).

In sum, RUPA's "reasonable compensation" rule undermines the Jewel doctrine, which applied the older "no compensation" rule. Nevertheless, California law may still recognize a dissolving firm's pending hourly fee matters as "assets." Specifically, to the extent that Robinson & Cole earned profits from former Thelen matters exceeding "reasonable compensation," California law dictates that those profits belong to Thelen. Accordingly, Robinson & Cole's motion to dismiss the Trustee's claims is denied.

V. Interlocutory Appeal

[The court sua sponte certified this order for interlocutory appeal.]

Conclusion

For the foregoing reasons, Seyfarth Shaw LLP's motion for judgment on the pleadings is granted, and Robinson & Cole LLP's motion to dismiss is denied. This Court certifies this order for interlocutory appeal pursuant to 28 U.S.C. §1292(b). Any party seeking leave for the Court of Appeals to hear an interlocutory appeal shall direct its application to the Court of Appeals within ten days. See 28 U.S.C. §1292(b). This Court hereby stays all proceedings in the district court pending a decision on certification from the Court of Appeals.

Questions:

- Why might departing partners find the unfinished business doctrine to be frustrating?
- How might the doctrine contradict the rules of professional responsibility and be disadvantageous to clients?

III. Conclusion

Compensation is a multi-variable consideration that lies at the heart of every law firm and many a partnership dispute. Aside from the amounts involved, you should appreciate that compensation choices can also drive and direct firm culture and evolution.

CHAPTER 7

MARKETING AND BUSINESS DEVELOPMENT

Without legal work, there is nothing for a law firm or its lawyers to do. Without paying legal work, a firm can't remain in business for very long.

There's a good chance that you recoiled at the very title of this chapter. Few law students profess to having come to law school to be salespeople. Indeed, the classic adage for lawyers was "just do good work, and the phone will ring." The ideal model involved clients seeking lawyers, not the other way around.

But lawyers have always had to pitch themselves, as if they were running for office. Very few lawyers have the luxury of waiting for business to come to them. Law is a service business, and lawyers must interact directly with their client-customers. The historical pillars of the profession—high standards, good work, reputation, and connections—still matter as much as they ever have. Yet today's competitive landscape—where rivalry among firms is intense—requires even more. In small firm environments, it is often crucial from the start, and even newly minted lawyers in law firms where most if not all business generation happens at the senior levels can benefit from an understanding of the underpinnings and goals of the process. In larger firm environments, there may be an institutionalized approach and there are a host of consultants and advisory firms available to provide customized planning and execution strategies.

This chapter is divided into three sections, entitled Marketing, Business Development, and Client Service. While each section relates to the others, and many lawyers conflate the three concepts discussed in these sections, they carry important distinctions.

I. Marketing

A. Outreach

According to the American Marketing Association, marketing is defined as "the activity, set of institutions, and processes for creating, communicating, delivering, and exchanging offerings that have value for customers, clients, partners, and society at large."[1] And identity in marketing is known as "brand"—that is, what identifies one firm as distinct from its competitors. Marketing in a law firm setting is outreach to prospective clients. The marketing process applies equally to both law firms and their individual lawyers. At the firm level, management will typically oversee these efforts at an organizational scale, and in furtherance of an overall strategic marketing plan. Larger firms may even have a dedicated marketing department. By comparison, at the individual attorney level this is largely done through profile-raising activities— to become a recognized authority in a particular area, for example, a lawyer might focus her efforts on providing expert analysis, commentary, and opinion through written articles, blog posts, speaking engagements, and presentations to industry groups and other lawyers (solid colleague referrals can be a good source of new business).

Most firms are engaged in some form of marketing or branding campaign. Because ethical rules place some restrictions on lawyer advertising and client solicitation, however, the channels available to law firms are fairly limited. Typical methods of law firm outreach include websites, search engine optimization, brochures and related collateral, advertising, events and sponsorships, directories and rankings, as well as generalized public relations.

B. Limits: Advertising and Solicitation

1. Advertising

There are vocal critics who draw the line at the very notion of lawyer advertising as beneath the dignity of a learned profession, with even its use marking the difference between a profession and a trade. Prior to 1977, lawyer advertising was taboo. Because states imposed and enforced disciplinary rules that restricted advertising by attorneys, lawyers marketed themselves indirectly, by serving on boards, joining clubs, chairing charity fundraisers, or by running for public office. Clients relied upon a lawyer's reputation in the community and word of mouth referrals.

This changed with the Supreme Court's decision in *Bates v. State Bar of Arizona*.[2] Reasoning that lawyer advertising informs society of the availability, nature, and cost of legal services, and aids in the process of informed decision making, the Court held that a state cannot prohibit attorneys from advertising true, factual information on First Amendment grounds. After *Bates*, the issue shifted from whether lawyers could advertise to what restrictions a state could impose to ensure accuracy and avoid misleading the public.

Model Rule 7.1 is part of the current regulatory scheme with respect to advertising as it attempts to give specific content to the permissible regulatory restrictions on "false, deceptive, or misleading" communications. It provides:

> A lawyer shall not make a false or misleading communication about the lawyer
> or the lawyer's services. A communication is false or misleading if it contains a

---

[1] American Marketing Association, *Definitions of Marketing*, https://www.ama.org/the-definition-of-marketing-what-is-marketing/.
[2] 433 U.S. 350 (1977).

material misrepresentation of fact or law, or omits a fact necessary to make the statement considered as a whole not materially misleading.

Model Rule 7.2(a) is the central provision relating to advertising; it provides, as amended:

A lawyer may communicate information regarding the lawyer's services through any media.

The Comment to Rule 7.2 adds:

This Rule permits public dissemination of information concerning a lawyer's name or firm name, address, email address, website, and telephone number; the kinds of services the lawyer will undertake; the basis on which the lawyer's fees are determined, including prices for specific services and payment and credit arrangements; a lawyer's foreign language ability; names of references and, with their consent, names of clients regularly represented; and other information that might invite the attention of those seeking legal assistance.

Thus, while states may regulate advertising by attorneys, they may not prevent attorneys from disseminating truthful and nondeceptive advertisements concerning the availability and terms of legal services. This kind of advertising is constitutionally protected commercial speech. However, states can impose limitations on attorney advertisements: Advertising that is false, deceptive, or misleading is subject to restraint, including regulation as to time, place, and manner. Categorically speaking, states generally regulate permitted media for advertising, retention requirements for advertising copy, referrals and related compensation arrangements, and identification disclosures for responsible lawyers.[3]

Today, with the rapid evolution of mass and social media, one need look no further than an Internet search to see the creativity and diversity of lawyer advertising on display. The scope of marketing platforms offers today's lawyers opportunities for both unlimited reach and perilous liability. The following case illuminates an example of the latter.

The Florida Bar v. Pape
918 So. 2d 240 (Fla. 2005)

Opinion
PARIENTE, C.J.

In this case we impose discipline on two attorneys for their use of television advertising devices that violate the Rules of Professional Conduct. These devices, which invoke the breed of dog known as the pit bull, demean all lawyers and thereby harm both the legal profession and the public's trust and confidence in our system of justice.

We conclude that attorneys Pape and Chandler ("the attorneys") violated Rules Regulating the Florida Bar 4-7.2(b)(3) and 4-7.2(b)(4) by

---

[3] *See, e.g.*, The Florida Bar, *Advertising Regulation and Information*, https://www.floridabar .org/ethics/etad/; State Bar of Texas, *Advertising Review*, https://www.texasbar.com/Content/ NavigationMenu/ForLawyers/GrievanceandEthics/AdvertisingReview/default.htm.

using the image of a pit bull and displaying the term "pit bull" as part of their firm's phone number in their commercial. Further, because the use of an image of a pit bull and the phrase "pit bull" in the firm's advertisement and logo does not assist the public in ensuring that an informed decision is made prior to the selection of the attorney, we conclude that the First Amendment does not prevent this Court from sanctioning the attorneys based on the rule violations. We determine that the appropriate sanctions for the attorneys' misconduct are public reprimands and required attendance at the Florida Bar Advertising Workshop.

Background and Procedural History

On January 12, 2004, The Florida Bar filed complaints against the attorneys, alleging that their law firm's television advertisement was an improper communication concerning the services provided, in violation of the Rules of Professional Conduct. The advertisement included a logo that featured an image of a pit bull wearing a spiked collar and prominently displayed the firm's phone number, 1-800-PIT-BULL. The Bar asserted that this advertisement violated the 2004 version of Rules Regulating the Florida Bar 4-7.2(b)(3) and 4-7.2(b)(4), which state:

> (3) Descriptive Statements. A lawyer shall not make statements describing or characterizing the quality of the lawyer's services in advertisements and written communications; provided that this provision shall not apply to information furnished to a prospective client at that person's request or to information supplied to existing clients.
> (4) Prohibited Visual and Verbal Portrayals. Visual or verbal descriptions, depictions, or portrayals of persons, things, or events must be objectively relevant to the selection of an attorney and shall not be deceptive, misleading, or manipulative.

The referee found that the attorneys did not violate rule 4-7.2(b)(3), relying on the distinction that the logo and telephone number "describe qualities of the respondent attorneys" but do not describe or characterize "the quality of the lawyer services." The referee also rejected the Bar's assertion that the ad violated rule 4-7.2(b)(4). After noting that pit bulls are perceived as "loyal, persistent, tenacious, and aggressive," the referee found these qualities objectively relevant to the selection of an attorney as they are informational, because these are qualities that a consuming public would want in a trial lawyer . . . and the ad is not improperly manipulative. . . . The advertisement is tastefully done, the logo is not unduly conspicuous in its replacement of an ampersand between respondents' names atop the TV screen, and the large print 1-800 number is an effective mnemonic [device] tailored to maximize responses from potential clients.

The referee also concluded that the ad was protected speech and therefore that an interpretation of rules 4-7.2(b)(3) and 4-7.2(b)(4) to prohibit the ad would render the rules unconstitutional as applied.

Analysis

Generally, a "referee's findings of fact regarding guilt carry a presumption of correctness that should be upheld unless clearly erroneous or without support in the record." Fla. Bar v. Senton, 882 So. 2d 997, 1001 (Fla. 2004) (quoting Fla. Bar v. Wohl, 842 So. 2d 811, 814 (Fla. 2003)). However, where there are no genuine issues of material fact and the only disagreement is whether the undisputed facts constitute unethical conduct, the referee's findings present a question of law that the Court reviews de novo. See Rykiel v. Rykiel, 838 So. 2d 508, 510 (Fla. 2003) (stating that if the issue presented in a decision is a pure question of law, the decision is subject to de novo review); Fla. Bar v. Cosnow, 797 So. 2d 1255, 1258 (Fla. 2001) (concluding that whether the attorney's admitted actions constitute unethical conduct is a question of law). The facts are not in dispute, and therefore our review is de novo.

A. Violation of Attorney Advertising Rules

As a preliminary matter, the pit bull logo and 1-800-PIT-BULL telephone number in the ad by the attorneys do not comport with the general criteria for permissible attorney advertisements set forth in the comments to section 4-7 of the Rules of Professional Conduct. The rules contained in section 4-7 are designed to permit lawyer advertisements that provide objective information about the cost of legal services, the experience and qualifications of the lawyer and law firm, and the types of cases the lawyer handles. See generally R. Regulating Fla. Bar 4-7.1 cmt. The comment to rule 4-7.1 provides that "a lawyer's advertisement should provide only useful, factual information presented in a nonsensational manner. Advertisements using slogans . . . fail to meet these standards and diminish public confidence in the legal system." The television commercial at issue here uses both a sensationalistic image and a slogan, contrary to the purpose of section 4-7.

More specifically, the attorneys' ad violated rule 4-7.2(b)(3), which prohibits the use of statements describing or characterizing the quality of the lawyer's services. In Florida Bar v. Lange, 711 So. 2d 518, 521-22 (Fla. 1998), we approved the referee's finding that an advertisement that stated "When the Best is Simply Essential" violated the predecessor provision to rule 4-7.2(b)(3) because it was self-laudatory and purported to describe the quality of the lawyer's services. In this case, the simultaneous display of the pit bull logo and the 1-800-PIT-BULL phone number conveys both the characteristics of the attorneys and the quality of the services they purport to provide. At the very least, the printed words and the image of a pit bull in the television commercial could certainly be perceived by prospective clients as characterizing the quality of the lawyers' services.

On this question we disagree with the referee, who distinguished the "quality of the lawyer's services" from the qualities (i.e., traits or characteristics) of the lawyer. We conclude that this is an artificial distinction which unduly limits the scope of the rule by interpreting "quality of the lawyer's services" in the narrowest sense. From the perspective of a prospective client unfamiliar with the legal system and in need of counsel, a lawyer's character and personality traits are indistinguishable from the quality of the services that the lawyer provides. A courteous lawyer can be expected to be well mannered in court, a hard-working lawyer well prepared, and a "pit bull" lawyer vicious to the opposition. In the attorneys' advertisement, the pit bull image appears in place of an ampersand between the attorneys' names, and the ad includes the use of the words "pit bull" in the attorneys' telephone number in large capital letters. The combined effect of these devices is to lead a reasonable consumer to conclude that the attorneys are advertising themselves as providers of "pit bull"-style representation. We consider this a characterization of the quality of the lawyers' services in violation of rule 4-7.2(b)(3).

We also conclude that the ad violates rule 4-7.2(b)(4), which requires that visual or verbal depictions be "objectively relevant" to the selection of an attorney, and prohibits depictions that are "deceptive, misleading, or manipulative." The comment to this rule explains that it prohibits visual or verbal descriptions, depictions, or portrayals in any advertisement which create suspense, or contain exaggerations or appeals to the emotions, call for legal services, or create consumer problems through characterization and dialogue ending with the lawyer solving the problem. Illustrations permitted under Zauderer v. Office of Disciplinary Counsel of the Supreme Court of Ohio, 471 U.S. 626, 105 S. Ct. 2265, 85 L. Ed. 2d 652 (1985), are informational and not misleading, and are therefore permissible. As an example, *a drawing of a fist, to suggest the lawyer's ability to achieve results, would be barred.* Examples of permissible illustrations would include a graphic rendering of the scales of justice to indicate that the advertising attorney practices law, a picture of the lawyer, or a map of the office location. (Emphasis supplied.) The logo of the pit bull wearing a spiked collar and the prominent display of the phone number 1-800-PIT-BULL are more manipulative and misleading than a drawing of a fist. These advertising devices would suggest to many persons not only that the lawyers can achieve results but also that they engage in a combative style of advocacy. The suggestion is inherently deceptive because there is no way to measure whether the attorneys in fact conduct themselves like pit bulls so as to ascertain whether this logo and phone number convey accurate information.

In addition, the image of a pit bull and the on-screen display of the words "PIT-BULL" as part of the firm's phone number are not objectively relevant to the selection of an attorney. The referee found that the qualities of a pit bull as depicted by the logo are loyalty, persistence, tenacity, and aggressiveness. We consider this a charitable set of associations that ignores the darker side of the qualities often also associated with pit bulls: malevolence, viciousness, and unpredictability. Further, although some may associate pit bulls with loyalty to their owners, the manner in which the pit bull is depicted in the attorneys' ad in this case certainly does not emphasize this association. The dog, which is wearing a spiked collar, directly faces the viewer and is shown alone, with no indication that it is fulfilling its traditional role as "man's best friend."

Pit bulls have a reputation for vicious behavior that is borne of experience. According to a study published in the Journal of the American Veterinary Medical Association in 2000, pit bulls caused the greatest number of dog-bite-related fatalities between 1979 and 1998. Jeffery J. Saks, et al.,

Breeds of Dogs Involved in Fatal Human Attacks in the United States Between 1979 and 1998, 217 J. Am. Veterinary Med. Ass'n 836, 837 (2000), available at http://www.cdc.gov/ncipc/duip/dogbreeds.pdf. The dangerousness of pit bulls has also been recognized in a number of court decisions. See, e.g., Giaculli v. Bright, 584 So. 2d 187, 189 (Fla. 5th DCA 1991) (recognizing that "[p]it bulls as a breed are known to be extremely aggressive and have been bred as attack animals"); Hearn v. City of Overland Park, 244 Kan. 638, 772 P.2d 758, 768 (1989) ("[P]it bull dogs represent a unique public health hazard not presented by other breeds or mixes of dogs. Pit bull dogs possess both the capacity for extraordinarily savage behavior and physical capabilities in excess of those possessed by many other breeds of dogs. Moreover, this capacity for uniquely vicious attacks is coupled with an unpredictable nature."); Matthews v. Amberwood Assocs. Ltd. Partnership, Inc., 351 Md. 544, 719 A.2d 119, 127 (1998) ("The extreme dangerousness of [the pit bull] breed, as it has evolved today, is well recognized.").

In State v. Peters, 534 So. 2d 760 (Fla. 3d DCA 1988), the Third District Court of Appeal upheld a City of North Miami ordinance imposing substantial insurance, registration, and confinement obligations on owners of pit bulls. The City of North Miami ordinance contained findings that pit bulls have a greater propensity to bite humans than all other breeds, are extremely aggressive towards other animals, and have a natural tendency to refuse to terminate an attack once it has begun. See id. at 764. The current Miami-Dade County ordinance provides that it is illegal to own a pit bull. See Miami-Dade County, Fla. Code, §5-17 (1992).

This Court would not condone an advertisement that stated that a lawyer will get results through combative and vicious tactics that will maim, scar, or harm the opposing party, conduct that would violate our Rules of Professional Conduct. See, e.g., R. Regulating Fla. Bar 4-3.4(g)-(h) (prohibiting threats to present criminal or disciplinary charges solely to gain an advantage in a civil matter). Yet this is precisely the type of unethical and unprofessional conduct that is conveyed by the image of a pit bull and the display of the 1-800-PIT-BULL phone number. We construe the prohibitions on advertising statements that characterize the quality of lawyer services and depictions that are false or misleading to prohibit a lawyer from advertising his or her services by suggesting behavior, conduct, or tactics that are contrary to our Rules of Professional Conduct.

Further, we reject the referee's finding that the use of the words "pit bull" in the phone number is merely a mnemonic device to help potential clients remember the attorneys' number. Phrase-based phone numbers are memorable because of the images and associations they evoke. The "1-800-PIT-BULL" phone number sticks in the memory precisely because of the image of the pit bull also featured in the ad, the association of pit bulls with the characteristics discussed herein, and the "go for the jugular" style of advocacy that some persons attribute to lawyers. In short, this is a manipulative and misleading use of what would otherwise be content-neutral information to create a nefarious association. Indeed, permitting this type of advertisement would make a mockery of our dedication to promoting public trust and confidence in our system of justice. Prohibiting advertisements such as the one in this case is one step we can take to maintain the dignity of lawyers, as well as the integrity of, and public confidence in, the legal system. Were we to approve the referee's finding, images of sharks, wolves, crocodiles, and piranhas could follow. For the good of the legal profession and the justice system, and consistent with our Rules of Professional Conduct, this type of non-factual advertising cannot be permitted. We therefore conclude that the 1-800-PIT-BULL ad aired by the attorneys violates rules 4-7.2(b)(3) and 4-7.2(b)(4).

B. First Amendment Protection of Lawyer Advertising

We also disagree with the referee's conclusion that the application of rules 4-7.2(b)(3) and 4-7.2(b)(4) to prohibit this advertisement violates the First Amendment. Lawyer advertising enjoys First Amendment protection only to the extent that it provides accurate factual information that can be objectively verified. This thread runs throughout the pertinent United State Supreme Court precedent.

The seminal lawyer advertising case is Bates v. State Bar of Arizona, 433 U.S. 350, 376, 97 S. Ct. 2691, 53 L. Ed. 2d 810 (1977), which involved the advertising of fees for low cost legal services. In *Bates*, the Supreme Court held generally that attorney advertising "may not be subjected to blanket suppression," and more specifically that attorneys have the constitutional right to advertise their availability and fees for performing routine services. Id. at 383-84, 97 S. Ct. 2691. The cost of legal services, the Supreme Court concluded, would be "relevant information needed to reach an informed decision." Id. at 374, 97 S. Ct. 2691.

In reaching this conclusion the Supreme Court recognized that "[a]dvertising is the traditional mechanism in a free-market economy for a supplier to inform a potential purchaser of the availability and terms of exchange." Id. at 376, 97 S. Ct. 2691. "[C]ommercial speech serves to inform the public of the availability, nature, and prices of products and services, and thus performs an indispensable role in the allocation of resources in a free enterprise system. In short, such speech serves individual and societal interests in assuring informed and reliable decisionmaking." Id. at 364, 97 S. Ct. 2691 (citation omitted).

The Supreme Court emphasized that advertising by lawyers could be regulated and noted that "because the public lacks sophistication concerning legal services, misstatements that might be overlooked or deemed unimportant in other advertising may be found quite inappropriate in legal advertising." Id. at 383, 97 S. Ct. 2691. The Supreme Court specifically declined to address the "peculiar problems associated with advertising claims relating to the quality of legal services," but observed that "[s]uch claims *probably are not susceptible of precise measurement or verification and, under some circumstances, might well be deceptive or misleading to the public, or even false.*" Id. at 366, 97 S. Ct. 2691 (emphasis supplied).

After *Bates*, the Supreme Court considered a Missouri rule that restricted lawyer advertising to newspapers, periodicals, and the yellow pages, and limited the content of these advertisements to ten categories of information (name, address and telephone number, areas of practice, date and place of birth, schools attended, foreign language ability, office hours, fee for an initial consultation, availability of a schedule of fees, credit arrangements, and the fixed fee charged for specified "routine" services). See In re R.M.J., 455 U.S. 191, 194, 102 S. Ct. 929, 71 L. Ed. 2d 64 (1982). Even the manner of listing areas of practice was restricted to a prescribed nomenclature. See id. at 194-95, 102 S. Ct. 929. In violation of the state restrictions, the lawyer advertised areas of practice that did not use the prescribed terminology, listed the states in which the lawyer was licensed, specified that he was admitted to practice before the United States Supreme Court, and did not restrict the recipients of announcement cards to lawyers, clients, former clients, personal friends, and relatives. See id. at 198, 102 S. Ct. 929.

Writing for a unanimous Court, Justice Powell summarized the commercial speech doctrine in the context of advertising for professional services:

> Truthful advertising related to lawful activities is entitled to the protections of the First Amendment. But when the particular content or method of the advertising suggests that it is inherently misleading or when experience has proved that in fact such advertising is subject to abuse, the States may impose appropriate restrictions. Misleading advertising may be prohibited entirely. But the States may not place an absolute prohibition on certain types of potentially misleading information, e.g., a listing of areas of practice, if the information also may be presented in a way that is not deceptive. Id. at 203, 102 S. Ct. 929.

In holding the Missouri restrictions per se invalid as applied to the lawyer, the Supreme Court concluded that the state had no substantial interest in prohibiting a lawyer from identifying the jurisdictions in which he or she was licensed to practice. See id. at 205, 102 S. Ct. 929. The Court noted that this "is *factual* and highly relevant information." Id. (emphasis supplied). Although the Court found the lawyer's listing in large capital letters that he was a member of the Bar of the Supreme Court of the United States to be "[s]omewhat more troubling" and in "bad taste," this alone could not be prohibited without a finding by the Missouri Supreme Court that "such a statement could be misleading to the general public unfamiliar with the requirements of admission to the Bar of this Court." Id. at 205, 102 S. Ct. 929. In short, the Supreme Court in *R.M.J.* was dealing with restrictions on clearly factual and relevant information that had not been found to be misleading or likely to deceive. As in *Bates*, the Supreme Court concluded that such restrictions violated the First Amendment.

In Zauderer v. Office of Disciplinary Counsel of the Supreme Court of Ohio, 471 U.S. 626, 629, 105 S. Ct. 2265, 85 L. Ed. 2d 652 (1985), the Supreme Court addressed whether a state could discipline a lawyer who ran newspaper advertisements containing nondeceptive illustrations and legal advice. One advertisement published the lawyer's willingness to represent women injured from the use of the Dalkon Shield intrauterine device. See id. at 630, 105 S. Ct. 2265. The parties had stipulated that the advertisement was entirely accurate. See id. at 633-34, 105 S. Ct. 2265.

In holding that the lawyer could not be disciplined on the basis of the content of his advertisement, the Supreme Court observed that the advertisement did not promise results or suggest any special expertise but merely conveyed that the lawyer was representing women in Dalkon Shield litigation and was willing to represent other women with similar claims. See id. at 639-40, 105 S. Ct. 2265. Turning to the lawyer's use of an illustration of the Dalkon Shield, the Court first held that illustrations are entitled to the same First Amendment protection as that afforded to verbal commercial speech. See id. at 647, 105 S. Ct. 2265. The Court then concluded that "[b]ecause the illustration for which appellant was disciplined is an accurate representation of the Dalkon Shield and has no features that are likely to deceive, mislead, or confuse the reader, the burden is on the State to present a substantial governmental interest justifying the restriction." Id. at 647, 105 S. Ct. 2265.

The most recent United States Supreme Court decision to address restrictions on the content of lawyer advertising involved an attorney who held himself out as certified by the National Board of Trial Advocacy (NBTA). See Peel v. Attorney Registration & Disciplinary Comm'n of Illinois, 496 U.S. 91, 110 S. Ct. 2281, 110 L. Ed. 2d 83 (1990). The state supreme court had concluded that the claim of NBTA certification was "misleading because it tacitly attests to the qualifications of [petitioner] as a civil trial advocate." Id. at 98, 110 S. Ct. 2281 (plurality opinion) (quoting In re Peel, 126 Ill. 2d 397, 128 Ill. Dec. 535, 534 N.E.2d 980, 984 (1989)) (alteration in original). The state court had not addressed "whether NBTA certification constituted *reliable, verifiable evidence of petitioner's experience as a civil trial advocate*." Id. at 99, 128 Ill. Dec. 535, 534 N.E.2d 980 (emphasis supplied). After applauding the development of state and national certification programs, a plurality of the Supreme Court concluded that the facts as to NBTA certification were "true and verifiable." Id. at 100, 128 Ill. Dec. 535, 534 N.E.2d 980 (plurality opinion). The plurality pointed out the important "distinction between *statements of opinion or quality and statements of objective facts that may support an inference of quality*." Id. at 101, 128 Ill. Dec. 535, 534 N.E.2d 980 (plurality opinion) (emphasis supplied). A majority of the Court concluded that the letterhead was not actually or inherently misleading, and thus that the attorney could not be prohibited from holding himself out as a civil trial specialist certified by the NBTA. See id. at 106, 128 Ill. Dec. 535, 534 N.E.2d 980 (plurality opinion); id. at 111-12, 128 Ill. Dec. 535, 534 N.E.2d 980 (Marshall, J., concurring in the judgment).

The pit bull logo and "1-800-PIT-BULL" phone number are in marked contrast to the illustration of the Dalkon Shield intrauterine device at issue in *Zauderer*, which the United States Supreme Court found to be "an accurate representation . . . and ha[ve] no features that are likely to deceive, mislead, or confuse the reader." 471 U.S. at 647, 105 S. Ct. 2265.

The Dalkon Shield illustration informed the public that the lawyer represented clients in cases involving this device. The "pit bull" commercial produced by the attorneys in this case contains no indication that they specialize in either dog bite cases generally or in litigation arising from attacks by pit bulls specifically. Consequently, the logo and phone number do not convey objectively relevant information about the attorneys' practice. Instead, the image and words "pit bull" are intended to convey an image about the nature of the lawyers' litigation tactics. We conclude that an advertising device that connotes combativeness and viciousness without providing accurate and objectively verifiable factual information falls outside the protections of the First Amendment.

C. Discipline

Because the referee found that the attorneys were not guilty of violating rules 4-7.2(b)(3) and 4-7.2(b)(4), the referee did not address the issue of discipline. The parties do not address the issue of discipline in their briefs to this Court. However, we have in the past approved public reprimands for attorneys who have been found guilty of violating the advertising rules. See Fla. Bar v. Herrick, 571 So. 2d 1303, 1307 (Fla. 1990); Fla. Bar v. Budish, 421 So. 2d 501, 503 (Fla. 1982). We have also required that attorneys attend the Florida Bar Advertising Workshop. See, e.g., Fla. Bar v. Zebersky, 902 So. 2d 793 (Fla. 2005) (No. SC04-1907) (table report of unpublished order). We conclude that similar discipline is warranted in this case.

Conclusion

We disapprove the referee's finding that the television commercial at issue is constitutionally protected speech that does not violate our attorney advertising rules. We find John Robert Pape and Marc Andrew Chandler guilty of violating rules 4-7.2(b)(3) and 4-7.2(b)(4) of the Rules Regulating the Florida Bar. We order that each attorney receive a public reprimand, which shall be administered by the Board of Governors of The Florida Bar upon proper notice to appear. We also direct Pape and Chandler to attend and complete the Florida Bar Advertising Workshop within six months of the date of this opinion.

It is so ordered.

WELLS, ANSTEAD, LEWIS, QUINCE, CANTERO, and BELL, JJ., concur.

Questions: This case is a study in restrictions on lawyer advertising driven largely by a desire to protect the dignity of the profession. A significant number of judicial pronouncements have followed the view that regulation of lawyer advertising may appropriately be grounded in the preservation of the dignity of the profession. While which cell-phone plan or car consumers choose may be a conceptually different decision from what

(continued)

kind of lawyer they choose, doesn't the regulation of lawyer advertising on the grounds that it is demeaning to the profession raise significant First Amendment concerns? Is "go for the jugular" advocacy somehow inherently unethical or illegal? What about the duty to zealously represent your client's interests?

2. Solicitation

Solicitation is lawyer outreach that crosses acceptable boundaries. Model Rules 7.3(a) to (d) currently provide:

(a) "Solicitation" or "solicit" denotes a communication initiated by or on behalf of a lawyer or law firm that is directed to a specific person the lawyer knows or reasonably should know needs legal services in a particular matter and that offers to provide, or reasonably can be understood as offering to provide, legal services for that matter.

(b) A lawyer shall not solicit professional employment by live person-to-person contact when a significant motive for the lawyer's doing so is the lawyer's or law firm's pecuniary gain, unless the contact is with a:

(1) lawyer;

(2) person who has a family, close personal, or prior business or professional relationship with the lawyer or law firm; or

(3) person who routinely uses for business purposes the type of legal services offered by the lawyer.

(c) A lawyer shall not solicit professional employment even when not otherwise prohibited by paragraph (b), if:

(1) the target of the solicitation has made known to the lawyer a desire not to be solicited by the lawyer; or

(2) the solicitation involves coercion, duress or harassment.

(d) This Rule does not prohibit communications authorized by law or ordered by a court or other tribunal.

Be wary of "creative" ways of expanding your law practice. In the following recent case, a lawyer was disciplined for solicitation through a non-lawyer intermediary:

In re Wray
91 N.E.3d 578 (Ind. 2018)

Attorney Discipline Action
PER CURIAM
We find that Respondent, Robert John Wray, engaged in attorney misconduct arising from his solicitation of clients through a nonlawyer intermediary. For this misconduct, we conclude that Respondent should be suspended from the practice of law in this state for at least nine months without automatic reinstatement.

This matter is before the Court on the report of the hearing officer appointed by this Court to hear evidence on the Indiana Supreme Court Disciplinary Commission's "Amended Verified Complaint for Disciplinary Action," and on the post-hearing briefing by the parties. Respondent's 1980 admission to this state's bar subjects him to this Court's disciplinary jurisdiction. See Ind. Const. art. 7, §4.

Procedural Background and Facts

The Commission filed a five-count "Verified Complaint for Disciplinary Action" on November 13, 2015, and later amended that complaint to add a sixth count. As set forth in more detail below, the amended complaint charged Respondent with a wide range of rule violations arising out of his professional relationship with Douglas Stephan, a nonlawyer. Following a hearing, the hearing officer filed a 64-page report finding Respondent committed violations as charged.

Respondent has represented several owners of allegedly defective modular or manufactured homes in actions against the homes' installers, builders, or manufacturers. One of those owners was Stephan, who purchased a home from Joseph Callaghan, d/b/a Fahl Manufactured Homes ("Callaghan"). Respondent and Stephan developed a relationship under which Stephan (through his company Stephan Consulting, Inc., which Respondent helped Stephan incorporate) would solicit other owners to become plaintiffs in Stephan's action and in other actions against Callaghan and other installers, builders, and manufacturers. Typically, Stephan would "cold call" the owners, offer to perform home inspections for them, and then ask those owners to sign an "Investor Agreement" and an "Attorney Agreement," both of which were drafted and/or approved by Respondent and included Respondent's name throughout. The owners, and subsequently Respondent, would sign the Attorney Agreements, frequently without any direct communication with one another or discussion about the merits of the claim.

The Investor Agreements included statements falsely representing that the owners already had entered into fee agreements with Respondent. The Investor Agreements also included several statements that inaccurately described how litigation costs would be advanced and how the risks of litigation would be assumed. For example, the Investor Agreements stated Stephan would advance the costs of litigation in exchange for 50% of the client's net recovery, but aside from the first few cases Stephan did not actually advance these costs. The Attorney Agreements provided that Respondent would receive a contingent fee of between 33% and 50%, and some Attorney Agreements also required a nonrefundable $1,000 retainer for costs.

Respondent entered into contracts with about 118 owners through his relationship with Stephan. One of these clients was David Lomperski, who—in exchange for a reduced contingent fee in his case—agreed to work with Stephan to identify other potential clients. Respondent helped draft an employment and noncompete agreement between Stephan and Lomperski.

The relationship between Respondent and Stephan eventually soured due to a dispute involving the advancement of costs, and Respondent proposed to Lomperski that they work together in the same capacity that Respondent had been working with Stephan. When they met to discuss this, Lomperski secretly recorded the conversation. Respondent also briefly entered into a similar relationship with David Blumenherst, who solicited at least two new clients using the same "Investor Agreement" template Respondent had provided Stephan.

In addition to the misleading representations in the Investor Agreements regarding the advancement of litigation costs, after cases settled Respondent drafted a "Disbursement Authorization and Acknowledgement" form for his clients that in some instances inaccurately reflected the actual distributions and advancement of costs. After the accounting dispute arose between Respondent and Stephan, Respondent represented to clients that he had paid Stephan his share and instructed them not to pay Stephan, when in fact Respondent merely had "allocated" Stephan's share against the amount Respondent believed Stephan owed him.

The Investor Agreements provided that Stephan "shall take the lead in communications with the attorney" and others and purported to grant Stephan the authority to advance the client's claims and to "arrange for settlement." Notwithstanding this language, Respondent did have a general practice of writing his clients to notify them of significant events in their cases. However, Respondent admitted there often were delays of several months between the time that Stephan had clients execute Attorney Agreements and the time that Respondent eventually received those Agreements, and Respondent admitted further that he never raised the issue of these delays with Stephan. These delays could have led to claims being time-barred, although there is no evidence this occurred in any of the cases.

Several clients testified about what they felt was a lack of adequate communication or explanation from Respondent. Several clients also testified that they agreed to settle a claim against one defendant (Callaghan) based, at least in part, on Respondent's representation that they could recover additional amounts against another defendant (Chilton). However, Chilton would have been among the parties covered by the release in the Callaghan settlement. The hearing officer found that Respondent misrepresented the viability of a potential claim against Chilton in order to motivate clients to settle claims against Callaghan.

During the Commission's investigation into the events described above, Respondent represented to the Commission that "Stephan Consulting did not 'solicit' clients for my law office. Stephan Consulting provided financing and consulting to various homeowners under separate and distinct agreements with homeowners." The hearing officer found this statement was false with respect to both solicitation and financing.

Finally, from 2008 through 2015, Respondent failed to keep adequate trust account records and separate ledgers for each client. Respondent also kept more than a nominal amount of personal funds in his trust account.

Discussion

The Commission alleged, and the hearing officer concluded following an evidentiary hearing, that Respondent violated the following Indiana Rules of Professional Conduct:

1.4(a)(2): Failing to reasonably consult with a client about the means by which the client's objectives are to be accomplished.

1.4(a)(3): Failing to keep a client reasonably informed about the status of a matter.

1.4(a)(4): Failing to comply promptly with a client's reasonable requests for information.

1.5(a): Making an agreement for, charging, or collecting an unreasonable fee or amount for expenses.

1.15(a): Failing to maintain and preserve complete records of client trust account funds.

5.3(b): Failing to make reasonable efforts to ensure that the conduct of a nonlawyer employee over whom the lawyer has direct supervisory authority is compatible with the professional obligations of the lawyer.

5.3(c): Ordering or ratifying the misconduct of nonlawyer assistants, or failing to take reasonable remedial action with respect to the misconduct of nonlawyer assistants under the lawyer's supervision.

5.4(a): Improperly sharing legal fees with a nonlawyer.

7.3(a): Improperly soliciting employment in-person, by phone, or by real time electronic contact from a person with whom the lawyer has no prior relationship when a significant motive is the lawyer's pecuniary gain.

7.3(e): Improperly giving something of value for a recommendation for employment.

7.3(f): Accepting employment when the lawyer knows, or reasonably should know, that the person seeking the lawyer's services does so as a result of lawyer conduct prohibited under Rule 7.3.

8.1(a): Knowingly making a false statement of material fact to the Disciplinary Commission in connection with a disciplinary matter.

8.4(a): Violating the Rules of Professional Conduct through the acts of another.

8.4(c): Engaging in conduct involving dishonesty, fraud, deceit, or misrepresentation.

The Commission also alleged, and the hearing officer concluded, that Respondent violated the following Indiana Admission and Discipline Rules:

23(29)(a)(2): Failing to create, maintain, or retain appropriate trust account records.

23(29)(a)(3): Failing to maintain a ledger with separate records for each client with funds deposited in a trust account.

Respondent has petitioned this Court to review the hearing officer's findings and conclusions. In his petition, Respondent admits the trust account violations but disputes the other charges. The Commission carries the burden of proof to demonstrate attorney misconduct by clear and convincing evidence. See Ind. Admission and Discipline

Rule 23(14)(g)(1). We review de novo all matters presented to the Court, including review not only of the hearing officer's report but also of the entire record. See Matter of Wall, 73 N.E.3d 170, 172 (Ind. 2017). While this Court reserves the right to make the ultimate determination, the hearing officer's findings receive emphasis due to the unique opportunity for direct observation of witnesses. Id.

The overarching issue in this case involves the nature of Respondent's relationship with Stephan. Respondent has contended throughout these proceedings that Stephan acted independently and that Respondent merely accepted referrals from him. The Commission has contended that Stephan was acting as Respondent's agent. The hearing officer acknowledged conflicting evidence on this point but ultimately concluded the Commission had proven the existence of an agency relationship. Upon review of the materials before us, we agree with the hearing officer.

In his petition for review, Respondent strenuously attacks Stephan's credibility. Indeed, the hearing officer in his report expressly questioned the credibility of both Stephan and Respondent, but ultimately found key portions of Stephan's testimony corroborated by independent evidence and logical inferences. This type of credibility determination was within the hearing officer's purview to make, and we find ample support for his findings in this case. Respondent helped Stephan incorporate Stephan Consulting, the business Stephan used to recruit other potential plaintiffs. The Investor Agreements and Attorney Agreements used by Stephan (and later by Blumenherst) were drafted and/or approved by Respondent and contained his name throughout. Stephan performed the client intake and, as the Agreements expressly contemplated, served as the primary point of contact for the clients. Respondent later drafted an employment and noncompete agreement between Stephan and Lomperski, who assisted Stephan in identifying potential plaintiffs. When Respondent's relationship with Stephan soured, Respondent attempted to persuade Lomperski to take Stephan's place in the recruitment scheme and discussed (in a conversation secretly recorded by Lomperski) the need for Lomperski to get out of the noncompete agreement Respondent had drafted. In sum, this was not merely a referral system, and Respondent's role in the client recruitment process was anything but passive. We find the evidence clearly and convincingly establishes an agency relationship between Respondent and Stephan. See Restatement (Third) of Agency §§1.01, 1.03 (2006).

As the issues have been framed in this case, many of the rule violations found by the hearing officer consequently follow from the finding of an agency relationship between Respondent and Stephan. See, e.g., Rules 7.3(a) (barring solicitation by a lawyer or the lawyer's employee or agent) and 8.4(a) (addressing violation of professional conduct rules through the acts of another). Respondent's remaining challenges to the hearing officer's findings and conclusions are not persuasive. With respect to the Rule 1.4 charges, Respondent attacks the credibility of those clients who testified to a lack of adequate communication or explanation from Respondent, and he points to the existence of some written correspondence between himself and those clients. Similar to Stephan's testimony though, the hearing officer found the clients' testimony largely corroborated by independent evidence and logical inferences, and we find ample support for the hearing officer's findings and reasoning.

With respect to the Rule 8.1(a) and 8.4(c) charges, Respondent contends he was not dishonest or deceitful with either his clients or with the Commission. For example, Respondent asserts there is little material difference between Stephan being "paid" and having funds "allocated" against Stephan's alleged debt to Respondent, but under the circumstances there plainly was a difference. Stephan disputed the alleged debt, and if Respondent did not pay him, Stephan presumably could seek payment from the clients (which likely is why the clients were seeking clarification and confirmation of payment from Respondent). And while Respondent argues that the solicitation component of his statement to the Commission was simply a good-faith defense to the matters being investigated by the Commission, he makes no argument about the financing component of his statement, which was objectively false. Notwithstanding the plain language (and asserted purpose) of the Investor Agreements, Stephan was not providing financing to the homeowners, and Respondent testified he knew Stephan was not advancing these funds and that Respondent was paying these costs out of his own trust account instead.

Finally, Respondent advances an alternative argument with respect to Rule 7.3. Respondent argues that even if Stephan was soliciting clients as Respondent's agent, and even though Rule 7.3(a) generally prohibits such solicitation, Rule 7.3(b)(3) provides a "safe harbor" in this case. Respondent is mistaken. Rule 7.3(b)(3) by its express terms addresses solicitation that "concerns an action for personal injury or wrongful death or otherwise relates to an accident or disaster . . . ." Allegedly defective workmanship in a manufactured or modular home, standing alone, is not the type of injury encompassed by this rule. And while Respondent advances a colorable policy argument in favor of expanding the scope of permitted solicitation under Rule 7.3, an attorney has the obligation to conform his practices to the applicable professional conduct rules as written, not whatever alternative rules the attorney believes would be better.

In sum, we find sufficient support for the hearing officer's findings and conclusions with regard to each of the charged rule violations. Accordingly, we find Respondent violated Professional Conduct Rules 1.4(a)(2), 1.4(a)(3), 1.4(a)(4), 1.5(a), 1.15(a), 5.3(b), 5.3(c), 5.4(a), 7.3(a), 7.3(e), 7.3(f), 8.1(a), 8.4(a), 8.4(c), and Admission and Discipline Rules 23(29)(a)(2) and 23(29)(a)(3). We turn now to the question of sanction.

Respondent's arrangement with Stephan shares some similarities with the type of business model we have confronted in disciplinary cases involving attorneys' association with corporations marketing "foreclosure assistance" or "debt relief" services to consumers. See, e.g., Matter of Mossler, 86 N.E.3d 387 (Ind. 2017); Matter of Dilk, 2 N.E.3d 1263 (Ind. 2014). To be sure, there are important distinctions. Respondent had much more substantive involvement in his clients' cases than did the attorneys in cases such as *Mossler* and *Dilk*, whose marginal roles in the business schemes at issue amounted to little more than creating the illusion of meaningful attorney involvement. Further, unlike the largely worthless services sold by the debt relief companies to consumers in those cases, Respondent's services provided some value for his clients, many of whom obtained recoveries they might not otherwise have obtained.

Nonetheless, the actual and potential harm resulting from this type of arrangement is readily apparent. In this case, Respondent's delegation of client intake responsibilities to Stephan led to impermissible solicitation of clients, misrepresentations to clients about financing and costs, and delays of several months before Respondent became involved with (or even aware of) the clients' cases. Clients, whose primary point of contact was Stephan, encountered difficulty communicating with Respondent and remaining sufficiently apprised about their cases. Although many clients did obtain some recovery, those recoveries were greatly reduced due to a second contingent fee owed to Stephan, a middleman who was not actually providing the financing services clients were paying him to provide. And when a financial dispute arose between Respondent and Stephan, clients were caught in the middle.

Throughout all of this, Respondent lied. Respondent provided Stephan with Investor Agreements for clients to execute that Respondent knew were false in several material respects. Respondent falsely told several clients at the conclusion of their cases that Respondent already had paid Stephan. And when the Commission began investigating Respondent's practices, Respondent falsely told the Commission that Stephan provided financing for clients, when Respondent knew Stephan was not doing so. Respondent's pattern of dishonesty elevates his problematic arrangement with Stephan into a much more serious offense. See Matter of Ellison, 87 N.E.3d 460, 462 (Ind. 2017).

Nor is this Respondent's first encounter with the disciplinary process. Respondent and two other attorneys were publicly reprimanded by this Court in 2009 for deceptive advertising and improper use of a trade name. Matter of Loomis, Grubbs and Wray, 905 N.E.2d 406 (Ind. 2009). Notably, Respondent undertook his unethical arrangement with Stephan around the same time he was being disciplined for a prior unethical scheme to attract clients. One would have hoped our reprimand would have prompted Respondent to consider his ethical obligations and business practices more carefully. See Matter of Powell, 76 N.E.3d 130, 135 (Ind. 2017) ("[I]n many instances an attorney will be chastened by discipline for a first offense, adequately remedy his or her professional shortcomings, and be unlikely to recidivate going forward"). Instead, Respondent continued his enterprise with Stephan for several years and then sought to pursue similar client solicitation arrangements with other middlemen. Under these circumstances, Respondent's prior discipline is a significant aggravating factor.

After careful consideration of this matter, we conclude that Respondent should be suspended for a period of at least nine months, after which he may be reinstated only after proving by clear and convincing evidence his remorse, rehabilitation, and fitness to practice. See Admis. Disc. R. 23(18)(b).

Conclusion

For Respondent's professional misconduct, the Court suspends Respondent from the practice of law in this state for a period of not less than nine months, without automatic reinstatement, effective April 9, 2018. Respondent shall fulfill all the duties of a suspended attorney under Admission and Discipline Rule 23(26). At the conclusion of the minimum period of suspension, Respondent may petition this Court for reinstatement to the practice of law in this state, provided Respondent pays the costs of this proceeding, fulfills the duties of a suspended attorney, and satisfies the requirements for reinstatement of Admission and Discipline Rule 23(18).

The costs of this proceeding are assessed against Respondent. The hearing officer appointed in this case is discharged.

RUSH, C.J., and DAVID, MASSA, and SLAUGHTER, JJ., concur.
GOFF, J., did not participate.

Questions: What specific actions led to the problems in Wray's case? How badly were they compounded by Wray's "pattern of dishonesty" in the disciplinary proceedings? Might those problems have been avoided?

II. Business Development

Business development is different from marketing in that business development is the process of trying to establish a relationship with a prospective client. New clients lead to new business.

Business development has become an essential skill at most firms. It is comprised of many things, such as leadership, public speaking, networking, and connections. Law school doesn't prepare you to be a salesperson, and part of your role as lawyer eventually will be selling yourself and your firm's capabilities. The market is filled with highly skilled lawyers for clients to choose from—you have to be able to convince people you are the lawyer they should hire. As law is a service business, clients cannot comparatively evaluate work products. Competence is presumed because our business is a learned profession subject to licensing requirements and, to a large degree, traditional indicia of lawyer pedigree (education, judicial clerkships and other accomplishments). However, the same is not true for service, where personal style and attention can make all the difference. Some firms provide new lawyers with baseline training or at least an overview of what they consider to be business development best practices. But many do not.

In brief, the business development process for lawyers starts by establishing a personal contact between the lawyer and the hoped-to-be client. Once initial contact is made, the relationship must be nurtured, but the timing, content, nature, and number of your follow-up communications may vary depending on your style and the prospective client's tolerance. Many successful lawyers adopt a specific system and discipline that they use to ensure that client development efforts are appropriate, routine, tracked, and followed up on in a timely manner and that contacts are appropriately managed. They distinguish "high value" contacts from those with less likelihood of success.

Do not feel left out or behind the curve in the business development area. The typical new associate has followed a path directly from a lifetime of schooling—high school, college, and law school—to their first professional job in a law firm. It would be highly unusual to find an associate with the existing skills required for successful business development. The skills will come with practice and experience. But every associate should be conscious of the fact that the day will come when they will need to establish and maintain relationships with clients. The essential criteria for success in this process will include simply learning how to listen, make and return phone calls and emails in a professional manner, ask for an appointment, network, run a meeting, deal with difficult people, and how to develop all the requisite tools possessed by a successful businessperson.

There are some enduring truths about business development: first, it is really nothing more than a series of conversations, and second, it's all about clients and their needs. The line between genuine outreach and opportunism can be a fine one, and you have to learn to balance the urge to sell or close too soon. There is an appropriate time in the client development cycle to promote your legal skills and ask for the business. Be patient and wait.

III. Client Service

Similar to but separate from business development, client service is focusing efforts on serving existing clients and their matters. Many consultants will say that improving your relationships with existing clients and contacts has a faster and more profitable payoff than developing new clients entirely. Of course, the reality is that you need both.

As with business development skills, client service skills must be learned by almost all new associates over time. They are not found in a playbook, and one size fits all does not apply here. Success in both areas largely relies on interpersonal skills, also known as people skills, soft skills, or emotional intelligence skills, which are related to the way you communicate and interact with others. Communication, conflict management, empathy, leadership, listening, positivity, and teamwork are all examples of interpersonal skills.

As a new associate, you can practice client service skills by thinking of the firm partners as your clients. Because you likely are not yet bringing in your own clients, your job is to do good work and keep the partners happy so they will continue to use you on their matters. Start by treating them like clients: Be responsive, responsible, and respectful, and meet (or at least manage) their expectations. Observe how they interact with the firm's clients and learn from the experience. And at the most basic level, you should strive to be enthusiastic, smile, show respect for others, practice humility, and avoid asking questions for which you can readily find answers yourself.

IV. Conclusion

Clients are the lifeblood of private practice. The concepts introduced in this chapter cut across most practices and should help sensitize you to the issues you may face as you grow your practice. Keeping clients in mind, and making smart and deliberate outreach, development, and service choices can help you distinguish yourself in an often difficult profession.

PART IV

In-House Counsel

Introduction

Businesses are the largest consumers of private legal services in the United States. Businesses large and small rely on lawyers across the whole spectrum of practices. From general transactional work and litigation to more specialized areas such as advertising, regulation, capital markets, intellectual property, insurance, tax, and employment, you are all but certain to encounter legal work for a business at some point in your career.

So far, this book has been oriented toward the business of being a lawyer in a law firm setting who does work for various clients. This is commonly referred to in the industry as "outside counsel" to denominate a relationship to a corporate client distinct from the law firm itself.

As businesses grow larger, they tend to "insource" at least part of their legal needs for the sake of efficiency. Insourced counsel are commonly referred to as "in-house" lawyers or legal departments. Such departments can range in size from one person to hundreds. In-house lawyers are also consistently found outside the private sector, in nonprofits and government agencies.

Understanding the structure and dynamics of in-house legal departments is important for at least two reasons: It will greatly enhance your role as outside counsel in a law firm environment, where those in-house lawyers "are" the client, and it provides some background should you consider pursuing an in-house position yourself. This part concludes with a look at special issues faced by in-house counsel with respect to the attorney-client privilege.

CHAPTER 8

CORPORATE LAW DEPARTMENTS

I. Overview of Corporate Law Departments and Roles

A. Nature

Hiring for in-house law departments is often done as a lateral matter—that is, lawyers typically migrate to companies after working in private practice. The conventional wisdom—that in-house is a preferred "lifestyle" choice over private practice—may be exaggerated. Many in-house lawyers work just as hard, and many harder, than their counterparts in law firms. That said, there is typically less schedule flux with an in-house position. It is perhaps fairer to say that the job is just a "different" one. Working in-house may simply suit different types of people. For example, the pressures of timesheets and business development in private practice may simply be swapped for the in-house pressures of configuring budgets for the finance department and quarterly reports for management.

Some common generalizations about working in-house are discussed below:

In-house employers heavily weigh legal experience, business sense, and interpersonal skills.

Many in-house lawyers are generalists who shift between practice areas and issues on a near-constant basis. For this reason, it is uncommon for in-house positions to be offered to new law graduates. The jobs are generally more suited for lawyers with at least several and often many years of experience in a law firm environment and exposure to both business and legal matters. Businesses tend to strongly favor lawyers with specialized knowledge of and expertise in their industry. There also tend to be more in-house opportunities in the transactional hemisphere (corporate, securities, mergers and acquisitions, real estate, and intellectual property), but opportunities for litigators are expanding. People skills and communication skills are at a premium in the in-house environment. And unlike a law firm, in a corporate legal department, you are paid for results, not your time. Your focus will almost always be on tasks that add value to the business.

Even more so than at law firms, in-house lawyers may have a variety of titles and duties, and those may vary by organization.
Smaller businesses may have one in-house lawyer. This lawyer will often double as the corporate secretary, and may have responsibility for all internal legal matters and oversight and coordination with outside law firms.

In departments of more than one lawyer, one will typically carry the apex title of General Counsel—referred to by the shorthand "GC." The GC commonly provides legal advice directly to management or the board of directors, and often reports directly to the chief executive officer or other senior management. As companies expand their legal departments, they often place the lawyers in a hierarchy of sorts (tiers, ranks, and bands are common examples), and they may divide lawyers into executive and non-executive levels. Ranks can impact salary, benefits, and bonus distributions. These ranks also typically correlate to similar ranks company-wide and may not be restricted to the legal department—for example, vice president, senior vice president, and executive vice president is a common three-stage title progression in a corporate hierarchy.

In-house legal teams are often comprised of junior lawyers of various ranks as well as paralegals and administrative personnel. Common titles for those lawyers on the tier below the GC may include "Associate" or "Assistant General Counsel." In larger departments, there may be additional tiers of attorneys with titles such as "Counsel," "Corporate Counsel," or "Staff Attorney." Further distinctions of rank may include "Senior" or "Managing." There is almost no limit to this expansion. In the largest legal departments, there may be various "Deputy GC" or "Division Counsel"—attorneys with substantial responsibility and differing direct reports.

Historically, corporate law departments were predominantly focused on broad subject matter areas like transactions, intellectual property management, employment, and routine litigation. As the business environment has grown increasingly complex, however, that focus has broadened considerably. Today, in-house departments may routinely handle matters involving risk management, corporate ethics, regulatory compliance, cybersecurity and privacy, and even crisis management and communications. And, in an overarching sense, the matters will largely be aligned however they will best advance the company's business objectives.

Moreover, law departments are increasingly managed and measured like any other business unit, subject to formal budgeting, forecasting, reporting, and performance requirements—all of which lead to constant pressure to perform and manage outside counsel in an increasingly efficient manner. The Outside Counsel Guidelines presented in Chapter 5 are an example of this.

As corporate law departments grow, they also bear administrative and operational responsibilities similar to any other division within the corporate structure. This leads to structural responsibility within the department for multiple non-legal functions, such as strategic planning and budgeting, personnel management, management of outside counsel spending, process improvement, project management, technology adoption, knowledge management, and general office administration. If this all sounds familiar, it should. These are all issues underlying the operation of a private law firm as well.

B. Structure

Knowing the structure of a given in-house department helps in understanding how a lawyer's role fits into the overall picture. There is no single or "correct" way to structure a law department. Many factors influence this decision, including business needs, efficiency, and corporate culture. Often, the structure of a company's legal function parallels the overall management philosophy of the company. Businesses with strong centralized management are more likely to have a centralized legal function. Businesses that operate in a more decentralized fashion are more likely to have decentralized legal responsibilities.

1. Centralized Model

A centralized legal department is commonly located at a company headquarters and provides legal services for the company across all business units and geographic locations. For purposes of illustration, assume a corporate parent company, "Newco," operates in three different lines of businesses and is organized into three quite unrelated business divisions: "Animals, Inc.," "Vegetables, Inc.," and "Minerals, Inc." The top-level corporate organization might look like this:

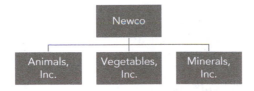

Presuming Newco would likely have a General Counsel, the GC's team could be structured in several ways. An example of a centralized law department at Newco might look like this:

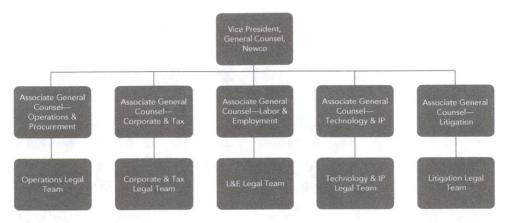

Under this model, the lawyers are aligned along substantive expertise, assisting all three divisions with matters that fall into the lawyers' areas of expertise. For example, if an issue involves technology and intellectual property for any business in the Newco family, its responsibility falls to the Associate General Counsel for Technology and IP. All of these lawyers might also be located at the company headquarters or other shared space.

2. Decentralized Model

In a decentralized model, the headquarters may have only one or a few lawyers, while the various business units and regional locations may have in-house lawyers of their own (or rely on their own outside counsel). An example for Newco might be:

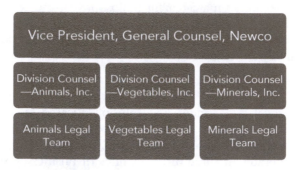

In this model, the lawyers for the business units may be more like generalists, helping their specific business units with whatever legal matters arise. For example, the Division Counsel for Animals might be responsible for the drafting and negotiation of contracts, dealing with employment issues, and the oversight of litigation, as well as anything else pertaining to Animals. Depending on the size of the company, the Animals legal team could also include specialists.

Larger legal departments are often structured in a corporate hierarchy. An example of this might be as follows:

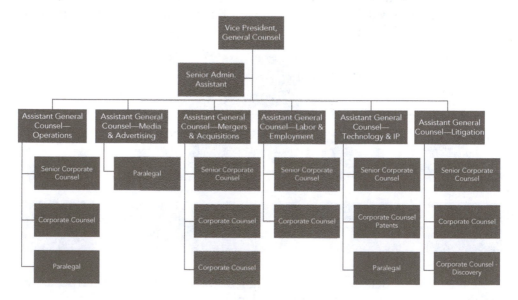

Whatever the structure, in-house lawyers at all levels provide points of contact for outside counsel.

II. Relationships with In-House Counsel

As companies grow and expand their in-house law departments and capabilities, outside lawyers find themselves in increasing competition for a diminishing pool of corporate legal work. Simple excellence in a practice area is rarely enough to land a major matter from a corporate client in today's environment. Larger corporate clients may use numerous law firms for various matters, and competition among those firms can be fierce. Decision makers may even presume that any firm under consideration will meet the substantive bar for performance and experience. What, then, makes the difference?

In some instances, it can be issues unrelated to expertise such as the ability to staff a matter with a diverse team; in others, it may be a simple matter of cost-effectiveness and, possibly, a firm's ability to offer an attractive rate structure or alternative fee arrangement.

A key variable is often the human one—a good relationship with in-house counsel. Law firms typically have a designated "relationship partner" who is responsible for the growth and maintenance of existing relationships with a corporate client and its legal department. The importance of this role cannot be overstated. As discussed in Chapter 7, relationship building takes time and a nuanced approach, as well as an advanced understanding of the client's business, operations, and goals, and industry trends. A simple news search about a company or a deep dive into its annual reports or SEC filings can provide lawyers with much detail and information, all from publicly available sources.

Knowing the law department's structure and chain of command can prove invaluable in building relationships with in-house counsel. Everyone has a boss. Helping in-house counsel provide timely and streamlined advice to their direct reports or executive counterparts (who often do not have time to focus on the details) makes them look good—which, in turn, makes outside counsel look good.

Further, you should understand that a corporate law department may be only one of many business units within an enterprise and faced with budgeting, forecasting, and reporting pressures like any other.

Finally, one differentiator in this area is the ability to keep legal advice framed in the context of practical realities of time, cost, and resource constraints. In short, successful relationship partners recognize the value of serving as a business partner to their corporate clients.

III. Attorney-Client Privilege in the Corporate Context

The role of an in-house lawyer is like that of an outside lawyer in some ways, but dramatically different in others. There are gray areas and questions concerning whether and how the attorney-client privilege may or may not attach in the corporate context, and therefore it is important that in-house and outside counsel who represent corporate clients understand when communications are privileged.

As you know from other studies, the attorney-client privilege is an embodiment of the time-honored tradition of confidentiality in the relationship between lawyer and client. It exists in large part to encourage clients to make full disclosures to their attorneys by providing an assurance that such disclosures will be held in confidence. Because the privilege was built on a traditional conception of the relationship, which largely assumed an individual client with a discrete legal problem and an individual lawyer or law firm, it has proven to be a challenging fit for the corporate context.

While the applicable law at issue may vary depending on the jurisdiction and case, for our purposes here we can simplify and conceptualize the issues into two broad considerations: who the client is, and whether the in-house lawyer is acting in a legal capacity.

A. Who Is the Client?

There is no dispute that the attorney-client privilege extends to corporations as well as individuals, and in-house counsel can certainly fulfill the role of client when communicating with outside counsel. An in-house lawyer's client, however, is her employer, and she owes the same ethical duties of loyalty to her employer as an outside representative would. Therefore, she may also fulfill the role of the attorney when communicating with personnel within her organization. The question arises as to which people within an organization are deemed to be her client for privilege purposes. Surely a company's customer service representative in the phone room of a far-flung division of a multinational corporation is not the "client" of staff counsel. Or is he?

Historically, many courts considered in-house lawyer communications with senior management to be the best approximation of the individual attorney-client model the privilege was founded upon, and they applied what is known as the "control" or "control group" test to determine whether a communication should be afforded the protection of the privilege. In practice, this test can require a complicated assessment of corporate governance issues and may not reach communications with lower-level employees, even if they were directly involved in the issue. Defenders of the test raise concerns that, without some boundaries, virtually all corporate communications could be swept into the privilege, resulting in an intolerable zone of secrecy around corporate operations.

The Supreme Court considered this question, at least in a federal context, in the 1981 *Upjohn* decision.[1] *Upjohn* involved an investigation by both in-house and outside counsel of payments by a foreign corporate subsidiary to foreign government officials. The company's general counsel sent questionnaires to corporate employees and then interviewed them. The IRS later sought discovery of both the questionnaires and the interview notes. In holding that these documents were protected by the privilege because the employees were "acting as [employees], at the direction of corporate superiors in order to secure legal advice from counsel[,]" the Supreme Court rejected a

---

[1] *Upjohn Co. v. United States,* 449 U.S. 383 (1981).

strict control group test in favor of a case-by-case determination based on a variety of factors, including

- whether the communications were made by employees to corporate counsel in order for the corporation to secure legal advice;
- whether the employees were cooperating with corporate counsel at the direction of corporate superiors;
- whether the communications concerned matters within the employees' scope of employment; and
- whether the information was not available from upper-echelon management.

With *Upjohn*, the Supreme Court ushered in a "subject matter" test, which expanded the control group inquiry to include a look at the actual communication involved and whether its subject matter brought the employee involved within the protective sphere of the client relationship.

An important practice for clients and counsel is to identify situations in which individual employees' interests conflict with those of the corporate client. In-house counsel conducting internal investigations should then make it clear to employees that communications are not privileged and that the attorney represents the company and not necessarily the employee.

This clarification of roles is sometimes called an "Upjohn warning" (or, perhaps more colorfully, a "corporate Miranda warning").

Importantly, *Upjohn*'s holding is also limited to the federal courts. Many states have not adopted the Upjohn test and rely instead on some form of the "control group" test, or different common law and statutory rules. This sphere of uncertainty creates considerations for all in-house lawyers when interacting with their company's mid- and low-level employees.

B. What Role Is the Lawyer Performing?

A communication between an in-house lawyer and her client is presumptively privileged—as with communications between outside counsel and the client. However, unlike outside counsel, in-house counsel often serve in several different roles within a company, and depending on the role a lawyer was playing at the time, the attorney-client privilege may or may not apply. Communications conveying business advice, rather than legal advice, are not protected by the privilege.

For many legal departments, their role is purely a legal function, ranging from that of a captive law firm to more advisory roles. A legal team can also encompass other roles, such as procurement, compliance, and risk management. Many in-house lawyers fulfill a business or executive function in addition to their legal duties. This brings legal background to the business context, but attorneys practicing in such a dual capacity must be vigilant in understanding and demarcating their role. When in-house counsel's job responsibilities involve business-oriented duties, communications pertaining to those duties may amount to no more than business advice and may fall outside the privilege. Perils can lurk with respect to attorney-client privilege failing to attach to business communications. Consider two cases addressing the question of whether a corporate attorney is acting in a business or a legal capacity, and the consequences that flow from that determination.

Rossi v. Blue Cross & Blue Shield of Greater N.Y.
73 N.Y.2d 588 (1989)

Opinion of the Court

KAYE, J.

An internal memorandum from a corporate staff attorney to a corporate officer communicating advice regarding a company form that was the subject of an imminent defamation action is protected from disclosure in that action by the attorney-client privilege.

As alleged in the complaint, in April 1984, plaintiff, a physician specializing in radiology, opened a facility for medical diagnostic testing through the use of a Diasonics NMR (nuclear magnetic resonance) Imaging Scanner. Over the next year and a half, plaintiff performed NMR scans on numerous patients, among them subscribers of defendant health insurer, Blue Cross and Blue Shield. Defendant allegedly rejected more than 2,000 claims by plaintiff's patients seeking reimbursement for the scans. In rejecting claims, defendant sent its subscribers a form containing the following statement: "Your contract does not cover procedures which are experimental or whose effectiveness is not generally recognized by an appropriate governmental agency." Apparently, the procedure had in fact been approved by the Federal Food and Drug Administration, National Center for Devices and Radiological Health.

After several times notifying defendant of the FDA approval and unsuccessfully seeking correction of the statement, on May 2, 1985, plaintiff drew up a summons and complaint for defamation. In the complaint, plaintiff pleaded that hundreds of his patients who had received defendant's rejection notice condemned him for using an unapproved, experimental nuclear procedure that could harm them physically. Plaintiff alleged that Blue Cross knew that the language used in rejecting his patients' claims was false and fraudulent, but that it nonetheless persisted in sending the statement to his patients, gravely damaging his practice and reputation.

The focus of this appeal is an internal Blue Cross memorandum dated May 2, 1985—the date of the summons and complaint—from Edward Blaney, Jr., to Dr. Mordecai Berkun. Blaney was a lawyer employed by Blue Cross on its counsel's staff, not a company officer; Berkun was an officer of Blue Cross and its Medical Director. Copies of the memorandum were indicated for C. Ammarati, Blue Cross Vice-President of Professional Affairs (Berkun's staff superior), and J. L. Shurtleff, Blue Cross Vice-President and General Counsel (Blaney's staff superior).

In response to discovery requests, defendant identified the Blaney memorandum but withheld production on grounds of attorney-client privilege, work product and material prepared for litigation. While the document has not been made public, defendant has described its contents, paragraph by paragraph, as follows. According to defendant, the first paragraph refers to conversations between Blaney and plaintiff's attorney regarding a possible defamation suit based on the rejection form; the second concerns conversations between Blaney and the FDA regarding plaintiff's NMR Imaging System; the third paragraph sets forth Blaney's understanding of Blue Cross' NMR reimbursement policy and his understanding of new language that was going to be used to deny NMR claims; and the final paragraph expresses Blaney's opinion and advice regarding the rejection language of the form, and requesting comments from the Medical Director.

On plaintiff's motion for production of the memorandum in its entirety, Supreme Court reviewed the document in camera and directed that it be turned over to plaintiff. A divided Appellate Division reversed, concluding that the memorandum was a privileged attorney-client communication as well as work product, and it granted plaintiff leave to appeal to this court on a certified question. The dissenters would have ordered production because the thrust of the memorandum "concerns the quality of a business judgment and does not in any significant way involve a lawyer's learning and professional skills reflecting legal research or theory." We now affirm on the ground that the memorandum is privileged, and therefore do not reach the alternative arguments advanced by defendant.

To begin with points of agreement, no one questions that corporations, as other clients, may avail themselves of the attorney-client privilege for confidential communications with attorneys relating to their legal matters. A corporation's communications with counsel, no less than the communications of other clients with counsel, are encompassed within the legislative purposes of CPLR 4503, which include fostering uninhibited dialogue between lawyers and clients in their professional engagements, thereby ultimately promoting the administration of justice. The privilege applies to communications with attorneys, whether corporate staff counsel or outside counsel. Finally, while the cases largely concern communications by clients to their attorneys, CPLR 4503 speaks of communications "between the attorney * * * and the client" (CPLR 4503 [a]), and the privilege thus plainly extends as well to the attorney's own communications to the client.

Beyond these points of agreement, the attorney-corporate client privilege has raised nettlesome questions—particularly as to communications from corporate agents to counsel (see, e.g., Waldman, Beyond Upjohn: The Attorney-Client Privilege in the Corporate Context, 28 Wm & Mary L Rev 473 [1987]; Saltzburg, Corporate and Related Attorney-Client Privilege Claims: A Suggested Approach, 12 Hofstra L Rev 279 [1984]; Sexton, A Post-Upjohn Consideration of the Corporate Attorney-Client Privilege, 57 NYU L Rev 443 [1982]). But even where the communication in issue is—as here—from the staff attorney to the corporate agent, difficult questions may arise.

For example, unlike the situation where a client individually engages a lawyer in a particular matter, staff attorneys may serve as company officers, with mixed business-legal responsibility; whether or not officers, their day-to-day involvement in their employers' affairs may blur the line between legal and nonlegal communications; and their advice may originate not in response to the client's consultation about a particular problem but with them, as part of an ongoing, permanent relationship with the organization. In that the privilege obstructs the truth-finding process and its scope is limited to that which is necessary to achieve its purpose, the need to apply it cautiously and narrowly is heightened in the case of corporate staff counsel, lest the mere participation of an attorney be used to seal off disclosure.

Obviously, not every communication from staff counsel to the corporate client is privileged. It is equally apparent that no ready test exists for distinguishing between protected legal communications and unprotected business or personal communications; the inquiry is necessarily fact-specific. However, certain guideposts to reaching this determination may be identified by looking to the particular communication at issue in this case. Here, as the Appellate Division noted, the "memorandum is clearly an internal, confidential document. Nothing indicates that anyone outside the defendant company had access to it." Moreover, there is no dispute as to the author's status or role. Blaney functioned as a lawyer, and solely as a lawyer, for defendant client; he had no other responsibility within the organization. His communication to his client was plainly made in the role of attorney.

For the privilege to apply when communications are made from client to attorney, they "must be made for the purpose of obtaining legal advice and directed to an attorney who has been consulted for that purpose." By analogy, for the privilege to apply when communications are made from attorney to client—whether or not in response to a particular request—they must be made for the purpose of facilitating the rendition of legal advice or services, in the course of a professional relationship. Here that test is met.

The subject of the memorandum was plaintiff's imminent defamation suit based on the language of defendant's rejection form. The memorandum, written the very day plaintiff's summons and complaint were drafted, began by referring to Blaney's conversations with plaintiff's counsel and went on to express the lawyer's views regarding the rejection language of the form. Communications from an attorney to a client dealing with the substance of imminent litigation generally will fall into the area of legal rather than business or personal matters. That the memorandum does not reflect legal research is not determinative, where the communication concerns legal rights and obligations and where it evidences other professional skills such as lawyer's judgment and recommended legal strategies.

So long as the communication is primarily or predominantly of a legal character, the privilege is not lost merely by reason of the fact that it also refers to certain nonlegal matters. Indeed, the nature of a lawyer's role is such that legal advice may often include reference to other relevant considerations. Here, it is plain from the content and context of the communication that it was for the purpose of facilitating the lawyer's rendition of legal advice to his client. While we are mindful of the concern that mere participation of staff counsel not be used to seal off discovery of corporate communications, here "[n]othing suggests that this is a situation where a document was passed on to a defendant's attorney in order to avoid its disclosure." It appears that Blaney was exercising a lawyer's traditional function in counseling his client regarding conduct that had already brought it to the brink of litigation.

Plaintiff finally asserts that even if the memorandum is privileged, the privilege should give way to "strong public policy considerations[.]" The "strong public policy considerations" are defendant's alleged massive fraud and Blaney's death. Neither the nature of the alleged wrong nor the attorney's unavailability rises to the level of subverting the lawful and honest purposes for which the privilege exists; indeed, were Blaney alive, the communication still would be shielded from discovery. Protecting this memorandum from disclosure in plaintiff's defamation action is, in the circumstances, consistent with the lawful and honest aims of the privilege to foster uninhibited communication between lawyer and client in the fulfillment of the professional relationship.

Accordingly, the order of the Appellate Division should be affirmed, with costs, and the certified question answered in the affirmative.

Chief Judge WACHTLER and Judges SIMONS, ALEXANDER, TITONE, HANCOCK, JR., and BELLACOSA concur.
Order affirmed, etc.

However, as seen in the next case, even advice that may be legal in nature is not always in a safe harbor.

Georgia Pacific Corp. v. GAF Roof Mfg. Corp.
1996 U.S. Dist. Lexis 671 (S.D.N.Y. Jan. 24, 1996)

Opinion and Order
ROBERT P. PATTERSON, JR., District Judge.

In this breach of contract action, plaintiff Georgia-Pacific Corporation ("GP") moves to compel answers to certain deposition questions addressed to Michael D. Scott, the negotiator of the environmental provisions of the contract and in-house environmental counsel for defendants GAF Roofing Manufacturing Corporation and G-I Holdings, Inc. (collectively, "GAF"). GAF opposes on the grounds of attorney-client privilege.

The contract involved the sale to GAF of GP properties and other assets related to GP's roofing business. The general issue raised by this motion is whether testimony of in-house counsel can be compelled if he acted as negotiator of terms and provisions of a contract or whether defendants may invoke the attorney-client privilege.

In February 1993, or possibly, January 1993, GAF asked Mr. Scott to review a proposed asset purchase agreement and related documents provided by GP and comment on the environmental issues raised by the proposed agreement. On March 12, 1993, Mr. Scott met with Kathy Rhyne and Ronald Allen, GP's environmental lawyers, to discuss the environmental provisions, and during the week March 15 to March 19, 1993, Mr. Scott served as a negotiator for GAF with respect to various environmental issues relating to the proposed transaction. During that period, Mr. Scott told Carl Eckardt, a senior GAF executive, and Barry Kirshner and Barry Simon, in-house counsel for GAF, prior to execution, that the environmental provisions of the proposed contract might not cover certain types of claims that would come up during an environmental audit and were "unusual" in nature. Mr. Scott made recommendations to Eckardt, Kirshner, and Simon as to how he might go about negotiating the agreement and negotiating changes in the contract.

GP and GAF signed an asset purchase agreement dated March 19, 1993 (the "Agreement") calling for a closing no later than July 31, 1993. Mr. Scott was present at the execution of the Agreement and had reviewed its disclosure schedule.

The Agreement contained several attachments, including a to-be-entered-into form of the Environmental Remediation and Indemnification Agreement (the "Environmental Agreement") pursuant to which GP would agree to remediate and assume liability for, to the extent not remediated as defined in the contract, various existing environmental conditions to be listed in an exhibit entitled "Schedule 1." Prior to the execution of the Agreement, GP provided GAF "with [a] proposed Schedule 1 to the [Environmental Agreement] listing Existing Conditions identified as a result of Seller's Environmental Audit that . . . Seller agrees to rectify as that term is defined in that agreement." Pursuant to the Agreement, GAF was then to conduct its own environmental audit of the properties and within 65 days propose "any additions to Seller's proposed Schedule 1 based on Buyer's Environmental Audit or Seller's Environmental Audit Update." Upon receipt of GAF's proposed additions, the parties were to negotiate, in good faith, from the perspective of a reasonably prudent site operator and identify those additional items for Schedule 1 that required "corrective measures or other action to achieve substantial compliance with applicable Environmental Laws." The prior execution of the Environmental Agreement with an agreed-on Schedule 1 was a condition of closing.

After execution of the Agreement, Mr. Scott notified GP of GAF's proposed environmental audit pursuant to Section 5.15 of the Agreement. In April and May 1993, Mr. Scott requested that GP agree that an issue relating to the detection of a hazardous substance, trichloroethylene ("TCE"), in subterranean well water in a well adjacent to or on GP's felt mill property in Franklin, Ohio, be carved out from the Environmental Agreement with the provision that GP not be required to do anything to remediate the condition until and unless regulatory agencies were to require it. GAF took the position through Mr. Scott that either this "carve out" provision or a "straight indemnification" provision should be used to eliminated from the asset purchase this problem for GAF. GP was opposed to both of these alternatives.

On June 7, 1993, Mr. Scott again met with Ms. Rhyne and Mr. Allen. He testified that in light of certain flexibility evidenced by GP, he attempted to signal to GP that if the parties could get agreement on all the other issues, he would be prepared to work within GAF to support a solution of the TCE issue. Mr. Scott stated, however, that the issue "ultimately would have to be resolved by Earl and Van Meter" (id.) and indicated that he did not have a particular solution in mind. Mr. Scott testified that he reported to Mr. Eckardt what had occurred at the meeting on June 7, 1993. Mr. Scott and Mr. Allen thereafter spoke periodically and planned another meeting for July 19 or July 20, 1993 in order to finalize their discussions on environmental matters. On July 19, 1993, however, GAF terminated the Agreement and the planned meeting never took place.

On July 23, 1993, GP commenced this action. Mr. Scott was deposed on April 27 and 28, 1995. On May 31, 1995, GP wrote the Court seeking an order to compel him to answer questions and to produce his diaries. GAF opposed the motion as premature and argued that the defense's repeated objections were justified on the basis of attorney-client privilege. After the Court cautioned that the attorney-client privilege would not apply if Mr. Scott were acting in a business capacity, the parties agreed to continue Mr. Scott's deposition and try to resolve those issues without the Court's assistance. On October 30 and 31, 1995, Mr. Scott's deposition continued. On December 4, 1995, GP wrote the Court requesting an order compelling Mr. Scott to testify in three areas:

1. What recommendations, if any, did Mr. Scott make to the GAF negotiators of the Agreement in February-March 1993 as to how the provisions of the proposed agreement could be changed and the impact of such changes on the proposed provisions.
2. Whether, after his June 7, 1993 meeting with GP, Mr. Scott made a recommendation to anyone in GAF's senior management that they should consider options other than "straight indemnification" or "carve out" as a negotiating strategy.
3. Whether Mr. Eckardt asked Mr. Scott to cancel Mr. Scott's planned meeting for July 19 or July 20, 1993 with Mr. Allen of GP.

The Court held a conference in response to this letter on December 19, 1995 and ordered Mr. Scott to comply with plaintiff's third request, i.e. to testify as to whether he had been ordered by Mr. Eckardt to cancel his scheduled meeting with Mr. Allen. The Court asked the parties to submit briefs on the other issues. Those briefs were submitted on January 5, 1996.

Discussion

New York law governs the attorney-client privilege in a diversity case such as this. Fed. R. Evid. 501; Agreement §10.2 (New York Choice of Law provision); Drummer v. Appleton, 628 F. Supp. 1249, 1250 (S.D.N.Y. 1986); Note Funding Corp. v. Bobian Investment Co., 1995 WL 662402 (S.D.N.Y., 1995). Under §4503(a) of the New York Civil Practice Law and Rules ("CPLR"), the attorney-client privilege may be invoked with respect to "evidence of a confidential communication between the attorney . . . and the client in the course of professional employment." CPLR §4503(a). "The burden is on a party claiming the protection of the privilege to establish those facts that are the essential elements of the privilege relationship." von Bulow by Auersperg v. von Bulow, 811 F.2d 136, 144 (2d Cir. 1987), cert. denied, 481 U.S. 1015 (1987).

The New York Court of Appeals has made it clear that the scope of the attorney-client privilege "is limited to that which is necessary to achieve its purpose." Rossi v. Blue Cross, and Blue Shield of Greater New York, 73 N.Y.2d 588, 592, 540 N.E.2d 703, 705, 542 N.Y.S.2d 508, 510 (N.Y. 1989).

Rossi involved an internal memorandum from Edward Blaney, a lawyer employed by Blue Cross on its counsel's staff. The memorandum was sent to Blue Cross medical director with copies indicated to its general counsel and vice president of professional affairs. Its contents referred to (1) conversations between Blaney and plaintiff's attorney regarding a possible defamation suit based on a rejection form used by Blue Cross which included the statement: "Your contract does not cover procedures which are experimental or whose effectiveness is not generally recognized by an appropriate governmental agency"; (2) conversations between Blaney and the FDA regarding plaintiff's NMR Imaging System; (3) Blaney's understanding of Blue Cross's NMR reimbursement policy and his understanding of new language that was going to be used to deny NMR claims; (4) Blaney's opinion and advice regarding the rejection language of the form; and (5) a request for the medical director's comments. *Rossi*, 542 N.Y.S.2d at 509.

Where the communication in issue—as in this case—is from an in-house attorney to management, difficult fact specific questions are involved. See Abel v. Merrill Lynch & Co., Inc., 1993 WL 33348, *3 (S.D.N.Y., 1993) (corporation not entitled to assert privilege in suit for civil rights violations by funneling all information concerning potential terminations in its work force to in-house counsel and then claiming that the data in the in-house counsel's files is privileged). In *Rossi*, the Court of Appeals observed that staff attorneys may serve as company officers with mixed business-legal responsibility; whether or not officers, their day-to-day involvement may blur the line between legal and non-legal communications; and their advice may originate not in response to the client's consultation about a particular problem but with them, as part of an on-going, permanent relationship with the organization. In that the privilege obstructs the truth-finding process and its scope is limited to that which is necessary to achieve its purpose, the need to apply it cautiously and narrowly is heightened in the case of corporate staff counsel, lest the mere participation of an attorney be used to seal off disclosure. *Rossi*, 508 N.Y.S.2d at 510.

The court then proceeded to weigh the facts relating to the genesis of the memorandum and found that Mr. Blaney was "exercising a lawyer's traditional function in counseling his client."

It is a general rule that "courts will not recognize the privilege when the attorney is acting . . . as a business advisor. . . ." 5 Weinstein New York Civil Practice, §4503.04 (1995). In Cooper-Rutter Associates, Inc. v. Anchor Nat. Life Ins. Co., the Second Department citing *Rossi* held that two handwritten memoranda prepared by "an individual who was both in-house counsel and corporate secretary to one of the defendants" were not shielded by the privilege. Although, the two memoranda dealt with "both the business and legal aspects of the defendant's on-going negotiations with plaintiff with respect to the business transaction out of which the underlying lawsuit ultimately arose," the documents were "not primarily of a legal character" and "expressed substantial non-legal concerns." Cooper-Rutter Associates, Inc. v. Anchor Nat. Life Ins. Co., 168 A.D.2d 663, 563 N.Y.S.2d 491 (N.Y.A.D. 2 Dept., 1990); *Rossi*, 542 N.Y.S.2d at 510.

Applying the reasoning in *Rossi* to Mr. Scott's role in March 1993, it is clear that Mr. Scott was not "exercising a lawyer's traditional function." *Rossi*, 542 N.Y.S.2d at 511. The record indicates that Mr. Scott was asked to review GP's proposed agreement with respect to the environmental provisions. He then negotiated the environmental provisions of the agreement, and after execution of the agreement, he served as negotiator of the matters to be included in Schedule 1. As a negotiator on behalf of management, Mr. Scott was acting in a business capacity. Mr. Scott's deposition testimony demonstrates that he recognized that the proposed contract would not protect GAF on certain environmental matters. Mr. Scott's discussion with management concerning these issues was prior to the Agreement being entered into and not in the context of imminent litigation.

Since Mr. Scott negotiated the environmental terms of the Agreement, GP is entitled to know what environmental matters he determined would not be covered in the proposed agreement; the extent to which they were covered in the provisions he negotiated in the Agreement; and whether Scott advised GAF management of the degree to which his negotiations had left GAF protected and unprotected. Only by such testimony can it be determined whether GAF, as a matter of business judgment, agreed to assume certain environmental risks when it entered the Agreement.

The deposition of Mr. Scott (Exs. A and B to GAF's memorandum in opposition) reveals that Mr. Scott was acting as a negotiator of the environmental provisions for GAF. The environmental provisions were substantive provisions. Mr. Scott's averment that he rendered legal advice to management, although considered, does not overcome the nature of his role in the transaction as revealed by his deposition. von Bulow by Auersperg v. von Bulow, 811 F.2d at 146 (affidavit consisting of conclusory and ipse dixit assertions insufficient to sustain privilege). Accordingly, Mr. Scott is ordered to answer questions pertaining to the matters within the scope of plaintiff's first request.

By June 1993, the parties had evidently met an impasse about how to handle the fact that there was some evidence of TCE in a well on or under the GP felt mill in Franklin, Ohio. Mr. Scott testified that at the June 7, 1993 meeting with Ms. Rhyne and Mr. Allen ". . . [they] had made very good progress on the other issues and that assuming that GP was willing to grant the sorts of concessions that [he] thought [he] heard Ron and Kathy say they were prepared to at least consider, that all options would be open and that [he] would work with [his] management to achieve a mutually acceptable resolution to the problem, which of course, could take one of many forms." Despite Mr. Scott's testimony, GAF counsel would not allow questions about whether he then advised management about the negotiating options that were open to them or about any advice the witness gave to Carl Eckardt thereafter with respect to how to handle environmental issues. It seems clear Mr. Scott acted as a negotiator of the terms of Schedule 1 and that his conversation with Eckardt as regards the status of the negotiations, the tradeoffs that Mr. Scott perceived GP was willing to make, and GAF's options, involved business judgments of environmental risks. Such reporting of developments in negotiations, if divorced from legal advice, is not protected by the privilege under New York law. Accordingly, Mr. Scott is directed to answer the questions raised in plaintiff's second request.

It is so ordered.

Questions: Note the high standard involved in claims of attorney-client privilege. Note, too, that many in-house lawyers walk a fine line in this area every day. Imagine yourself as an in-house lawyer within a medium-sized company. In addition to your legal duties, you are often pulled into general business and strategy meetings. What steps might you consider to clearly delineate your comments and advice among your many roles in the company?

PRACTICE NOTE: MULTIPLE THEORIES OF PRIVILEGE ARGUABLY PROTECT CORPORATE FAMILY COMMUNICATIONS

What about communications by and between separate corporate divisions such as Animals, Inc., Vegetables, Inc., and Minerals, Inc. from the Newco example? Courts have now long recognized that communications between corporate clients and their attorneys are indeed privileged. The court in *In re Teleglobe Commc'ns Corp.*, 493 F.3d 345, 360 (3d Cir. 2007), explored this concept in some detail, stating that the general rule has been that "when a corporation's managers require its employees to give information to attorneys in the course of providing legal advice, those communications also are protected." The court provided three primary rationales to support application of the attorney-client privilege to communications between entities within a corporate family: (1) joint client or co-client representation, (2) the common interest privilege, or (3) the treatment of a corporate family as one client for privilege purposes.

Joint Client or Co-Client Representation. An in-house counsel or legal department may represent multiple entities within a corporate family as joint or co-clients. Communications between co-clients and their common attorneys can be considered to be made in confidence for privilege purposes. Generally, a co-client relationship is limited by the extent of the legal matter of common interest.

The Common Interest Privilege. When different counsel represent different entities within a corporate family, the common interest privilege may protect communications. The common interest privilege protects all communications shared within a proper "community of interest." This privilege allows attorneys representing different clients with similar legal interests to share information without having to disclose it to others.

The Corporate Family as One Client. Another rationale for application of the privilege, particularly when subsidiaries are wholly owned, is that all members should be considered one client for privilege purposes. This rationale has parallels in other legal contexts, such as the inability of parent companies and subsidiaries acting together to form a conspiracy.

Of course, even in the corporate context, the privilege will not apply if it has been waived—either intentionally or inadvertently—and will not reach communications in furtherance of an ongoing crime or fraud. There are also more nuanced exceptions in certain matters such as shareholder derivative actions. This is an area for serious consideration by in-house lawyers and assumptions should not be made. You should understand that this represents an additional pressure lawyers on the "inside" face as part of the job.

IV. Conclusion

Corporate law departments may vary, but their core priorities remain effectiveness, efficiency, and protecting the company's interests. While this has been only a brief glimpse into a complex and evolving environment, it should be clear that lawyers must pay constant attention to stay in step and aligned with their corporate clients.

NEW LAW

Introduction

Contrary to common perception, the legal profession is not immune to innovation. The practice is now infused with, and some would say transformed by, an array of technology and tools that impact almost every facet of the practice, including core business models.

In Part V, Chapter 9 will touch on three areas of change in the "new law" environment, each with its own controversy. We will first briefly explore virtual firms. Once considered a fringe concept, "virtual" law firms have gained traction, both with clients and lawyers, and have become normalized as "new model" practices.

Next, we discuss litigation finance, whereby third parties underwrite the costs of litigation in exchange for a percentage of any recovery, which is a growing force in the litigation business model. Once considered wholly taboo and even illegal, it remains an evolving and controversial topic.

And third, the online delivery of legal services, such as LegalZoom, remains a subject of deeply divided opinion and creates a balancing act between access to legal services and the unauthorized practice of law.

In Chapter 10, our final chapter, we conclude with an overview of the current state of the legal technology sector. As technology evolves faster than this book can be updated and because many law schools have courses dedicated solely to the topic, we will focus on higher order issues and leave details of particular technological implementation to the province of your particular classroom environment and professor's discretion.

CHAPTER 9

EMERGING MODELS AND PLATFORMS

As the business of private practice undergoes dynamic change and expansion, it tends to remain at its core a quite static institution. Why change? Change is largely driven by efficiencies and economics, but at root, change is driven by market, or more pointedly, client demand. In this chapter, we will explore three developing areas in private practice: virtual firms, litigation finance, and online delivery of legal services. While none of these areas are truly "new"—their roots stretch back 20 years or more—each has recently reached a state of maturity that allows for topical discussion. A core argument underlying the growth and promotion of each is the concept of the expansion of access to legal services. As you work through this chapter, balance this concept with the countervailing view that the profession, and clients, must be protected, at least in some senses, from unchecked expansion in the name of commerce and at the loss of the lawyer's independent judgment.

I. "Virtual" Firms

Emerging law firm models are an important part of any future-of-the-profession conversation.

The concept of "virtual law practices" originated in the early days of the Internet, whereby sole practitioners started serving clients through websites and client portals. Today, "virtual" law firms have grown to encompass a variety of practice environments, now better known as "new model," "hybrid," or "distributed" law firms.[1] At root, these are practices comprised of experienced lawyers

---

[1] *See, e.g.*, Culhane Meadows PLLC, www.culhanemeadows.com ("BigLaw for the New Economy"); FisherBroyles, LLP, www.fisherbroyles.com ("Lawfirm2.0"); Potomac Law Group, PLLC, www.potomaclaw.com ("A New Model Law Firm"); Rimon PC, www.rimonlaw.com ("Law Firm Redesigned").

where the overhead costs of brick-and-mortar office space are removed or dramatically reduced. But new model firms can take many different forms: Lawyers and other firm personnel might work out of their homes or personal office spaces, or they might work in smaller firm satellite offices. Often these firms have lawyers and personnel in several different states. Lawyers may never meet clients in person, or they might meet them occasionally in spaces rented for client meetings. The COVID-19 pandemic experience, which began in 2020, helped to normalize both the acceptability and the experience of remote working for lawyers, and virtual firms gained footing and experienced growth.

Commonly understood advantages to running a virtual law firm over a traditional one include, primarily, lower overhead and lawyer flexibility. As discussed previously, office space and related expenses are a substantial part of a law firm's budget. Additionally, virtual firms tend to use cloud-based software, which lowers high IT expenses. By reducing costs, virtual firms are able to offer their services at rates substantially below those of their traditional rivals. A new model firm can also provide a more flexible work platform for its attorneys. Many of these firms employ a graduated compensation model that is directly tied to hours worked and business generated, which leaves the pressures of performance and income largely to the lawyers themselves.

Of course, there are challenges to running a new model firm as well. It is not for everyone—maintaining focus and work-life balance when working from a home office takes a fair degree of self-discipline, and if you're used to working in a traditional law office, the transition can be challenging and, in some instances, isolating. New model firms have to work hard at creating a cohesive culture through social events and other interactions. Training is limited or nonexistent, as many of the larger new model firms are comprised solely of lawyers with many years of experience and thus are not well suited for junior lawyers.

II. Litigation Finance

A. What Is Litigation Finance?

Litigation finance is a form of underwriting in which an entity or individual that is not a party to a lawsuit finances one of the parties' litigation costs. It is sometimes referred to as "alternative litigation finance," "third-party financing," or "litigation funding." Funders do not make loans, do not charge interest, and have no recourse. Rather, in exchange for providing the capital they receive a portion of any recovery—like a contingency fee. Thus, these funders are in effect investors. Indeed, some funders have now evolved to become publicly traded companies themselves, so there are investors in the investors.[2]

---

[2] *See, e.g.*, Burford Capital LLC, www.burfordcapital.com; in October 2020, Burford listed on the New York Stock Exchange. Sara Merken, *Burford Capital Touts Litigation Funding's Inroads as Its Stock Makes NYSE Debut* (Oct. 19, 2020), https://www.reuters.com/article/burford-research-nyselisting/burford-capital-touts-litigation-fundings-inroads-as-its-stock-makes-nyse-debut-idUSL1N2HA1CA.

The nature of funding agreements varies, but typically the provided capital will directly pay some of the startup and ongoing costs of the litigation, including attorney and expert fees, as well as court costs and other expenses. In some instances, the funders may even provide working capital or financial support for the businesses and individuals involved. As discussed throughout this book, businesses and corporate clients are under intense pressure to reduce legal costs; thus, they may find litigation finance an attractive alternative to pay for otherwise unaffordable legal costs or to simply free up capital for present business needs that would have otherwise been consumed by legal expenses. In the current market, litigation finance is primarily found on the plaintiff or affirmative-claim side of litigation, but there are small inroads into defense-side arrangements as well.

There are three players in a typical financed litigation: plaintiffs, investors, and law firms. The plaintiffs are the holder of the claim(s)—often businesses with commercial contract or intellectual property issues, who lack the resources to press their claims in court. The investors are purchasing a portion of the future proceeds of the litigation in exchange for up-front, and often ongoing, cash payments. The law firms handle the case in the traditional way, but also provide up-front evaluative advice to the plaintiff and the investors. In effect, the law firm is outsourcing the funding aspect of the traditional contingency fee model.

Critics of the practice complain that financed litigation converts the justice system into a stock market, claiming that it disrupts the attorney-client relationship through handcuffing the lawyer. Beholden to the financiers, the lawyer cannot act as a true legal advisor because the financiers control the litigation and settlement. The resulting arrangement intolerably stresses the loyalty and independence of counsel. Critics also suggest as an overarching matter that allowing outside investors into the litigation market breeds excessive and frivolous litigation.

Proponents counter that the practice does just the opposite, helping to equalize access to the justice system by unlocking the asset value of meritorious claims that would have otherwise never been brought due to lack of resources. Complex litigation can involve high costs, which are prohibitive barriers to entry for many would-be plaintiffs. Proponents contend that access to justice under the current litigation structure is, in two words, too expensive.

B. Legal Issues and Ethical Considerations

Historically, practices such as litigation funding were barred by the doctrines of maintenance, champerty, and barratry—each with their roots in medieval England.[3] The continued viability of these doctrines varies by jurisdiction, but in many instances the doctrines have now been largely diluted or deemed obsolete. The following case involves the recent consideration and abolishment of Minnesota's common law prohibition on champerty in the context of a litigation funding agreement.

---

[3]The doctrines are distinct, but for present purposes they may be considered as a whole. Cases of maintenance and champerty are founded on the principle that no encouragement should be given to litigation by the introduction of parties to enforce those rights that others are not disposed to enforce. *Papageorge v. Banks*, 81 A.3d 311 (D.C. 2013). Barratry encompasses the encouragement of another to bring or persist in a litigation.

Maslowski v. Prospect Funding Partners LLC
944 N.W.2d 235 (Minn. 2020)

Opinion

HUDSON, Justice.

This appeal arises from a contract between appellant Prospect Funding Holdings LLC and respondent Pamela Maslowski whereby appellant purchased an interest in respondent's personal injury suit. When respondent settled her suit and did not abide by the terms of the contract, appellant sued respondent to enforce the contract. Both the district court and the court of appeals held that appellant could not enforce the contract because it violated Minnesota's common law prohibition against champerty. We reverse and remand to the district court for further proceedings consistent with this opinion.

Facts

Appellant Prospect Funding Partners LLC ("Prospect") is a litigation financing company. Respondent Pamela Maslowski is a Minnesota resident who was injured in a car accident in Woodbury in 2012. Following the accident, she retained Schwebel, Goetz & Sieben, P.A. to represent her concerning a possible claim against both the driver and owner of the other car involved in the accident.

While her personal injury claim was pending, Maslowski contacted Prospect regarding the company's litigation financing services because she needed money to pay her living expenses. On May 21, 2014, Prospect and Maslowski executed a "Sale and Repurchase Agreement." Maslowski was the "seller" and Prospect was the "purchaser" under the contract. Maslowski sold to Prospect the right to receive a portion of the proceeds of any settlement that she received from her personal injury suit. As consideration for the sale, Maslowski received $6,000 from Prospect that was essentially a cash advance on her prospective settlement. Under the contract's fee schedule, the amount Maslowski owed to Prospect increased by 30 percent every 6 months, starting from a baseline of the $6,000 plus fees, with a cap at $25,245.00. But if Maslowski did not receive a settlement, she owed Prospect nothing. The contract also provided that Maslowski's obligation to Prospect would not exceed the amount of her settlement. Maslowski's attorney in the personal injury suit discussed the contract with her and signed the last page of the agreement certifying that he had reviewed the terms with Maslowski and acknowledged the payment directions in the event of a settlement.

On June 22, 2015, Prospect contacted Maslowski to inform her that she would owe Prospect $14,108.00 if her personal injury claim settled and she made payment to Prospect before September 22, 2015. Maslowski's attorney then informed Prospect that he believed that the litigation financing agreement between Maslowski and Prospect was unenforceable.

Maslowski settled her personal injury suit in July of 2015. When Maslowski did not pay Prospect according to the terms of their agreement,

Prospect filed suit in New York against Maslowski, her attorney, and her attorney's law firm for breach of contract and other related claims.

Maslowski served a complaint for declaratory relief on Prospect on August 6, 2015, seeking a ruling from the Hennepin County District Court that the New York forum-selection clause in the Maslowski-Prospect agreement was invalid. Litigation over the proper forum went on for two years, concluding with decisions in appellate courts of both New York and Minnesota. The New York Supreme Court, Appellate Division, held that the New York action should have been dismissed because the choice-of-forum provision was "unreasonable and should not be enforced." Prospect Funding Holdings L.L.C. v. Maslowski, 43 N.Y.S.3d 904, 905, 146 A.D.3d 535 (2017). The Minnesota Court of Appeals agreed that any litigation over the agreement should occur in Minnesota. Maslowski v. Prospect Funding Partners LLC, 890 N.W.2d 756, 769 (Minn. App. 2017) ("The district court did not abuse its discretion by refusing to enforce the forum-selection clause in the parties' agreement based on Minnesota's local interest against champerty."), rev. denied (Minn. May 16, 2017).

The litigation as to the validity of the agreement itself proceeded in Minnesota, with both the district court and the court of appeals holding that Prospect could not enforce the agreement against Maslowski because Minnesota law applied to the agreement and the agreement violated Minnesota's common-law prohibition against champerty. See Maslowski v. Prospect Funding Partners LLC, No. A18-1906, 2019 WL 3000747 (Minn. App. July 8, 2019). Prospect petitioned for review of the court of appeals' decision. We granted review only on the question of whether the agreement violates Minnesota's prohibition against champerty.

Analysis

This case concerns the common-law prohibition against champerty. Champerty is "an agreement to divide litigation proceeds between the owner of the litigated claim and a party unrelated to the lawsuit who supports or helps enforce the claim." Champerty, Black's Law Dictionary (11th ed. 2019). It is closely related to the concept of maintenance. See Maintenance, Black's Law Dictionary (11th ed. 2019) ("Improper assistance in prosecuting or defending a lawsuit given to a litigant by someone who has no bona fide interest in the case; meddling in someone else's litigation."). The issue before us is whether we should affirm the court of appeals' decision on the ground that the contract between Prospect and Maslowski is void as against public policy, or reverse the decision and abolish, under Minnesota law, the common-law doctrine that champertous agreements are unenforceable.

The common law's disapproval of champerty and maintenance traces back many centuries. See Max Radin, Maintenance by Champerty, 24 Calif. L. Rev. 48, 48 (1935) (explaining that laws in both ancient Greece and Rome prevented a third party from intervening in the legal dispute of another). In medieval England, those with means played "the game of writs" to increase their power and harass their rivals through the medieval court system. R. D. Cox, Champerty as We Know It, 13 Mem. St. U. L. Rev. 139, 142 (1983). Part of this practice included the maintenance by a lord of a lawsuit against a landowner in exchange for a share of the proceeds of land. Id. at 143-44.

To address this problem, English statutes and common law prohibited third parties from taking a financial interest in litigation. Id. at 153-54. The law against champerty explains the early prohibitions against assignment of claims and against contingency fees for attorneys in both England and the United States, because both practices were seen as champertous. Radin, supra, at 68-70. Although these attitudes were very strong in England, the adoption of the prohibition against champerty in the United States was uneven. Id. at 68, 70; Cox, supra, at 160 ("Judicial opinion on the question whether a rule against champerty would be good or bad ran from the view that it would be intolerable to the view that it was required for the happiness of mankind.").

We addressed champerty as it applies to an agreement to finance litigation in our decision in Huber v. Johnson, 68 Minn. 74, 70 N.W. 806 (1897). We explained that the "general purpose of the law against champerty and maintenance was to prevent officious intermeddlers from stirring up strife and contention by vexatious or speculative litigation which would disturb the peace of society, lead to corrupt practices, and pervert the remedial process of the law." Id. at 807. We subsequently applied the principle articulated in *Huber* to void contracts between attorneys and laypersons to instigate litigation for a profit. See, e.g., Holland v. Sheehan, 108 Minn. 362, 122 N.W. 1, 2-3 (1909) (involving an agreement between a layperson and an attorney to find potential plaintiffs for personal injury suits in exchange for a percentage of the settlements); Gammons v. Johnson, 76 Minn. 76, 78 N.W. 1035, 1037 (1899) (involving a plan by an attorney to "hunt up claims" against a railroad company and fund the lawsuits at no expense to the plaintiffs in return for a share of the recovery).

We most recently considered the status of champertous agreements in Hackett v. Hammel, 185 Minn. 387, 241 N.W. 68 (1932). Hammel was involved in a lawsuit over a stake in an iron mine in northern Minnesota. 241 N.W. at 69. Hackett "advanced $705 to aid [Hammel] in the prosecution of the case" pursuant to a contract that promised Hackett "ten times the amount so advanced" if Hammel prevailed in the suit involving the iron mine. Id. If Hammel lost, he owed Hackett nothing. Id. When Hammel won the suit, he paid Hackett only $700, and Hackett sued. Id. We held that the contract between Hackett and Hammel was void: "Such speculation in litigation in which the adventurer has no interest otherwise, and where he is in no way related to the party he aids, is champertous." Id.

Under the rule of law articulated by these cases, the contract between Prospect and Maslowski is champertous because Prospect is a stranger to the lawsuit who agreed to provide Maslowski with financial support during her personal injury litigation in exchange for a right to recover from the proceeds of the settlement of her lawsuit. The lower courts therefore did not err in determining that, under our prior decisions, the contract was unenforceable.

We decline, however, to hold that the contract between Maslowski and Prospect is void as against public policy as we understand it today. Champerty is a common law doctrine, and the development of the common law is "determined by the social needs of the community which it governs." Tuttle v. Buck, 107 Minn. 145, 119 N.W. 946, 947 (1909). We have previously explained that, as society changes, "the common law must also evolve" with it. Lake v. Wal-Mart Stores, Inc., 582 N.W.2d 231, 234 (Minn. 1998). Our review of changes in the legal profession and in society convinces us that the ancient prohibition against champerty is no longer necessary.

We first recognized the prohibition against champerty in the years before we adopted formal rules of ethics and before we adopted Minnesota's Rules of Civil Procedure. Today, the rules of professional responsibility and civil procedure address the abuses of the legal process that necessitated the common-law prohibition. Although attorneys may advertise to the general public, there are strict limits on solicitation. See Minn. R. Prof. Conduct 7.2 (generally permitting, but regulating, attorney advertisements); Minn. R. Prof. Conduct 7.3 (limiting solicitation of clients); see also Lester Brickman, Of Arterial Passageways through the Legal Process: The Right of Universal Access to Courts and Lawyering Services, 48 N.Y.U. L. Rev. 595, 645 (1973) (explaining that the "historical antecedents" of restrictions on advertising and solicitation by lawyers "are found in common law proscriptions against barratry, champerty, and maintenance"). Attorneys who file frivolous claims or use the legal system for harassment are subject to discipline and sanctions. See Minn. R. Prof. Conduct 3.1 (prohibiting lawyers from asserting frivolous claims); Minn. R. Civ. P. 11.02 (requiring attorneys who submit pleadings, motions, or other documents to the court to certify that they present the materials for a proper and nonfrivolous purpose); Minn. R. Civ. P. 11.03 (providing sanctions for attorneys, law firms, and parties who violate Rule 11.02).

Along with the increase in regulation, another important development in the law has been the narrowing or abolition of other common law prohibitions based on concerns about champerty and maintenance. Although contingency fees were disfavored under early common law, all American jurisdictions now allow attorneys to take cases on contingency. Lester Brickman, Contingent Fees Without Contingencies: Hamlet Without the Prince of Denmark, 37 UCLA Law Rev. 29, 38-39 (1989); see also Minn. Stat. §549.01 (2018) ("A party shall have an unrestricted right to agree with an attorney as to compensation for services, and the measure and mode thereof . . . ."). Today, we understand contingent fee agreements as a way to facilitate access to justice by incentivizing attorneys to take cases that they might otherwise decline because the client cannot afford their services on an hourly or fixed-fee basis. Brickman, Contingent Fees Without Contingencies, supra, at 43-44; see also Hollister v. Ulvi, 199 Minn. 269, 271 N.W. 493, 497 (1937) ("Contracts for contingent fees are as much for the benefit of the client as for the attorney, because if the client has a meritorious cause of action, but no means with which to pay for legal services unless he can . . . make a contract for a contingent fee to be paid out of the proceeds of the litigation, he cannot obtain the services of a law-abiding attorney . . . ." (internal quotation marks omitted) (citation omitted)).

Similarly, attitudes have shifted concerning the assignment of choses in action. See Leuthold v. Redwood County, 206 Minn. 199, 288 N.W. 165, 167 (1939) ("The law of this state is that an assignment of a chose in action is valid and complete in itself upon the mutual assent of the assignor and assignee without notice to the debtor." (internal quotation marks omitted) (citation omitted)); Anthony J. Sebok, The Inauthentic Claim, 64 Vand. L. Rev. 61, 72-74 (2011) (explaining that fears of champerty and maintenance underlie the traditional common law rule of nonassignability of claims, but the rule has generally been abandoned across the United States in favor of a more modern approach).

Societal attitudes regarding litigation have also changed significantly. Many now see a claim as a potentially valuable asset, rather than viewing litigation as an evil to be avoided. Radin, supra, at 72. The size of the market for litigation financing reflects this attitudinal change. See Investing in Legal Futures: The Rise of the Litigation Finance Firm, The Practice, Sept./Oct. 2019, at 1 (citing an estimate of the litigation finance market's value at $50 to $100 billion). Businesses often seek financing to mitigate the risks associated with litigation and maintain cash flow for their operations. Victoria A. Shannon, Harmonizing Third-Party Litigation Funding Regulation, 36 Cardozo L. Rev. 861, 869 (2015). It is also possible that litigation financing, like the contingency fee, may increase access to justice for both individuals and organizations. Maya Steinitz, Follow the Money? A Proposed Approach for Disclosure of Litigation Finance Agreements, 53 U.C. Davis L. Rev. 1073, 1085 (2019).

Maslowski argues that these changes do not justify an abolition of the common law prohibition against champerty. She raises three specific points in support of her argument. First, she contends that the rules of professional responsibility and civil procedure are insufficient because they do not regulate the substance of champertous agreements. Second, she argues that litigation financing agreements have the potential to strip tort victims of their recovery. Third, she claims that champertous agreements will deter plaintiffs from settling their claims because they will need larger settlements to offset the cost of litigation financing. We address these objections in turn.

It is true that the rules of professional responsibility and civil procedure do not specifically regulate champertous agreements. But, as we have explained, the rules of professional responsibility and civil procedure prevent both attorneys and parties from profiting off of frivolous litigation—which is the type of behavior that we took issue with in *Huber*, *Holland*, and *Gammons*. It is also unlikely that companies like Prospect will fund frivolous claims because they only profit from their investment if a plaintiff receives a settlement that exceeds the amount of the advance—an unlikely result in a meritless suit. See David Tyler Adams, Note, Laissez Fair: The Case for Alternative Litigation Funding and Assignment of Lawsuit Proceeds in Georgia, 49 Ga. L. Rev. 1121, 1148-49 (2015). Litigation financing companies have claim valuation procedures to avoid this very problem. Id.

We are likewise unpersuaded by Maslowski's argument that concern for tort victims requires us to maintain an ancient prohibition. Although it is important that the victims of torts receive compensation for their injuries, they nonetheless have the freedom to contract, and we must not lightly disregard that basic principle. See Jepson v. Gen. Cas. Co. of Wis., 513 N.W.2d 467, 472 (Minn. 1994) ("[H]owever significant Minnesota's interest in the compensation of tort victims, we have other interests which in situations like this one are in conflict with the value we place on victim compensation. For example, we also believe that people should get the benefit of the contracts they enter into, nothing less and nothing more."). Maslowski's argument ignores the many sophisticated parties to whom this reasoning does not apply, such as those who seek commercial litigation financing and understand the risks involved with such agreements.

Regarding Maslowski's argument that litigation financing "under-incentivizes settlement," she cites no empirical evidence to support her claim. There is also a well-reasoned argument to the contrary made by scholars considering the same issue. See, e.g., Ronen Avraham & Abraham Wickelgren, Third-Party Litigation Funding—A Signaling Model, 63 DePaul L. Rev. 233, 235 (2014) (explaining that the decision to fund a plaintiff may create a "credible signal" that the plaintiff's case has merit, which can affect a defendant's incentives to settle). And, as Prospect points out, contingent fee agreements arguably affect a plaintiff's calculation regarding settlement in a similar manner because they reduce the plaintiff's ultimate recovery. Yet we permit such arrangements because they allow plaintiffs who would otherwise be priced out of the justice system to assert their rights. We believe the same is true of litigation financing, as explained above.

Finally, we note that district courts may still scrutinize litigation financing agreements to determine whether equity allows their enforcement. See, e.g., Osprey, Inc. v. Cabana Ltd. P'ship, 340 S.C. 367, 532 S.E.2d 269, 278 (2000) ("Our abolition of champerty as a defense does not mean that all such agreements are enforceable as written."). Parties like Maslowski retain the common law defense of unconscionability. See Abernethy v. Halk, 139 Minn. 252, 166 N.W. 218, 220 (1918) (observing that a court "may decline to enforce an unconscionable contract"). Courts should carefully review uncounseled agreements, particularly between parties of unequal bargaining power or agreements involving an unsophisticated party. Courts and attorneys should likewise be careful to ensure that litigation financiers do not attempt to control the course of the underlying litigation, similar to the "intermeddling" that we described in our early champerty precedent. See Huber, 70 N.W. at 808 (stating that "it is difficult to conceive of any stipulation more against public policy" than a contract term requiring the litigation financier's permission to settle the underlying litigation). There is also the possibility of further regulation by the Legislature, although this prospect is an issue beyond the scope of our review.

For these reasons, we abolish Minnesota's common-law prohibition against champerty.

Conclusion

For the foregoing reasons, we reverse the decision of the court of appeals and remand this case to the district court for further proceedings consistent with this opinion.

Reversed and remanded.

Questions:

- Does third-party funding promote access to justice? Or is it merely a means for sophisticated parties to engage in financial manipulation?
- How might the presence of a third-party funder affect the independent judgment of counsel?
- What about the application of confidentiality and the attorney-client privilege in connection with a third-party funder who is neither attorney nor client? *See, e.g., Mondis Tech. Ltd. v. LG Electronics, Inc.*, 2011 WL 1714304 (E.D. Tex. 2011).

III. Online Delivery of Legal Services

One of the most prolific and controversial technological innovations affecting the legal industry in the past few decades is the do-it-yourself model for the creation of binding legal documents such as wills, divorce documents, and business incorporation documents.

Of particular interest is a central question about the gray area in which these providers operate: Does the online legal service provider simply enhance the self-help abilities of pro se customers who were traditionally priced out of the traditional legal market, or is the company instead in the business of providing legal advice without the licenses required in the jurisdictions in which it operates? The answer to this question is likely "both," which creates tension between the positive social justice policy of expanding access to legal resources and the legal industry's protective ethical limitations on the practice of law.

A. LegalZoom

LegalZoom is at the forefront of the online delivery of legal services sector and has grown in large part by taking risks.[4] LegalZoom's business offerings have become more complex in recent years, and the company now offers services such

---

[4]For more on the history and background of LegalZoom, see Alejandro Cremades, *This Entrepreneur Built a $2 Billion Business with 1,000 Employees by Disrupting the Legal Industry* (June 11, 2019), https://www.forbes.com/sites/alejandrocremades/2019/06/11/this-entrepreneur-built-a-2-billion-business-with-1000-employees-by-disrupting-the-legal-industry/#31cc0a204b3c; Matthew T. Ciulla, *Mapping LegalZoom's Disruptive Innovation*, 11 J. Bus. Entrepreneurship & L. 53 (2018) (applying *Inventor's Dilemma* framework).

as bankruptcy filing and patent and trademark searches, filing, and monitoring, services traditionally performed exclusively by attorneys in law firms.

Another way in which LegalZoom's business model has shown movement is the shift from the "new market" model to the "low market" model. These labels pertain to the extent to which the business disrupts the business of competitors, if any. New market disruption involves creating a new market for a product—here, by providing legal services to customers who otherwise could not afford the product offered by the traditional law firm market. LegalZoom essentially created a market for online, low-cost forms, thereby meeting unmet demand—thus it was a "new" company.

By providing increasingly complex legal services, however, LegalZoom's model begins to morph into the "low market" model, which provides products that are designed to compete with the low end of the established market. The offered products in the low market model are designed to be low cost, but sufficient—or "good enough"—to meet the customer's basic needs. Thus, LegalZoom is best considered a "hybrid disruptor," showing tendencies of both models. Its goal of rerouting customers from the traditional legal industry, one of the oldest and most politically involved industries in the country, illustrates LegalZoom's ambitious and risk-tolerant approach to business.

B. Legal Issues and Ethical Considerations

LegalZoom's risk tolerance has created considerable conflict with traditional practitioners and state bar associations.

Legalzoom.com, Inc. v. North Carolina State Bar
Wake County Business Court, No. 11 CVS 15111 (2014 WL 1213242, Mar. 24, 2014)

This Matter is before the court on LegalZoom.com, Inc.'s Motion for Partial Judgment on the Pleadings ("LegalZoom's Motion") and The North Carolina State Bar's Motion for Judgment on the Pleadings ("State Bar's Motion"). For the reasons stated below, LegalZoom's Motion is Denied, and the State Bar's Motion is Granted in part and Denied in part.

Order and Opinion
   GALE, Judge.

I. Procedural History

LegalZoom, Inc. ("LegalZoom") filed its Complaint on September 30, 2011 seeking declaratory and injunctive relief. The matter was designated a complex business case and assigned to the undersigned on November 7, 2011. The North Carolina State Bar ("State Bar") moved to dismiss the Complaint on February 22, 2012. By its August 27, 2012 Order, the court denied the State Bar's Motion to Dismiss in part, but deferred ruling on the issue of whether LegalZoom is engaged in the unauthorized practice of law until the State Bar elected whether to file a counterclaim seeking to enjoin LegalZoom. The State Bar filed its Answer, Counterclaim, and Motion for Preliminary and Permanent Injunction on September 21, 2012, and an Amended Answer and Counterclaim on October 1, 2012, including a request that LegalZoom be enjoined. LegalZoom replied to the counterclaim on October 31, 2012.

LegalZoom filed its Motion for Partial Judgment on the Pleadings on December 20, 2012, which was limited to the issue of whether the State Bar must register LegalZoom's prepaid legal services plans. The State Bar filed its Motion for Judgment on the Pleadings on January 17, 2013. The Motions have been fully briefed, a hearing was held on June 18, 2013, and the Motions are ripe for disposition.

II. Factual Background

The court does not make findings of fact in ruling upon a Rule 12(c) motion, and in considering the motion, the nonmovant's factual averments are assumed to be true. Ragsdale v. Kennedy, 286 N.C. 130, 137, 209 S.E.2d 494, 499 (1974) (internal citations omitted).

The court is permitted, when assessing a Rule 12(c) motion, to consider exhibits attached to and referenced in the nonmovant's pleadings, and exhibits attached or referred to in the movant's pleadings so long as the nonmovant has made admissions regarding those exhibits. See Reese v. Charlotte-Mecklenburg Bd. of Educ., 196 N.C. App. 539, 545-46, 676 S.E.2d 481, 486 (2009). The court may further consider facts of which it may take judicial notice, so long as any such fact is "not subject to reasonable dispute in that it is either (1) generally known within the territorial jurisdiction of the trial court or (2) capable of accurate and ready determination by resort to sources whose accuracy cannot reasonably be questioned." N.C. R. Evid. 201(b) ("Rule 201"); see also Hope—A Women's Cancer Ctr., P.A. v. State, 203 N.C. App. 593, 597, 693 S.E.2d 673, 676 (2010).

In its Complaint, LegalZoom pleads that its services are "available on the Internet at www.LegalZoom.com." (Compl. for Declaratory and Injunctive Relief ("Compl.") ¶9.) The court concludes that it may take judicial notice of the information provided on LegalZoom's website pursuant Rule 201. See Blackburn v. Bugg, No. COA11-1349, 2012 N.C. App. LEXIS 485, at * 11-12, 723 S.E.2d 585, 2012 WL 1332728 (N.C. App. Ct. 2012); Doron Precision Sys., Inc. v. FAAC, Inc., 423 F. Supp. 2d 173, 179 n. 8 (S.D.N.Y. 2006) ("For purposes of a 12(b)(6) motion to dismiss, a court may take judicial notice of information publicly announced on a party's website, as long as the website's authenticity is not in dispute and 'it is capable of accurate and ready determination.'") (quoting Fed. R. Evid. 201(b)).

The factual statement provides context for these pending motions in accordance with these standards.

LegalZoom, through its website, www.LegalZoom.com, offers two services: (1) a legal document preparation service; and (2) in those states where permitted, prepaid legal services plans. (Compl. ¶9; Am. Answer ¶9.) LegalZoom currently offers its document preparation service nationwide, including in North Carolina, and offers its prepaid legal services plans throughout much of the United States. (Compl. ¶9.) Its prepaid legal services plans are not presently offered in North Carolina because they have not yet been registered.

A. The State Bar's Inquiry into LegalZoom's Online Legal Document Preparation Service

In March 2003, the State Bar's Authorized Practice Committee ("APC") opened an inquiry into whether LegalZoom's online legal document preparation service constituted the unauthorized practice of law ("UPL"). (Compl. ¶20, Ex. 1; Am. Answer ¶20.) On August 26, 2003, the APC advised LegalZoom by letter that it had "voted to dismiss this complaint because the evidence was insufficient to support a finding of probable cause that [LegalZoom was] engaged in the unauthorized practice of law." (Compl. Ex. 3; Am. Answer ¶23.)

On January 30, 2007, the APC notified LegalZoom by letter that it had again opened an inquiry into whether LegalZoom's activities constitute UPL. (Compl. Ex. 4; Answer ¶24.) A number of letters followed. LegalZoom responded to the APC's letter on February 13, 2007, explaining its contention that LegalZoom did not furnish legal advice or guidance, and did not engage in UPL. (Compl. Ex. 5; Am. Answer ¶25.) On May 5, 2008, the APC sent LegalZoom a letter, captioned "LETTER OF CAUTION—Cease and Desist" ("Cease and Desist Letter"), which states that the APC "concluded that there is probable cause to believe that LegalZoom's conduct constituted the unauthorized practice of law . . . [and] voted to issue this Letter of Caution to notify you of its decision and to demand that you stop engaging in your activities now." (Compl. Ex. 6; Am. Answer ¶26.) The letter concludes that, "Legalzoom's conduct as described above is illegal in North Carolina and must end immediately," and requests that LegalZoom "provide a response with evidence that [it has] have complied with the Committee's decision within 15 days of [its] receipt of this letter." (Compl. Ex. 6.)

LegalZoom responded to the Cease and Desist Letter on June 13, 2008 challenging the APC's conclusions, (Compl. Ex. 7; Am. Answer ¶27,) and providing a legal opinion drafted by LegalZoom's North Carolina counsel which concludes that the "document preparation and filing service provided by Plaintiff does not constitute the 'organizing' of a corporation, and therefore is not the unauthorized practice of law. . . ." (Compl. ¶30, Ex. 8; Am. Answer ¶8.)

By letter dated June 17, 2008, the APC acknowledged receipt of LegalZoom's June 13, 2008 response letter. The State Bar did not thereafter institute any legal proceeding against LegalZoom until filing its Counterclaim in this action. (Compl. Ex. 9; Am. Answer ¶¶31-32, 34.)

The State Bar has made copies of its Cease and Desist Letter and LegalZoom's June 13, 2008 response letter publicly available upon request, including to bar officials in other states who referenced the letter in their own investigations, and the APC's meeting minutes reflecting the decision to issue the Cease and Desist Letter were posted on the State Bar website for some period of time. (Compl. ¶35; Am. Answer ¶35.) LegalZoom avers that the State Bar's Counsel has also made statements to third parties expressing his opinion that LegalZoom's conduct is illegal in North Carolina. (Compl. ¶36; Am. Answer ¶36.)

B. LegalZoom's Attempts to Register Its Purported Legal Services Plans

LegalZoom has two legal service plans: one for consumers and one for business users. On July 14, 2010, LegalZoom sent a letter to the State Bar seeking to register its consumer "Advantage Plus Plan" as a prepaid legal services plan. (Compl. Ex. 10; Am. Answer. ¶45.)

The APC responded on September 30, 2010 by letter, (Compl. Ex. 11; Am. Answer ¶¶41-42.), informing LegalZoom that its initial registration statement was deficient in three respects: (1) it did not include the required "list of the names, addresses, and telephone numbers of all North Carolina licensed attorneys who have agreed to participate in the plan"; (2) it did not include the required "notarized certification forms from each attorney who has agreed to participate in the plan"; and (3) it did not include the marketing material the APC needed to review. (Compl. Ex. 11.) The letter raised an additional concern regarding the lack of a membership plan for individuals who plan to purchase the Advantage Plus Plan. (Compl. Ex. 11.) Finally, the APC stated that:

> It appears from the material you submitted for LegalZoom [Advantage Plus Plan] that LegalZoom continues to conduct business in a way that the [APC] prohibited in its May 5, 2008 cease and desist letter. You are offering plan members an opportunity to get a 10% discount off the price of legal documents prepared by LegalZoom. This service in your plan violates the very essence of a prepaid legal services plan, which is that a North Carolina licensed attorney must provide the legal services. Please respond to that concern.

(Compl. Ex. 11.)

LegalZoom responded on October 14, 2010 with two letters. The first contends that the Cease and Desist Letter did not and could not prohibit any activity, and, that, in any event, the State Bar does not itself have power to declare LegalZoom's practices to be illegal and must rather seek court action, such that the Cease and Desist Letter or the State Bar's unilateral determination is not a basis for refusing to register the Advantage Plus Plan. (Compl. Ex. 12; Am. Answer ¶44.) The second letter: (1) provided the name, address, and telephone number of one attorney who would provide the plan's legal services; (2) clarified that LegalZoom was attempting to register two plans: the Business Advantage Pro Plan (available to businesses) and the Legal Advantage Pro Plan (available to individuals); and (3) included what LegalZoom contends is the certification for the attorney and additional marketing materials for the plans. (Compl. Ex. 13; Am. Answer ¶41.)

The APC, through its legal counsel, responded on November 18, 2010 that, after considering the initial registration statement at its October 27, 2010 meeting, the APC "declined to register LegalZoom [Advantage Plus Plan] as it had several concerns about the plan as offered." (Compl. Ex. 14; Am. Answer ¶45.) First, the APC still had concerns that the plan offered its participants a discount on LegalZoom's legal document preparation services, which the APC believed rendered it unable to register the plan "since a component of it does not satisfy the definition of a prepaid legal service plan and violates [North Carolina's] unauthorized practice statutes." (Compl. Ex. 14.) Second, because LegalZoom desired to register two separate plans, each plan must be registered separately. (Compl. Ex. 14; Am. Answer ¶45.) Third, the APC was concerned that LegalZoom identified only one attorney to provide all plan services, and noted that an attorney certification had not been submitted for that attorney. (Compl. Ex. 14; Am. Answer ¶45.) The APC requested a response by December 10, 2010, and requested notice by January 7, 2011 if LegalZoom desired to appear before the APC at its next meeting on January 19, 2011. (Compl. Ex. 14; Am. Answer ¶45.)

LegalZoom responded on December 29, 2010. (Compl. Ex. 15; Am. Answer ¶46.) LegalZoom represented that it had removed the discount on the legal document preparation service from the prepaid legal service plans it was seeking to register; that it did want to register two separate plans and would submit separate applications if necessary; and that it had obtained a second attorney who agreed to provide services for the plans. (Compl. Ex. 15; Am. Answer ¶46.) On March 24, 2011, the APC responded that LegalZoom needed to submit separate applications for the two plans. (Compl. Ex. 16; Am. Answer ¶47.) The APC also raised its concern regarding how LegalZoom would notify North Carolina residents that the discount on the legal document preparation services was not available to them, noting that the discount was still listed on LegalZoom's website. (Compl. Ex. 16; Am. Answer ¶47.)

The APC met again to consider LegalZoom's applications on April 20, 2011. (Compl. Ex. 17; Am. Answer ¶47.) By letter dated April 28, 2011, the APC informed LegalZoom that an additional concern had been raised at the meeting: whether North Carolina residents would still have access to the legal document preparation service from the same website through which they would be accessing the prepaid legal services plans, and asked LegalZoom to respond by May 28, 2011. (Compl. Ex. 17; Am. Answer ¶47.)

LegalZoom responded on July 8, 2011 that both the document preparation service and the prepaid legal services would be available via its website, but insisted that "there is no legal basis to deny registration of the pre-paid plans based on the legal document service." (Compl. Ex. 18; Am. Answer ¶48.)

Sometime before August 18, 2011, counsel for LegalZoom telephoned the president of the State Bar to request a meeting regarding the registration of LegalZoom's prepaid legal services plans. (Comp. Ex. 19; Am. Answer ¶50.) The State Bar responded by email on August 18, 2011 that it did "not believe such a meeting would be productive at this time" and that it would "provide a more detailed written response to [LegalZoom's] issues very soon." (Compl. Ex. 19; Am. Answer ¶50.)

The APC's next meeting was scheduled for October 18, 2011. (The North Carolina State Bar's Br. in Opp'n to LegalZoom's Mot. for Partial J. on the Pleadings ("State Bar Opp'n Br.") 18.) Prior to this meeting, the State Bar had not issued a final determination whether it would register the plans, and if so, its basis for doing so.

LegalZoom filed its Complaint on September 30, 2011. It has never appeared before a meeting of the APC. It has not demanded a hearing before the State Bar.

Two things remain unclear after a review of the correspondence: first, the basis for the State Bar's doubts that LegalZoom's legal services plans do not meet the statutory definition of a prepaid legal service plan and whether those doubts would ultimately lead to a final decision to refuse to register them; and second, whether the State Bar separately contends it can refuse to register the plans based on its opinion that the document preparation service with which they are offered constitutes UPL.

C. The Nature of LegalZoom's Document Preparation Services

A customer using the LegalZoom internet document preparation program chooses the document he wishes to prepare. He then interacts with the software and provides information that is incorporated into templates.

LegalZoom indicates that the form language included in its templates was prepared before any customer interaction and does not change or vary depending upon what information the customer provides. (Compl. ¶10.)

LegalZoom calls its process "LegalZip," and refers to it as a "branching" technology. (Compl. Ex. 5.) As the customer proceeds, the pre-existing templates are populated with information the customer provides, and LegalZoom equates the software to the modern technological equivalent of a printed form book or do-it-yourself kit. (Compl. ¶¶10, 13.) It contends that it exercises no discretion or independent legal judgment in response to customer choice. (Compl. ¶16.)

A number of LegalZoom's templates are based on or are verbatim recitations of forms issued by North Carolina state agencies. Others are prepared or approved by North Carolina licensed attorneys before being made available online. (Compl. ¶13.)

The State Bar, in contrast, contends that the branching process is more akin to the practice of law, including professional judgment, and should be compared to the manner in which a lawyer interviews a client and chooses portions of a form depending on the client response, such that the choice of which part of the form to use or omit depends upon the exercise of judgment. LegalZoom contends that the absence of its exercise of judgment is evidenced by the fact that the software would always prepare an identical document for any customer providing the same responses.

In connection with its briefing, the State Bar prepared ten attachments taken from screenshots from the LegalZoom website. These include pages representing documents relating to incorporating a business (The

North Carolina State Bar's Br. Supp. Mot. J. on the Pleadings ("State Bar Supp. Br.") Attachs. 4, 5,) preparing a will (State Bar Supp. Br. Attach. 7,) preparing for an uncontested divorce (State Bar Supp. Br. Attach. 8,) and completing a real estate transaction (State Bar Supp. Br. Attachs. 9, 10.) Others include statements expressing opinions regarding the quality or nature of efforts developing the program, including, for example, statements that documents related to forming a business were "developed by attorneys from some of the most prestigious law firms in America," (State Bar Supp. Br. Attach. 1,) that the "documents are trial-tested and have been accepted by courts and governmental agencies in all 50 states," (State Bar Supp. Br. Attach. 2,) and that LegalZoom's "team of experienced attorneys have [sic] designed the LegalZoom Last Will to meet the specific laws and requirements of each U.S. state[,]" (State Bar Supp. Br. Attach. 3.) Other attachments relate to certain assurances, such as that incorporation packages are "backed by a 100% Satisfaction Guarantee[,]" (State Bar Supp. Br. Attach. 6,) that LegalZoom's documents are finalized with a "Peace of Mind Review", and that wills are "backed by our $50,000 Guarantee[,]" (State Bar Supp. Br. Attach. 7.)

LegalZoom also offers screenshots of its website to highlight disclaimers stated at various points throughout the software that LegalZoom is not a law firm and does not provide legal advice, and encourages consulting a lawyer for further legal questions or inquiries. (Compl. ¶17, Ex. 5.) The State Bar offers other statements within the software for context such as "we create and file your incorporation papers," (State Bar Supp. Br. Attach. 1,) "LegalZoom can complete all of these required documents for you, including personalized bylaws and organizational resolutions," (State Bar Supp. Br. Attach. 4,) "[s]imply answer a few questions and we'll create your divorce papers," (State Bar Supp. Br. Attach. 8,) and "[w]e complete your real estate deed[,]" (State Bar Supp. Br. Attach. 10.)

LegalZoom makes certain statements within the software program regarding legal requirements, such as, for example, a listing of legal criteria necessary for a valid will, (State Bar Supp. Br. Attach. 3,) the consequences of dying intestate, (State Bar Supp. Br. Attach. 3,) the steps required for valid incorporation, (State Bar Supp. Br. Attach. 4,) the advantages of incorporation, (State Bar Supp. Br. Attach. 5,) and requirements for uncontested divorce eligibility (State Bar Supp. Br. Attach. 8.)

Other details regarding the software may be referred to as necessary during the court's following analysis.

III. Standard of Review

"A motion for judgment on the pleadings is the proper procedure when all the material allegations of fact are admitted in the pleadings and only questions of law remain." *Ragsdale*, 286 N.C. at 137, 209 S.E.2d at 499. On a 12(c) motion,

> The trial court is required to view the facts and permissible inferences in the light most favorable to the nonmoving party. All well pleaded factual allegations in the nonmoving party's pleadings are taken as true and all contravening assertions in the movant's pleadings are taken as false. . . . All allegations in the nonmovant's pleadings, except conclusions of law,

legally impossible facts, and matters not admissible in evidence at the trial, are deemed admitted by the movant for purposes of the motion.

Id. (internal citations omitted).

IV. Analysis

LegalZoom's Motion asserts that the court can and should declare, on the present record, that the State Bar must register LegalZoom's prepaid legal service plans because it has no authority to decline that registration. The State Bar's Motion asserts the court can and should declare that LegalZoom is engaged in the unauthorized practice of law and is, therefore, not entitled to any of the relief sought in the Complaint. Each contends that at least certain aspects of the other's Motion is not yet ripe because its resolution depends upon contested fact issues. ((Pl. LegalZoom's Br. Opp'n North Carolina State Bar's Mot. J. on the Pleadings ("LegalZoom Opp'n Br.") 2; State Bar Opp'n Br. 3.)

The court will first address LegalZoom's Motion, followed by its discussion of the State Bar's Motion.

. . .

[The court first concluded that LegalZoom had failed to exhaust administrative remedies.]

B. The State Bar's Motion for Judgment on the Pleadings

1. The court's declaration on the primary issue of unauthorized practice of law should await a more developed factual record.

LegalZoom's Complaint presents several claims, but each either depends on or involves consideration of the central issue: whether LegalZoom engages in the unauthorized practice of law by offering its internet-based document preparation service. Both LegalZoom and the State Bar seek the court's declaration on that issue. LegalZoom contends that the declaration needs a more developed record. The State Bar contends the court can resolve the issue on the present record.

The court concludes that a more developed record is appropriate, even if some specific instances of claimed UPL can be isolated for review based on the current record. This decision follows long and careful review of pleadings, briefs, and cited authorities, oral argument presented, and a number of efforts to draft a dispositive ruling consistent with Rule 12(c) standards. Accordingly, the State Bar's Motion for Judgment on the Pleadings should be Denied in part, as it relates to the unauthorized practice of law issue, without prejudice to the potential later consideration of issues raised by the Motion pursuant to Rule 56. The court further elaborates on its reasoning below.

The context for deciding the ultimate issue of UPL may vary depending on the particular document or use to which a LegalZoom customer may put the software. The court's interaction with LegalZoom's website during the course of its further consideration amplified this contextual variance which it first recognized when reviewing the briefs. Considering these varying contexts, the court hopes to be able to apply the governing statutes through a standard that can be consistently applied to the various functions that may arise from use of LegalZoom's software, as well as other forms of software or self-help programs or texts to which LegalZoom's software might be compared.

The court approaches the matter as one in which it must apply the existing statutes and regulations. There is a current policy-oriented dialogue in which some urge that the practice of law should be substantially deregulated in favor of market forces. Proponents of such deregulation argue, in part, that strict application of statutes prohibiting the unauthorized practice of law has yielded economic inefficiency, including but not limited to causing basic legal services to be outside the reach of many or most consumers. Unless such policy arguments become a necessary part of a constitutional analysis the court is required to undertake, such policy changes are more appropriately addressed to the Legislature and are not now before the court.

In addition to the variables noted above, the court has also become generally but not specifically aware that LegalZoom may have modified its program or practices from state to state in response either to litigation, as in Missouri or South Carolina, or to regulatory inquiry, as in Ohio or Pennsylvania. Such distinctions, if they in fact have been made, are not dispositive, but may inform the court's analysis.

Ultimately, the court looks to the factual record to inform how it must apply the governing North Carolina statutes. The general prohibition against the unauthorized practice of law is stated in section 84-4 which provides:

> Except as otherwise permitted by law, it shall be unlawful for any person or association of persons, except active members of the Bar of the State of North Carolina admitted and licensed to practice as attorneys-at-law, to appear as attorney or counselor at law in any action or proceeding before any judicial body, including the North Carolina Industrial Commission, or the Utilities Commission; to maintain, conduct, or defend the same, except in his own behalf as a party thereto; or, by word, sign, letter, or advertisement, to hold out himself, or themselves, as competent or qualified to give legal advice or counsel, or to prepare legal documents, or as being engaged in advising or counseling in law or acting as attorney or counselor-at-law, or in furnishing the services of a lawyer or lawyers; and it shall be unlawful for any person or association of persons except active members of the Bar, for or without a fee or consideration, to give legal advice or counsel, perform for or furnish to another legal services, or to prepare directly or through another for another person, firm or corporation, any will or testamentary disposition, or instrument of trust, or to organize corporations or prepare for another person, firm or corporation, any other legal document. . . . The provisions of this section shall be in addition to and not in lieu of any other provisions of this Chapter.

N.C. Gen. Stat. §84-4 (2013). Chapter 84 does not define various terms, including "hold out," "legal advice or counsel," "legal document(s)," or "legal services."

Section 84-2.1 defines the "practice of law" as:

> performing any legal service for any other person, firm or corporation, with or without compensation, specifically including the preparation or

aiding in the preparation of deeds, mortgages, wills, trust instruments, inventories, accounts or reports of guardians, trustees, administrators or executors, or preparing or aiding in the preparation of any petitions or orders in any probate or court proceeding; abstracting or passing upon titles, the preparation and filing of petitions for use in any court, including administrative tribunals and other judicial or quasi-judicial bodies, or assisting by advice, counsel, or otherwise in any legal work; and to advise or give opinion upon the legal rights of any person, firm or corporation[.]

N.C. Gen. Stat. §84-2.1 (2013).

Section 84-5 further prohibits corporations from practicing law, and in doing so, lists additional activities which may supplement the definition of "the practice of law." It provides:

It shall be unlawful for any corporation to practice law or appear as an attorney for any person in any court in this State, or before any judicial body or the North Carolina Industrial Commission, Utilities Commission, or the Department of Commerce, Division of Employment Security, or hold itself out to the public or advertise as being entitled to practice law; and no corporation shall organize corporations, or draw agreements, or other legal documents, or draw wills, or practice law, or give legal advice, or hold itself out in any manner as being entitled to do any of the foregoing acts, by or through any person orally or by advertisement, letter or circular. The provisions of this section shall be in addition to and not in lieu of any other provisions of Chapter 84.

N.C. Gen. Stat. §84-5 (2013).

The court discerns at least three intersecting principles arising from these statutes, that, when considered in light of case precedent both within and without North Carolina, must be accommodated in the overall analysis. Two of these principles represent the reasoning in reported cases recognizing what has been referred to as "exceptions" on UPL prohibitions. The first has been referred to as either "self-help" or the "self-representation" exception, essentially meaning that one can legally undertake activities in his own interests that would be UPL if undertaken for another, or to "practice law" to represent oneself. The second exception has been referred to as a "scrivener's exception," essentially meaning that unlicensed individuals may record information that another provides without engaging in UPL as long as they do not also provide advice or express legal judgments. The third, less-litigated principle arises from the statutory prohibitions on "holding out." Applying this principle may become entangled with First Amendment issues.

Analyzing LegalZoom's software requires consideration of each of these three principles. The respective briefs concentrate most heavily on whether LegalZoom's software is protected by the two exceptions. That is, whether or not the software acts as a mere scrivener or appropriately assists customers who are engaged in self-representation. The briefs do recognize the First Amendment considerations at play, but do not include as extensive an effort to apply the "holding out" prohibitions specifically in the context of how LegalZoom's software works and how it is marketed to encourage customers more confidently to engage in self-representation. For example, they do not extensively discuss (1) how LegalZoom's own statements embodied in the website should regulate or qualify the application of the two recognized exceptions, if those statements are intended to, and actually do, instill greater customer confidence in self-representation, or (2) how such statements should be read together against the backdrop of the public policies promoted by the statutory prohibitions on "holding out."

A useful summary of the "self-help exception" or "self-representation exception" may be found in the oft-cited opinion in The Florida Bar v. Brumbaugh, 355 So. 2d 1186 (Fla. 1978). *Brumbaugh* recognizes that (1) each person has a fundamental constitutional right to represent themselves, and (2) individuals may sell sample legal forms and "type up" instruments that clients have filled out without engaging in the practice of law. *Brumbaugh*, 355 So. 2d at 1194.

The North Carolina Supreme Court recognized this right of self-representation and further extended the right to allow corporate agents to prepare certain legal documents on behalf of the corporation so long as the efforts were to advance a matter in which the corporation had a primary interest. State v. Pledger, 257 N.C. 634, 127 S.E.2d 337 (1962). The defendant in *Pledger* was an employee of a company engaged in the sale and construction of homes, but was not licensed to practice law or a member of The North Carolina Bar. Id. at 634, 127 S.E.2d 337. The defendant prepared several deeds of trust, and saw to the execution, acknowledgement, and recordation of those deeds, for homes that the company sold. Id. The Supreme Court held that the defendant did not engage in the unauthorized practice of law, because "[a] person, firm or corporation having a primary interest, not merely an incidental interest, in a transaction, may prepare legal documents necessary to the furtherance and completion of the transaction without violating [the law]." Id. at 637, 127 S.E.2d at 339.

LegalZoom champions *Pledger* as granting its customers the right of self-help. LegalZoom does not assert that it has a primary interest in its customer's legal affairs. LegalZoom's position is rather that it lawfully assists its customer in self-representation and in the process of recording the customer-supplied information, LegalZoom does not make legal judgments or offer customer advice tailored to the customer's individual circumstance. LegalZoom's contention is that its recording of information falls comfortably within the recognized "scrivener" exception.

The "scrivener exception" has not, to the court's knowledge, been considered by the North Carolina state appellate courts. It has been considered in a federal bankruptcy court sitting in North Carolina, which described the exception as "merely typing or 'scrivening' a petition or legal document for another person." In re Graham, No. 02-81930C-7D, 2004 Bankr. LEXIS 1678, 2004 WL 1052963 (M.D.N.C. Feb. 10, 2004); see also In re Lazarus, No. 05-80274C-7D, 2005 Bankr. LEXIS 1093, 2005 WL 1287634 (Bankr. M.D.N.C. Mar. 14, 2005). While recognizing the exception, these cases are also careful to caution scriveners against going further so as to provide advice. In *Lazarus*, the Bankruptcy Court held that a petition preparer, Ms. Couch, engaged in the unauthorized practice of law in violation of §110 of the Bankruptcy Code. In re Lazarus, 2005 Bankr. LEXIS at *14-15, 2005 WL 1287634. Ms. Couch was found to have exceeded the limited scrivener exception because "the evidence reflected that the Debtor had no understanding [of the matters in the bankruptcy forms] and that Ms. Couch counseled and advised the Debtor regarding such matters and that in some instances actually decided what information would be inserted in the forms." Id. at *15.

The petition preparer in *Graham* was also held to have engaged in the practice of law as it is defined by section 84-2.1, In re Graham, 2004 Bankr. LEXIS 1678, at *36-40, 2004 WL 1052963[,] where she provided clients with a workbook, a pamphlet providing a step-by-step guide to filling out the workbook, and information on filing for Chapter 7 bankruptcy. Id. at *5-6. The Bankruptcy Court held that

> [t]he Workbook and Guide are intended to clarify the information required on the official forms for the petition, schedules and statement of financial affairs. A review of these documents reveals that they constitute legal advice when provided by a petition preparer to a customer for whom bankruptcy documents are being prepared. The Workbook to be completed by the customer is not merely a blank copy of the official forms. Rather, it is a document prepared by We The People USA which, together with the Guide and Overview, contains advice to the customer concerning bankruptcy law and how the blanks in the Workbook should be completed. . . . While §110 allows a bankruptcy petition preparer to type bankruptcy forms, it does not allow the petition preparer "to provide documents that explain bankruptcy or how to complete the required information that the preparer is then to transfer to the Official Forms."

Id. at *38-39 (citing In re Moore, 283 B.R. 852, 863 (Bankr. E.D.N.C. 2003)). The court continued that, by taking the information the customer filled out in the Workbook and entering it into an official form on a computer, which differed from the Workbook the customer filled out, the preparer had engaged in the practice of law. Id. at *39.

In some instances, LegalZoom's software operations may comfortably remain within the permissible boundaries of these cases, such as where a legal form closely tracks a state agency form, the information a customer supplies is routine, and no significant part of the form is added or omitted based on customer responses. There are other aspects of the LegalZoom program that may not comfortably fit the scrivener exception, such as instances where LegalZoom may, either by itself or in association with another, go beyond recording information, for example, in obtaining or approving legal descriptions for deeds, reviewing and assessing potentially interfering trademarks, or taking actions to finalize incorporation.

The court is not yet comfortable that it understands the overall process of preparing more complex documents, and hopes to develop a greater understanding of how the branching software process is implemented in preparing such documents, including whether and how a customer's answer to one question effects what further parts of the template are offered and what further choices the customer is asked to make. Questions include, for example, if a customer makes one choice presented to him by the branching software, are there portions of the template that are then never shown to the customer? If so, what is the reasoning behind and the legal significance of the software's determination not to present that portion of the form? If *Pledger* teaches that an unlicensed individual has the right to "practice law" on his own behalf, *Pledger*, 257 N.C. at 636, 127 S.E.2d at 339, does its premise require that only the unlicensed individual make choices in drafting a legal document, and that the choice or risk of an incorrect choice about which portions of a form to include must belong exclusively to the individual? Is there then a legally significant difference between how one engaging in self-representation uses a form book versus LegalZoom's interactive branching software? A form book presents the customer with the entire form, often accompanied by opinions or directions on how to use the form, but any choice and its implications are solely the customer's. Does the LegalZoom software effectively make choices for its customer? Do responses depend in any part on the effects of statements embodied in the software, either those that promote the program or those that disclaim legal advice being given?

The court does not by any means suggest these are the controlling or only relevant questions or that they have certain answers. Rather, they are examples of questions the court is not comfortable answering based on the current record alone.

As to the statutory prohibitions on "holding out," the court will be required to seek a balance between the public interest being protected, and the corresponding First Amendment rights LegalZoom may have. The court remains uncertain how the interplay of those potentially competing rights and interests should affect the court's overall interpretation of UPL statutes, including application of recognized exceptions.

In sum, the court determines that a greater factual record will help shape and answer these and other questions. The court then concludes that the issue of unauthorized practice of law should not be decided at this juncture pursuant to the State Bar's Motion, and the State Bar's Motion in that regard should be Denied without prejudice to revisiting the issues pursuant to Rule 56.

. . .

Questions:

- Is the online delivery of legal services a boon to increase underserved access to legal services? Or a bane in the form of the unauthorized practice of law?
- Is it ironic for the "access to justice" concept that many online providers' terms of use include a binding arbitration clause and a class action waiver clause?
- Further, should online providers be exempt from malpractice liability because they are not technically involved in the practice of law?

IV. Conclusion

Virtual firms, litigation finance, and online delivery of legal services each offer a view into how market forces can drive change within the legal profession. The process of finding the way through the present into the future remains murky, however, and as these forms of change take root, more will surely follow, grow, and, ultimately, displace them. This also echoes the persistent question of whether the practice of law is a business or a profession. Perhaps it is simply both.

CHAPTER 10

LEGAL TECHNOLOGY AND INFORMATION

Law is fundamentally an information-dependent business. Understanding where legal information resides within a law firm and how it can be analyzed, manipulated, and communicated are important foundational concepts for the business of any law practice.[1] Moreover, law firms must be aware of the ethical and legal risks and obligations associated with this information.

Consider all of the information that typically flows in and out of a law firm: email, confidential client communications, internal communications, billing and time entries, files, documents, masses of work product, financial and personnel records, confidential and proprietary client information, etc. What technology is helpful, or even necessary, in harnessing and managing that information, and, moreover, will it ultimately help transform that information into advice and work product that the firm can monetize in the form of revenue?

Technology is by no means an elixir, but the practice of law is now infused with, and in many instances, wedded to it. The pace of change is rapid, and the field crowded with competitors—some veteran players in the industry, but many startups hoping to disrupt the establishment. We will not delve too deeply into any particular product, but with an eye toward a future of tech-savvy lawyers, we will touch on current trends and future possibilities in this area to help orient you to the contemporary, and next-generation, practice environment.

---

[1]There remain numerous unanswered questions—academic, philosophical, and practical— surrounding the proper legal and ethical framework around the boundaries between humans and machines in the implementation of legal functions. We will largely leave this deep and varied aspect of the subject to other courses dedicated to computational technology and the law.

I. Legal Technology, Analytics, and Tools

Any Internet search related to legal tech will return a trove of up-to-date information and reporting on the current state of this part of the industry.[2] It will also reveal many private businesses hoping to sell their products. The Law Practice Division of the American Bar Association publishes periodic "Tech Report" updates, which provide a relatively neutral, non-sales-oriented, point of introduction.[3]

Stepping back, consider what we mean when we use the term "legal technology." It is likely a combination of things, but comprised of technology: that is used by lawyers, built or adapted for the specialized needs of lawyers or their clients, or that performs a traditional legal role function, at least in part.

Many technology tools used by lawyers are not industry-specific: word processing software, calendaring and email, videoconferencing apps, electronic signature verification, and the other staples of the typical office environment. Next come the familiar stalwarts of the profession, such as LexisNexis, Westlaw, Bloomberg, and others in the legal research field. While not exclusively used by lawyers, these databases largely have their origins in the law field and are so widely adopted in the profession as to be functionally indispensable.

Automation, management, and efficiency tools are designed to help law firms operate more efficiently with the information they have. Examples include practice management software for billing, time management, accounting and invoicing, conflicts management, case intake and management, business development, and client relations (CRM);[4] document assembly, storage, and automation tools;[5] and clause libraries for contract drafting. Further examples are tools designed for litigation and compliance support, e-discovery, and case assessment.[6]

There are numerous marketplace tools, such as referral networks, and lawyer rating and matching services.[7]

Many tools provide support for legal analytics, which includes efforts to gain insight into litigation dynamics, court opinions, and expert witnesses.[8] Some tools may be practice-area specific.[9]

---

[2] *See, e.g.*, Samantha Lee, *Tech Is Revolutionizing the Old-School Legal Industry. How Law Firms Are Partnering Up to Cut Costs and the Startups Set to Benefit* (Nov. 27, 2020), https://www.businessinsider.com/legal-tech-disruption-biglaw-innovation-venture-capital-startups-2020-9.

[3] *See, e.g.*, American Bar Association, *ABA Tech Report 2020*, https://www.americanbar.org/groups/law_practice/publications/techreport/2020/.

[4] *See, e.g.*, Nicole Black, *The Ins and Outs of Law Practice Management Software* (Jan. 11, 2019), https://www.abajournal.com/news/article/the-ins-and-outs-of-law-practice-management-software; American Bar Association, *Legal Technology Buyer's Guide*, https://buyersguide.americanbar.org/sites/Practice+Management; *Legal Practice Management Software*, https://www.clio.com/law-practice-management-software/.

[5] *See, e.g.*, Nicole Black, *These Document Assembly Tools Will Keep Your Law Firm on Track* (June 25, 2019), https://www.abajournal.com/news/article/these-document-assembly-tools-will-keep-your-firm-on-track; AbacusNext, www.hotdocs.com.

[6] *See, e.g.*, Relativity, https://www.relativity.com/data-solutions/ediscovery/; Quantivate, https://quantivate.com/solutions/regulatory-compliance-management-software/.

[7] *See, e.g.*, Martindale-Avvo, www.martindale.com (ratings and reviews), www.avvo.com (referral network); Paladin, www.joinpaladin.com (pro bono portal).

[8] *See, e.g.*, Lex Machina, www.lexmachina.com; Ravel, www.ravellaw.com.

[9] *See, e.g.*, Intelligize, www.intelligize.com (Securities); Lexis Advance Legislative Outlook, www.lexisnexis.com (bill tracking).

Another office staple is digital signature software, which helps verify the digital identity of each signer, maintains the chain of custody for the documents, and can provide audit trails.[10]

The options for technology tools available to practitioners are numerous and robust. It is well worth investing some time in exploring those options that may be best suited to your particular practice.

II. Artificial Intelligence

For our purposes in the law business context, we will consider artificial intelligence (AI)—sometimes referred to as "cognitive computing" or "machine learning"—to be computer technology with the ability to simulate human thought and learning.[11] There are many questions surrounding the automation of human legal activities. Detractors suggest the robots will come for the lawyers! Proponents advocate that AI enhances rather than replaces lawyering, and the automation of lower-level tasks provides lawyers with the time and freedom to focus on analysis and client interaction.[12]

The fact is, we live in a vast and ever-expanding sea of information that requires more analytical power than human lawyers possess. Conceptually, this may require rethinking what a lawyer "is"—good lawyers are no longer defined by how much knowledge they can hold. Instead, being the best methodological users of legal information may be a core trait for good lawyers going forward. Moreover, a good lawyer may become, at least in part, one who can efficiently find relevant, impactful data without incurring substantial time delays in the process.

Some areas in which AI may have a direct impact in law practice include legal research, e-discovery, contract review, compliance, and litigation strategy and early case analysis.

While AI is not perfect, and privacy and other concerns are warranted, the appeal of AI as a cost-effective substitute for at least some legal work functions and tasks will inevitably lead to market and client pressures for law firms to adapt and adopt.

Questions: What legal functions are amenable to automation, and why? What impact may this have on staff and support roles in law firms?

---

[10] *See, e.g.*, DocuSign, www.docusign.com; PandaDoc, www.pandadoc.com.

[11] For a good overview of the use of AI within the legal profession, see Lauri Donahue, *A Primer on Using Artificial Intelligence in the Legal Profession* (Jan. 3, 2018), https://jolt.law.harvard.edu/digest/a-primer-on-using-artificial-intelligence-in-the-legal-profession.

[12] *See, e.g.*, William J. Connell, Esq., *Artificial Intelligence in the Legal Profession—What You Might Want to Know*, R.I. B.J. (May/June 2018); Neil Sahota, *Will A.I. Put Lawyers Out of Business?* (Feb. 9, 2019), https://www.forbes.com/sites/cognitiveworld/2019/02/09/will-a-i-put-lawyers-out-of-business/?sh=231e333231f0.

III. Risks for Law Firms

The constant flux and adoption of new technology also requires an ongoing assessment of lawyers' ethical obligations. Ethics opinions, case law, data breach notification requirements, and disciplinary cases will continue to illuminate the specifics of a lawyer's ethical obligations concerning technology in this evolving landscape.[13] There are also practical and business risks associated with cybersecurity, privacy, and data breaches.

Model Rule 1.1 specifies that "a lawyer should keep abreast of changes in the law and its practice, including the benefits and risks associated with relevant technology," and Model Rule 1.6 requires the lawyer to "make reasonable efforts to prevent the inadvertent or unauthorized disclosure of, or unauthorized access to, information relating to the representation of a client."[14]

Because law firms collect and store large amounts of confidential and sensitive client data, often including trade secret and confidential business information, they have become targets for hackers and data breaches. Many law firms, however, still lack robust (or any) cybersecurity measures.[15] Reported decisions remain few, but the decision presented below involves a former client suing his law firm for legal malpractice, breach of fiduciary duty, and breach of contract after a hacking incident resulted in the release of personal information on the Internet.

Wengui v. Clark Hill, PLC
440 F. Supp. 3d 30 (D.D.C. 2020)

Memorandum Opinion

James E. Boasberg, United States District Judge

This case features an asylum-application process gone awry, accompanied by alleged professional misconduct, foreign-government cyber hacking, and social-media propaganda campaigns. After Plaintiff Guo Wengui, a Chinese businessman and prominent political dissident, retained the services of the law firm Clark Hill, PLC to assist him with an asylum petition, someone—whom the parties presume to be associated with the Chinese government—hacked into the firm's computer servers. The hacker thereby gained access to Plaintiff's confidential information and then published that information on the Internet. Compounding Wengui's

---

[13]For an in-depth analysis and examination of ethical obligations and risks surrounding a firm's use of client data to build an AI tool, see Daniel W. Linna Jr. & Wendy J. Muchman, *Ethical Obligations to Protect Client Data When Building Artificial Intelligence Tools: Wigmore Meets AI* (Oct. 2, 2020) https://www.americanbar.org/groups/professional_responsibility/publications/professional _lawyer/27/1/ethical-obligations-protect-client-data-when-building-artificial-intelligence-tools-wigmore-meets-ai/.

[14]John G. Loughnane, ABA Tech Report 2019: Cybersecurity (Oct. 16, 2019), https://www .americanbar.org/groups/law_practice/publications/techreport/abatechreport2019/ cybersecurity2019/.

[15]*See* John G. Loughnane, ABA Tech Report 2020: Cybersecurity (Oct. 19, 2020), https://www .americanbar.org/groups/law_practice/publications/techreport/2020/cybersecurity/. Less than half of survey respondents utilized security measures.

problems, the firm withdrew its representation in response to the attack. Plaintiff asserts that in making his information vulnerable to a targeted hacking and subsequently withdrawing from the matter, Defendants Clark Hill and its attorney Thomas Ragland are liable for legal malpractice, breach of fiduciary duty, and breach of contract. Defendants now move to dismiss all claims.

To succeed on his tort claims, Wengui must "point to an act (or omission)" that "resulted in a loss" to him. See Seed Co., Ltd. v. Westerman, 840 F. Supp. 2d 116, 127 (D.D.C. 2012). Plaintiff has successfully pleaded that the alleged mishandling of his information and subsequent cyber attack resulted in damages. The withdrawal, however, may have added insult, but it did not add *injury*. In addition, he cannot establish that the withdrawal breached Defendants' contractual obligations to him. The Court therefore will dismiss all of Plaintiff's claims to the extent they rely on the theory that Defendants' withdrawal constituted a legally remediable wrong, but it will permit those claims to go forward that allege misrepresentations surrounding and mishandling of his confidential information. Finally, it dismisses the demand for punitive damages, as Plaintiff has not satisfied the high bar necessary for seeking such relief.

I. Background

A. Factual Background

As it must at this juncture, the Court draws the facts from the Complaint. *See* Sparrow v. United Air Lines, Inc., 216 F.3d 1111, 1113 (D.C. Cir. 2000). Plaintiff is a "highly successful businessman" and "well-known Chinese dissident." ECF No. 1 (Complaint), ¶10. While living in China, he exposed "systemic corruption" and "widespread abuse of human rights" being perpetrated by the Communist Party of China (CCP), China's ruling political party. Id., ¶15. These activities naturally caught the attention of the CCP, which allegedly threatened his livelihood and that of his family in order to put an end to his subversive activities. Id., ¶¶18-19. Fearing further persecution, Plaintiff fled his native country in 2015, and he now resides in New York. Id., ¶10. Wengui's escape from China has not prevented further harassment. The Chinese government has, for example, sent emissaries to demonstrate against him outside of his home as part of a larger "malicious negative propaganda campaign" organized against him. Id., ¶¶23-24. In response to this cross-continental maltreatment, Plaintiff set about applying for political asylum in the United States.

The source of this dispute dates back to Plaintiff's negotiations with Defendant Thomas Ragland, an attorney and partner at Defendant Clark Hill, PLC—a firm comprising about 650 lawyers—regarding potential assistance with his asylum petition. Id., ¶¶11-12. Hoping to secure Plaintiff as a client, Ragland assured him that both he and the firm more broadly "were qualified, capable, and competent to represent plaintiff and to protect his interests fully and professionally." Id., ¶28. At a subsequent meeting in August 2016, Wengui conveyed to Ragland and other Clark Hill attorneys "his standing and visibility as a prominent Chinese political dissident" and "the risks associated with and attendant to plaintiff's position as a prominent visible critic of the Chinese regime." Id., ¶31. Plaintiff also "warned of the persistent and relentless cyber attacks that he and his associates had endured." Id.

In further meetings with the firm, Wengui continued to warn Defendants that they should "expect to be subjected to sophisticated cyber attacks." Id., ¶32. In taking on Plaintiff's case, Defendants accordingly agreed to "take special precautions to prevent improper disclosure of plaintiff's sensitive confidential information." Id., ¶33. These precautions would include distinct measures to impede or evade cyber attacks, by, for example, "not placing any of plaintiff's information on the firm's computer server," as doing so would make the information more vulnerable to hackings. Id. Relying on the firm's commitments regarding the protection of his confidential information, Plaintiff hired Defendants, executing a letter of retention and paying the firm a retainer fee of $10,000. Id., ¶36.

Unfortunately for all parties involved, Plaintiff's warnings of a cyber attack, apparently as unheeded as Cassandra's, proved prescient. On September 12, 2017, the firm's computer system was "hacked"—again, both parties assume that the hacking was orchestrated by the Chinese government—"apparently without great difficulty." Id., ¶41. The hacker obtained a substantial amount of Plaintiff's and his spouse's personal information, such as their passport identification numbers, as well as Plaintiff's application for political asylum. Id., ¶43. This information, including the contents of Wengui's asylum petition, was then published and disseminated on social media. Id., ¶44.

Following the attack, the parties' relationship quickly dissolved. On September 19, Clark Hill's General Counsel, Edward Hood, informed Plaintiff that the firm was terminating its involvement with his case. Id., ¶49. Hood explained that the attack might require Ragland, along with other members of the firm, to serve as witnesses at Plaintiff's asylum proceeding, as the hacking provided evidence of the political persecution from which Plaintiff sought asylum in the United States. Id. Hood posited that because the Rules of Professional Conduct bar attorneys from playing the dual role of witness and advocate, Defendants were required to withdraw from the matter. Id., ¶¶49-50. At the time of that withdrawal, Plaintiff had filed an asylum application and was awaiting a hearing. Id., ¶51.

B. Procedural History

On September 19, 2019, Wengui filed this action against Defendants in the Superior Court of the District of Columbia. Defendants then removed the case to this Court on diversity-jurisdiction grounds. See ECF No. 1 (Notice of Removal) at 1-2. Plaintiff's Complaint asserts four counts: (1) breach of fiduciary duty; (2) breach of contract; (3) legal malpractice; and (4) punitive damages. See Compl., ¶¶66-93. Defendants now move to dismiss all counts, maintaining that they fail to state plausible claims for relief.

II. Legal Standard

Federal Rule of Civil Procedure 12(b)(6) provides for the dismissal of an action where a complaint fails to "state a claim upon which relief can be granted." Although "detailed factual allegations" are not necessary to withstand a Rule 12(b)(6) motion, Bell Atl. Corp. v. Twombly, 550 U.S. 544, 555, 127 S. Ct. 1955, 167 L. Ed. 2d 929 (2007), "a complaint must contain sufficient factual matter, accepted as true, to state a claim to relief that is plausible on its face." Ashcroft v. Iqbal, 556 U.S. 662, 678, 129 S. Ct. 1937, 173 L. Ed. 2d 868 (2009) (internal quotation omitted).

In evaluating Defendants' Motion to Dismiss, the Court must "treat the complaint's factual allegations as true and must grant plaintiff 'the benefit of all inferences that can be derived from the facts alleged.'" *Sparrow*, 216 F.3d at 1113 (citation omitted) (quoting Schuler v. United States, 617 F.2d 605, 608 (D.C. Cir. 1979)) (citing Leatherman v. Tarrant Cty. Narcotics Intelligence & Coordination Unit, 507 U.S. 163, 164, 113 S. Ct. 1160, 122 L. Ed. 2d 517 (1993)). The Court need not accept as true, however, "a legal conclusion couched as a factual allegation" nor an inference unsupported by the facts set forth in the Complaint. See Trudeau v. FTC, 456 F.3d 178, 193 (D.C. Cir. 2006) (quoting Papasan v. Allain, 478 U.S. 265, 286, 106 S. Ct. 2932, 92 L. Ed. 2d 209 (1986)). Finally, even at the Rule 12(b)(6) stage, a court can review "documents attached as exhibits or incorporated by reference in the complaint" or "documents upon which the plaintiff's complaint necessarily relies." Ward v. D.C. Dep't of Youth Rehab. Servs., 768 F. Supp. 2d 117, 119 (D.D.C. 2011) (internal quotation marks and citations omitted).

III. Analysis

In seeking dismissal here, Defendants argue that neither the cyber attack nor the withdrawal constitutes a ground for a viable claim of legal malpractice, breach of fiduciary duty, or breach of contract. In particular, they assert that their conduct surrounding these two events did not breach any duty owed to Plaintiff. They also argue that their actions, even if improper, did not cause him to suffer any actual damages. The Court will consider the two relevant events in turn, examining the separate counts in that context, albeit slightly out of sequence.

A. The Cyber Attack

As recounted above, the Complaint alleges that: Plaintiff warned Defendants of the risk of an impending cyber attack; Defendants misrepresented the manner in which they would protect Plaintiff's confidential information from such an attack; and Defendants then failed to protect this information, allowing it to be retrieved and then publicly disseminated by a third-party hacker. Defendants dispute that they made such representations and argue that, in any event, the cyber attack did not actually harm Plaintiff. The Court, however, rejects Defendants' premature attempt to litigate disputed facts at the pleading stage and will deny their Motion to Dismiss as it pertains to the cyber attack.

1. Breach of Fiduciary Duty

Count I asserts that Defendants breached various fiduciary duties owed to Plaintiff, including the duty of good faith, the duty of loyalty, and the duty to protect Plaintiff's confidential records. See Compl., ¶68. To succeed on a claim of breach of fiduciary duty in the District of Columbia—the relevant jurisdiction here—Plaintiff must establish "(1) the existence of a fiduciary duty and (2) a violation of that duty that (3) proximately causes injury." Council on Am.-Islamic Relations Action Network, Inc. v. Gaubatz, 82 F. Supp. 3d 344, 353 (D.D.C. 2015) (citing Shapiro, Lifschitz & Schram, P.C. v. Hazard, 24 F. Supp. 2d 66, 75 (D.D.C. 1998)). It is axiomatic that the attorney-client relationship is fiduciary in nature. See Thomas v. Nat'l Legal Prof'l Assocs., 594 F. Supp. 2d 31, 34 (D.D.C. 2009) ("[T]here is an ever present fiduciary responsibility that arches over every aspect of the lawyer-client relationship.") (quoting Connelly v. Swick & Shapiro, P.C., 749 A.2d 1264, 1268 (D.C. 2000)). Defendants argue, however, that they did not breach any recognized fiduciary duties owed to Plaintiff and, in any event, did not cause any actual injury to him.

First, as to breach of duty, Wengui does not allege, contrary to Defendants' assertion, simply that "because there was a cyber incident, Defendants must have put up . . . 'unreasonable' security measures." ECF No. 12 (Def. MTD) at 12. It is true that some courts have gone so far as to hold that corporations maintain a duty to consumers to "'protect against a criminal act of a third person,' which could include hacking into a private data system, 'if it is alleged that the entity had reason to anticipate the criminal act.'" Attias v. CareFirst, Inc., 365 F. Supp. 3d 1, 21 (D.D.C. 2019) (quoting In re Arby's Restaurant Group Inc., Litig., 2018 WL 2128441, at *5 (N.D. Ga. Mar. 5, 2018)). As a result, those courts have held that if a corporation fails to prevent a foreseeable cyber attack, it thereby breaches fiduciary duties owed its customers. Id. This Court, however, need not go so far as to find that any corporation's failure to protect against any foreseeable cyber attack, standing on its own, constitutes a breach of fiduciary duty.

A fiduciary relationship—like that between a lawyer and client—"is founded upon trust or confidence reposed by one person in the integrity and fidelity of another." Democracy Partners v. Project Veritas Action Fund, 285 F. Supp. 3d 109, 121 (D.D.C. 2018) (quoting Bolton v. Crowley, Hoge, & Fein, P.C., 110 A.3d 575, 584 (D.C. 2015)). The duty of loyalty in this context "has been described as one of 'uberrima fides,' which means, most abundant good faith, requiring absolute and perfect candor, *openness and honesty, and the absence of any concealment or deception.*" Herbin v. Hoeffel, 806 A.2d 186, 197 (D.C. 2002) (emphasis added) (quotation marks omitted); see also Seed Co., 840 F. Supp. 2d at 126-27 (attorney breaches fiduciary duties when providing clients with "incorrect and misleading" advice); *Herbin*, 806 A.2d at 197 ("Disclosure of client confidences is contrary to the fundamental principle that the attorney owes a fiduciary duty to her client and must serve the client's interest with the utmost loyalty and devotion.") (quotation marks omitted).

Plaintiff has sufficiently pleaded that Defendants breached their duties of loyalty and good faith by misrepresenting the manner in which they would protect his confidential information in order to secure his business. Although they promised to take special precautions, they placed that information, including his asylum application, on their server and conveyed it via a firm email account—in direct contravention of his instructions—leaving Plaintiff vulnerable to the precise sort of machinations he had forewarned counsel about. *See* Compl., ¶¶2-3, 40-43. He further alleges that the firm breached the applicable duty of care in its treatment of his information by utilizing security measures that were "inadequate, unreasonable, and fell woefully far short of [D]efendants' promises, assurances, obligations, and commitments to provide adequate security measures." Id., ¶42. Discovery may reveal that Defendants never made any such misrepresentations to Plaintiff and were not negligent in their handling of his confidential information, but the well-pleaded allegations in the Complaint preclude granting Defendants' Motion to Dismiss.

Defendants argue in the alternative that even if they misled Plaintiff and were negligent in handling his confidential information, the cyber attack did not actually cause him any cognizable harm. Under D.C. law, not surprisingly, a breach of a fiduciary duty requires a showing of injury or damages. *See* Headfirst Baseball LLC v. Elwood, 239 F. Supp. 3d 7, 14 (D.D.C. 2017) (canvassing D.C. caselaw); *see also* Becker v. Colonial Parking, Inc., 409 F.2d 1130, 1136 (D.C. Cir. 1969) ("A simple breach of duty having no causal connection with the injury, we have admonished, cannot produce legal responsibility.") (quotation marks omitted). In arguing that Plaintiff has not made such a showing, Defendants rely on Randolph v. ING Life Insurance & Annuity Company, 973 A.2d 702 (D.C. 2009), where the District of Columbia Court of Appeals held that an "increased risk of future identity theft" does not qualify as an "actionable" injury "required to maintain a suit for common-law breach of fiduciary duty." Id. at 708.

Although this case, like *Randolph*, concerns a data breach, the similarities end there. In *Randolph*, an unknown burglar stole a laptop computer owned by the employee of an insurance company, which contained the plaintiffs' insurance information, including their names, addresses, and social-security numbers. Id. at 704. The DCCA reasoned that the plaintiffs had failed to plead "actual harm" because they had not alleged that the burglar stole the laptop in order to access their information or that their information had even been accessed since the laptop was stolen. Id. at 706-08. Instead, they simply alleged "the anticipation of future injury [identity theft] that has not materialized." Id. at 708; see also In re Sci. Applications Int'l Corp. (SAIC) Backup Tape Data Theft Litig., 45 F. Supp. 3d 14, 19 (D.D.C. 2014) (dismissing case where plaintiffs' information, along with other items, was allegedly stolen from parked car because "mere loss of data—without evidence that it has been either viewed or misused—does not constitute an injury sufficient to confer standing").

Plaintiff, however, has gone well beyond pleading the anticipation of future injury and has instead alleged an *actual* injury resulting from

Defendants' conduct. According to the Complaint, the Chinese government or someone associated with it hacked Defendants' server for the express purpose of stealing Plaintiff's information. The hacker then "published" the confidential material, including Plaintiff's application for political asylum and passport identification number, on social media. See Compl., ¶¶43-44. This chain of events occurred in the context of a broader propaganda campaign orchestrated by the CCP, one that included utilizing social-media platforms to spread information about Plaintiff and mobilizing demonstrators to protest his presence in the United States. Id., ¶¶22-24. Wengui therefore does not "speculate" as to potential uses of the stolen information; it has *already* been employed as part of the CCP's persecution and harassment of him. The Court therefore rejects Defendants' invitation to find that the cyber attack did not actually harm Plaintiff as a matter of law.

2. Legal Malpractice

Count III alleges legal malpractice, asserting that Defendants breached their "common law" and "professional and ethical duties and obligations to plaintiff . . . by failing to use the required degree of professional care and skill in representing plaintiff," and in failing to maintain "reasonable security measures to secure their computer system from unauthorized access, as required and promised to plaintiff." Id., ¶¶82-85.

The elements of a legal-malpractice claim are similar to, but slightly distinct from, those for breach of fiduciary duty. See Hickey v. Scott, 738 F. Supp. 2d 55, 67 (D.D.C. 2010) (quoting Shapiro, Lifschitz & Schram, 24 F. Supp. 2d at 74). As Justice O'Conner has commented, "Lawyers are *professionals,* and as such they have greater obligations." Zauderer v. Office of Disciplinary Counsel, 471 U.S. 626, 676, 105 S. Ct. 2265, 85 L. Ed. 2d 652 (1985) (O'Connor, J., concurring). To succeed on a legal-malpractice claim in the District of Columbia, "the plaintiff must show that (1) the defendant was employed as the plaintiff's attorney, (2) the defendant breached a reasonable duty, and (3) that breach resulted in, and was the proximate cause of, the plaintiff's loss or damages." Beach TV Props., Inc. v. Solomon, 306 F. Supp. 3d 70, 93 (D.D.C. 2018) (quoting Martin v. Ross, 6 A.3d 860, 862 (D.C. 2010)).

For the reasons recounted above, this count may also proceed as to the cyber attack because the Complaint identifies a breach of the duty of reasonable care owed by attorneys to their clients and actual damages. To be sure, attorneys cannot be held "liable for mistakes made in the honest exercise of professional judgment." Biomet Inc. v. Finnegan Henderson LLP, 967 A.2d 662, 665 (D.C. 2009). Honest mistakes, however, are a far cry from the conduct alleged here: misrepresentations made in order to secure a prospective client, the failure to follow promised procedures to adequately secure confidential information, and damages. *See* Swann v. Waldman, 465 A.2d 844, 846 (D.C. 1983) (finding plaintiff's allegations that attorney lied to him about attempting to obtain continuance and was negligent in failing to obtain expert witness sufficient to withstand motion for summary judgment on legal-malpractice claim).

3. Breach of Contract

Plaintiff also brings a claim for breach of contract in Count II, alleging that the firm violated its contractual obligation to provide "competent representation" by undertaking a matter beyond its "professional or technical competence" and "neglecting to undertake reasonable security measures." Compl., ¶76. "To prevail on a claim of breach of contract, a party must establish (1) a valid contract between the parties; (2) an obligation or duty arising out of the contract; (3) a breach of that duty; and (4) damages caused by breach." United States Conference of Mayors v. Great-W. Life & Annuity Ins. Co., 327 F. Supp. 3d 125, 129 (D.D.C. 2018), aff'd, 767 F. App'x 18 (D.C. Cir. 2019) (quoting Tsintolas Realty Co. v. Mendez, 984 A.2d 181, 187 (D.C. 2009)). Defendants concede that the parties entered into a valid contract (in this case, an engagement letter) that set forth their "respective obligations and expectations." See Def. MTD at 14. They dispute, however, that Plaintiff has alleged a breach of that contract.

Accepting the facts in the Complaint as true, Wengui has met his pleading burden—if just barely—of establishing that Defendants did not meet their contractual obligations. In particular, he alleges that they violated their obligations to provide "competent representation" and keep Plaintiff "reasonably informed about the status of the matter," Def. MSJ, Exh. A (Retainer Agreement) at 2, by misleading him as to the manner in which his information would be handled in the future, and then by failing to inform him when they eventually placed that information on their server. For the reasons stated in regard to the prior counts, this claim can proceed on the basis of failing to safeguard his information, which could amount to incompetent representation.

Going forward, however, Plaintiff may need to clarify this count because he appears to be exploring several different theories as to how Defendants breached the retainer agreement. First, he seems to be laying the groundwork for the introduction of extrinsic evidence. This evidence might demonstrate that Defendants orally amended the terms of the contract in making representations regarding higher-level protection of Plaintiff's personal information. See Segal Wholesale, Inc. v. United Drug Serv., 933 A.2d 780, 784 (D.C. 2007) (extrinsic evidence "*consistent* with the terms of a *partially* integrated agreement is permissible"); see also Stamenich v. Markovic, 462 A.2d 452, 455 (D.C. 1983) (extrinsic evidence permissible to demonstrate "a contemporaneous agreement in addition to and not inconsistent with or a variation of the written agreement between the same parties, which was an essential inducement of the written contract" or where "fraud, mistake, or duress is alleged").

Alternatively, Plaintiff also appears to be seeking to demonstrate that Defendants violated a general obligation to provide competent representation in providing insufficient protection of client materials. See Compl., ¶76. Or, finally, he may be asserting that Defendants breached the "implied duty of good faith and fair dealing" that D.C. courts have found to be contained within all contracts, one that prohibits "evad[ing] the spirit of the contract" or "willfully render[ing] imperfect performance." Murray

v. Wells Fargo Home Mortg., 953 A.2d 308, 321 (D.C. 2008) (internal quotation marks omitted). Plaintiff will have to choose among these theories, and provide much more substantial support for them, should he decide to defend this count against further dispositive motions.

4. Duplicative Nature of Claims

Finally, the Court rejects Defendants' argument that the three claims chronicled above are *necessarily* "duplicative" of one other and thus that only one can proceed past the pleading stage. Under D.C. law, when a plaintiff's breach-of-fiduciary-duty claim rests on the same factual allegations and requests the same relief as his professional-malpractice claim, a court "as a matter of judicial economy, should dismiss" one of the claims as duplicative. *See* N. Am. Catholic Educ. Programming Found., Inc. v. Womble, Carlyle, Sandridge & Rice, PLLC, 887 F. Supp. 2d 78, 84 (D.D.C. 2012) (collecting cases). The same holds true for tort claims that arise out of the same factual circumstances as a breach-of-contract claim. *See Attias*, 365 F. Supp. 3d at 18 ("Under D.C. law, for a plaintiff to recover in tort for conduct that also constitutes a breach of contract, 'the tort must exist in its own right independent of the contract, and any duty upon which the tort is based must flow from considerations other than the contractual relationship.'") (quoting Choharis v. State Farm Fire & Cas. Co., 961 A.2d 1080, 1089 (D.C. 2008)).

Down the line, Plaintiff may indeed have to choose among his three common-law claims. At this early stage, however, it would be premature to dismiss any of the three as duplicative, given the fact-dependent nature of such an inquiry. While the counts all relate to the cyber attack *generally*, they may be predicated on distinct wrongs surrounding the attack. Defendants' conduct may have, for example, violated a Rule of Professional Responsibility—potentially creating liability for legal malpractice—which does not necessarily give rise to a breach of fiduciary duty. *See, e.g., Hickey*, 738 F. Supp. 2d at 67-68 (finding fee-related fiduciary-duty claim distinct from legal-malpractice claim concerning breach of Rule of Professional Responsibility in dispute over fees).

Finally, considerations of judicial economy do not weigh in favor of dismissal of any claims here. Allowing all three to proceed will not expand the scope of the case or potential avenues of discovery. At this juncture, therefore, the Court will decline Defendants' invitation to narrow Plaintiff's potential theories of relief. In sum, the Court will deny Defendants' Motion to Dismiss Counts I, II, and III to the extent that they rely on the theft of his personal information via cyber attack and Defendants' misrepresentations relating to protections from that attack.

B. The Withdrawal

By contrast, Defendants' withdrawal from Plaintiff's asylum process—or, as Plaintiff labels the incident, their "firing" of him—does not provide grounds for a viable legal claim. As described above, Defendants terminated their representation of Wengui following the cyber attack. They explained in a letter to him that the attack had created "several ethical complications" related to their representation. *See* ECF No. 12-5 (Clark Hill Termination Letter) at 1. Defendants' "primary concern" was that "the cyberattack would require Mr. Ragland—and possibly other members of the Firm—to be a witness in [Plaintiff's] asylum proceeding" because they now had first-hand knowledge of China's prior persecution of Plaintiff, a factor relevant to that proceeding. Id.

In their Motion to Dismiss, Defendants argue that not only did their withdrawal not breach any duty owed to Wengui, but that it was in fact *required* by the Rules of Professional Conduct. *See* D.C. R. Prof. Conduct 1.16(a)(1) (D.C. Bar 2010) (attorney must withdraw from representing client if ongoing representation would violate Rule of Professional Conduct). Defendants again rely on Rule of Professional Conduct 3.7(a), which states that an attorney "shall not" act as an advocate for a client when she is "likely to be a necessary witness" in the proceeding. They also invoke Rule 1.7(b)(4), which requires withdrawal if the lawyer's ability to represent a client "reasonably may be adversely affected by the lawyer's responsibilities to or interests in a third party or the lawyer's own financial, business, property, or personal interests." Defendants explain that following the cyber attack, they had their "own interests in investigating and mitigating the incident—which conflicted with their representation of Plaintiff." Def. MTD at 8.

Regarding Rule 3.7(a), Plaintiff counters that Defendants' withdrawal was premature at best, given that Wengui "did not have an asylum interview, let alone any hearing" and "had not asked that Mr. Ragland be a witness." ECF No. 14 (Pl. Opp.) at 8. Additionally, Plaintiff argues that Rule 1.7(b)(4) raises "inherently factual issues" as to whether the cyber attack created a conflict of interest, issues that cannot be resolved at this stage. Id. at 21.

The Court need not settle these disputes because Wengui's fiduciary and malpractice claims run aground on a different shoal. Plaintiff has not sufficiently pled that Defendants' conduct, even if improper, damaged or prejudiced him. Both of these claims require a showing of damage or loss. *See, e.g., Seed Co.,* 840 F. Supp. 2d at 126 (plaintiff bringing malpractice claim "must point to an act (or omission) by the . . . [D]efendants that resulted in a loss" to him); *Randolph,* 973 A.2d at 708-09 (same regarding breach of fiduciary duty). As one court in this district described the applicable test when considering legal malpractice, the claim " 'does not accrue until the plaintiff-client has sustained some injury from the malpractice[,]' and the 'mere breach of a professional duty, causing only nominal damages, speculative harm, or the threat of future harm—not yet realized—does not suffice to create a cause of action for negligence.' " Venable LLP v. Overseas Lease Grp., Inc., 2015 WL 4555372, at *2 (D.D.C. July 28, 2015) (quoting Knight v. Furlow, 553 A.2d 1232, 1235 (D.C. 1989)).

Plaintiff's claims predicated on the withdrawal do not plead damages that rise above the "speculative" or "nominal" level. Wengui does not dispute, for example, that at the time of Defendants' withdrawal, his asylum application had already been filed and he was awaiting an initial interview, which can take years to schedule. *See* Def. MTD at 20. He also does not claim to have experienced difficulties in finding a successor counsel with immigration-law expertise. As a result, Wengui has failed to factually substantiate his conclusory allegations that Defendants' withdrawal caused him "undue delay and complications," reputational harm, and prejudiced the outcome of his case. *See* Compl., ¶60; *see also* Hinton v. Stein, 278 F. Supp. 2d 27, 33 (D.D.C. 2003) (rejecting legal-malpractice claim where "[a]lthough there was a brief attorney-client relationship between the parties, defendant was justified in seeking to withdraw[,] . . . [h]er motion to withdraw was filed promptly[,] and there is no indication that plaintiff suffered any injury as a result of her withdrawal"). Put differently, the Complaint does not allege that Plaintiff "suffered any injury because of Defendant[s'] failure to represent him," and the Court will therefore dismiss his fiduciary-duty and malpractice claims to the extent that they rely on the withdrawal as the purported harm. Id.

Plaintiff's breach-of-contract claim based on the withdrawal is somewhat different, but also merits dismissal. A party may prevail on such a claim even if he "fails to prove actual damages," although he will be "entitled to no more than nominal damages." Wright v. Howard Univ., 60 A.3d 749, 753 (D.C. 2013) (quoting Bedell v. Inver Housing Inc., 506 A.2d 202, 205 (D.C. 1986)). With regard to the withdrawal, however, Plaintiff has failed to even gesture at provisions of the contract that Defendants breached in terminating their representation or at extrinsic evidence that might support such a claim. *See* Retainer Agreement at 2, 4 (attorney may terminate agreement for reasons permitted under Rules of Professional Conduct or if any conflict of interest arises).

C. Punitive Damages

The Court last tackles Count IV, which asserts a claim of punitive damages. Specifically, the Complaint alleges that Defendants violated Plaintiff's "rights" in an "intentional deliberate, [and] outrageous" manner. *See* Compl., ¶90. To begin, punitive damages are a form of relief, not a stand-alone cause of action. Although the count cannot survive independently, the Court considers whether such damages are available to Wengui at all. "To recover punitive damages," a plaintiff must establish that "the tortious act was committed with 'an evil motive, actual malice, deliberate violence or oppression' or in support of 'outrageous conduct in willful disregard of another's rights.'" Embassy of Nigeria v. Ugwuonye, 297 F.R.D. 4, 14 (D.D.C. 2013) (quoting Robinson v. Sarisky, 535 A.2d 901, 906 (D.C. 1988)). The imposition of punitive damages thus requires conduct that is "replete with malice." *See* Dalo v. Kivitz, 596 A.2d 35, 40 (D.C. 1991); *see also* Hendry v. Pelland, 73 F.3d 397, 400 (D.C. Cir. 1996) ("District of Columbia law allows punitive damages only if the attorney acted with fraud, ill will, recklessness, wantonness, oppressiveness, or willful disregard of the clients' rights.").

The Complaint does not plead such "outrageous" activity. Instead, if true, Wengui's allegations suggest that Defendants' failure to protect his information against hacking may mean that the firm acted "imprudently or incompetently, but they fall far short of showing the blatant wrongdoing necessary for a jury to infer that [Defendants] acted either with deliberate malice or conscious disregard of [their client's] rights." *Hendry*, 73 F.3d at 400; *see also Embassy of Nigeria*, 297 F.R.D. at 14 (rejecting punitive-damages claim where attorney stole client's tax refund and deposited it in firm's account). Plaintiff does not allege, for example, that Defendants *intentionally* left their server vulnerable to third-party hackings or stood to profit from such an event in any way. The Court therefore dismisses Count IV of the Complaint.

For the foregoing reasons, the Court will grant in part and deny in part Defendants' Motion to Dismiss. A separate Order consistent with this Opinion will be issued this day.

Law firms should be keenly aware of the risks involved in use of technology and develop robust information security protocols, controls, and procedures; have cyber incident response plans; keep an eye on vendors and personnel; and lastly, invest in cyber insurance.

IV. Conclusion

The adoption and use of technology is an existential issue for lawyers and law firms. You should endeavor to remain current and vigilant in this aspect of your practice. This is also a growth area within law firms and, perhaps more dramatically, for their service and support companies. Undoubtedly, there will be tremendous nontraditional career opportunities in this area.